ELEMENTARY STATISTICS

Elementary Statistics

BENTON J. UNDERWOOD
CARL P. DUNCAN
JANET A. TAYLOR
JOHN W. COTTON

Northwestern University

42175

NEW YORK

Appleton-Century-Crofts, Inc.

Preface

For several years we have felt some dissatisfaction with available elementary statistics texts. This dissatisfaction stemmed solely from the fact that these texts did not fit the kind of course we wished to teach at Northwestern University. At Northwestern the Department of Psychology teaches the elementary statistics course at the sophomore level; it is a one-quarter course required of all majors and is a prerequisite for many courses in the department, including experimental psychology. In this context we tie our statistics to research problems, trying to show the student how statistics are used in evaluating research results not only in psychology but in other social sciences. Our problems thus include the application of statistics not only to test evaluation but also to the evaluation of data obtained by the experimental approach and other techniques of research. We limit our consideration to a relatively small number of statistical concepts which we believe are currently most widely employed in describing distributions and testing differences between sets of data. In the present book it may appear at times that we labor unduly long over certain concepts; our only defense for this is that our experience tells us that this is necessary for adequate teaching of students at the sophomore level.

We have included a chapter on simple analysis of variance and one on chi square. With the average class we do not normally have time to include this material in the one-quarter course. There are two reasons for including these two chapters. We frequently use one or both of these techniques in advanced courses, particularly experimental psychology, and we have found that it

is advantageous for the students to have these chapters available
when needed. Secondly, we feel that if the course were one
semester long, as it is in many schools, sufficient time would be
available for inclusion of these chapters.

The book is distinctly a joint effort. Each of us was originally
responsible for preparing two to four chapters, but from that
point on each chapter became the responsibility of all. Session
after session was devoted to reaching agreement on the specific
contents of chapters and endeavoring to make the approach consistent throughout, as well as trying to develop a common language of expression. A small printed edition was developed to get
student reaction and was used later as the basis for our final re-
vision. This book, being truly a coöperative effort, with responsibility shared equally by the four of us, should have the authors'
names listed in circular form. A number of factors finally led us
to list the names in order of seniority, a decision which we will
not defend with vigor.

Invaluable criticisms have been received from the editor of the
Century Psychology Series, Professor R. M. Elliott, as well as
from Drs. Kenneth MacCorquodale and Kenneth Clark, all of the
University of Minnesota. Drs. E. L. Clark and Donald J. Lewis,
of Northwestern University, were kind enough to use the early
printed edition in their classes and contributed many worth-while
suggestions. Mrs. Irene Nolte has been largely responsible for
typing the manuscript.

We are grateful to a number of authors and publishers for
granting us permission to abridge or reproduce their materials:
The American Psychological Association for its several journals;
Dr. Carl Murchison for the *Journal of Psychology;* the Williams
& Wilkins Company for the *Journal of Comparative Psychology.*
Table A in the appendix is included through the courtesy of Cam-
bridge University Press and Houghton Mifflin Company; Table
B, through the courtesy of the Houghton Mifflin Company. We are
indebted to Sir Ronald A. Fisher, Cambridge, to Dr. Frank Yates,
Rothamsted, and to Messrs. Oliver and Boyd, Limited, Edinburgh,
for permission to abridge Tables III, IV, and VI from their book,
*Statistical tables for biological, agricultural, and medical re-
search.* Data from these tables make up Tables C, G, and a por-

tion of D. The remainder of Table D is with the permission of the Iowa State College Press and Professor George Snedecor. Table E is through the courtesy of the Institute of Mathematical Statistics and Professor E. G. Olds, and Table F is through the courtesy of Professor E. S. Pearson, editor of *Biometrika*. Finally, we are grateful to John Wiley & Sons, Inc., for allowing us to reproduce certain materials appearing in Chapter 13.

B.J.U.
C.P.D.
J.A.T.
J.W.C.

Contents

12

ELEMENTARY STATISTICS

1

Why Statistics?

An experiment,[1] recently reported in a psychological journal,
was designed to determine whether anxiety or tenseness might
interfere with performance on certain types of tasks which were
part of an intelligence test, thus, in effect, lowering the IQ score.
The subjects used in the study were college students who had
previously taken an individual intelligence test for another purpose. The investigators first divided their subjects into two groups
that were approximately equal in their scores on this intelligence
test. Next each subject was retested individually on certain subtests of the original intelligence test battery. Each member of one
group was told that on his first test his IQ had been incredibly
low, and that the experimenters were trying to give him an opportunity to improve his score. In addition, the testing was carried
out in a rather stiff, formal atmosphere that was hardly calculated
to reassure or comfort the student. The behavior and verbal comments of these subjects indicated that most of them were tense,
worried, and generally uncomfortable, just as the investigators
intended they should be.

The second group was treated quite differently: the subjects in
this group were told that the experimenters were merely interested
in the retest performance of persons who had been tested before.
In this instance the retesting itself was carried out in an emo-
tionally neutral atmosphere.

When they had finished testing all their subjects, the investigators had secured a series of numbers for every subject, each

[1] Moldawsky, S., and Moldawsky, P. C. Digit span as an anxiety indicator.
J. consult. Psychol., 1952, 16, 115-118. Raw data courtesy of the authors.

1

of which represented a measure of performance on a specific subtest. In one sense, we might say that having studied all their subjects and measured their responses, the psychologists had almost completed their research. In another, more important, sense we could say that the study had just begun. Remember that the investigation was carried out in the first place to answer certain questions; before it could be considered finished, there remained the major job of examining the mass of data in order to extract from it the information that would answer these questions.

Although the primary purpose of this particular study was to compare the two groups, let us first examine the performance on one of the subtests of the control ("neutral atmosphere") group alone to see what kind of information might interest us. The group's scores on a vocabulary test are shown in Table 1.1. We might first inquire how well the group was able to do this task. Were these students better than a non-college group? We see from the table that all the subjects were not equally good, so that these questions might better be phrased: What score best characterized the whole group (what was the typical or average score)? Did the average student in this experiment have a better vocabulary than the average non-college-trained individual?

TABLE 1.1

Scores Obtained by the 16 Neutral Subjects on the Vocabulary Subtest

12	13
11	13
14	13
13	13
14	14
13	15
14	12
13	13

But we might also be interested in the variability of the scores. How good was the brightest student? How low the poorest subject? Were the students quite similar in their scores or were there large differences in spite of the highly selected nature of the college population? Suppose you had been a subject in this experiment (in the neutral group, remember). How well did you do in comparison with the others? Scrutiny of the data from this group would tell us some of the answers to these questions, but very likely these answers would be vague, inaccurate, and awkward to convey to others (e.g., most of them scored such and such; the subjects didn't vary much; John Jones did better than most of the students).

There are more questions which we might ask that are even more fundamental to this specific research. Most basic, of course, is the question the experimenters set out to answer: Did anxiety have any effects on performance? Consider the data from both groups in Table 1.2, containing scores on another subtest, memory span for a series of numbers. Was the average person in the neutral group superior in memory span to the average anxious subject? Was one group more variable than the other? Suppose that we found that the average score was actually lower for the anxious subjects than for the neutral group. Could this inferiority be attributed to their treatment in the experiment? Even the neutral subjects didn't perform exactly as they had during the original testing. Was the difference between the two groups in the experiment perhaps due merely to the same kind of uncontrolled and unidentified variations rather than to anxiety? In other words, if the experiment were repeated with a different group of subjects, would we expect the results to come out the same way? Again, simply staring at the scores made by the subjects would not be a very satisfactory way of solving such questions. We would find that few or none of the answers just pop out at us.

TABLE 1.2

Scores Made by the Neutral and the Anxious Group on Memory Span
for Digits

NEUTRAL GROUP		ANXIOUS GROUP	
11	11	9	13
10	11	10	4
16	14	16	10
13	16	10	11
11	13	10	13
9	10	10	11
13	13	17	13
17	17	14	11

What we obviously need, then, is a more exact method that will enable us to extract information from our raw data. We need some way to discover and describe the relationships that are hidden in a mass of numbers. This is where statistics comes in. By performing arithmetic and algebraic manipulations with our scores we are able to abstract group trends and relationships and express them in a precise, accurate manner. Only with such information are we able to throw light on the problems the experiment was originally designed to investigate.[2]

So we can see from the preceding discussion that in experiments of the type just described, statistics is indispensable. As a matter of fact, in any research involving the testing of people or objects, be it a sort of Gallup poll, a classroom examination, or a formal laboratory experiment, statistics is a necessary tool if we hope to accomplish our objectives. Knowledge of statistics is as essential to the individual who would perform or even understand research as training in drafting is to the architect or drawing to the dress designer.

In teaching statistics or in writing a textbook on the subject our emphasis might be on statistical methods as such, a full explanation of the rationale of various techniques, the derivation of equations, and so on, without any reference to the concrete data to which these techniques can be applied. Such thorough knowledge of statistical methods requires an extensive background in advanced mathematics which, unfortunately, few in the social sciences possess.

Since we fully recognize these limitations in mathematical training, and further, since we are more concerned with statistics as a tool to be applied to actual research situations, this type of abstract approach will not be followed in this text. Our emphasis will be on the description and interpretation of concrete experimental data by statistical methods; our most fundamental concern is research—the results of controlled observation in the field

[2] By this time you may be curious about the conclusions the investigators drew from their study on anxiety. The results of their statistical analysis showed that performance on the vocabulary subtest was unaffected by anxiety. Memory span for numbers, however, was adversely affected, subjects in the anxious group scoring lower in comparison with the neutral group than would be expected by chance variation.

or the laboratory. This is not to imply that true sophistication in the application of statistical techniques may be had without a thorough mathematical understanding of them. However, it is possible within limits to learn the intelligent use of such methods without a complete knowledge of their mathematical derivation. Our aim, then, is to provide an understanding of certain statistical techniques that may be used to extract information from the types of experimental results frequently encountered in psychology and the other social sciences, methods by which we may answer such questions as those posed earlier in this chapter. It is to these questions that we now turn.

2

Frequency Distributions

The basic data resulting from any research are a series of numbers. These numbers usually represent measurements of some characteristic, measurements obtained from a group of objects or individuals. We might secure, for example, the mid-term test scores from a statistics class, the number of Rorschach ink blot responses made by a group of psychotic patients, or the batting averages made by major league players during the current season.

Unfortunately we can seldom make much sense out of the jumble of numbers obtained from such situations when we leave them in this raw form. As we said in the first chapter, we use statistical procedures to enable us to answer questions we have raised about our basic data. On the simplest level we usually want to know what the performance of a group has been: what the highest and lowest measures are, what measure occurs most frequently, whether scores tend to be concentrated about the middle or are distributed in some other fashion. A baseball enthusiast might be quite concerned, for example, with finding out the highest batting average in the major leagues this year. Or he might ask: What was the worst batting record this season? Did most players fall midway between the best and worst?

SIMPLE FREQUENCY DISTRIBUTION

A first step in obtaining information from any data that will aid us in answering such questions as those asked above is to bring some kind of order into our collection of numbers. One method of doing this that will probably occur to you immediately is to arrange the measures in order from their highest to lowest value. This tells us more about our data, but it is still not immediately obvious how many times a particular score occurs, or whether it occurs at all. One additional step in our procedure will, however, give us this extra information. All possible reported score values between the highest and lowest measures can be listed in one column and the number of individuals receiving each score in an adjacent column. An illustration of this procedure is shown in Table 2.1. The numbers represent scores received by a group of 100 mental patients on a 50-item personality test of anxiety, high scores indicating extreme anxiety.[1] As can be seen, the first column is labeled *score*. The order of highest to lowest,

TABLE 2.1

Simple Frequency Distribution of Anxiety Scores for 100 Mental Patients

SCORE	f	SCORE	f	SCORE	f
50	1	34	4	18	1
49	0	33	2	17	0
48	2	32	2	16	1
47	1	31	2	15	2
46	5	30	5	14	1
45	4	29	2	13	1
44	3	28	2	12	1
43	3	27	1	11	2
42	2	26	1	10	1
41	1	25	3	9	1
40	2	24	1	8	0
39	7	23	3	7	0
38	4	22	1	6	1
37	5	21	4	5	0
36	4	20	1	4	1
35	6	19	3		$N = 100$

seen in the score column, is the standard arrangement and should always be followed. The second column, labeled *frequency* (commonly abbreviated as f), contains the number of cases, in this instance the number of patients, receiving each score. For example, five patients received a score of 46 and two a score of 28. At the bottom of the frequency (f) column you will observe the

[1] Taylor, J. A. Unpublished data.

letter N, which is simply a symbol for the total number of cases in a group. N is 100 in the present illustration. *Such a table in which all score values are listed in one column and the number of individuals receiving each score in the second is called a frequency distribution.*

Arranging the measures into a frequency distribution makes interpretation of group performance easier. In our example we find that certain scores stand out as occurring frequently and, more important, that the scores are heavily concentrated towards the high anxiety end of the scale, not a surprising result considering that these are mental patients. Collecting scores into a frequency distribution, then, allows us to see these characteristics of group performance more easily than would a simple listing of scores in order.

TABLE 2.2

Simple Frequency Distribution of Anxiety Scores for 100 Normal Individuals

SCORE	f	SCORE	f	SCORE	f
38	1	25	2	12	6
37	1	24	0	11	4
36	0	23	3	10	7
35	1	22	0	9	6
34	0	21	2	8	6
33	2	20	1	7	5
32	0	19	2	6	4
31	1	18	2	5	5
30	1	17	2	4	8
29	2	16	7	3	1
28	2	15	5	2	1
27	2	14	4	1	1
26	3	13	0		N = 100

As an interesting contrast to the scores of the patients, the scores of 100 normal individuals on the same anxiety scale are shown in Table 2.2.[2] An arrangement of these results in a frequency distribution shows us something about the distribution of scores for normal individuals and permits a comparison of the two groups.

[2] Ahana, E. Y. A study on the reliability and internal consistency of a manifest anxiety scale. M.A. thesis, Northwestern Univ., 1952.

GROUPED FREQUENCY DISTRIBUTIONS

In many instances, particularly those in which the range of the measures (highest minus lowest score) is small, a frequency distribution of the type just described yields a compact table which shows the pattern formed by a group of scores. But when the measures are scattered over a wide range, the frequency distribution is long and bulky. We can see this from the three long columns in Tables 2.1 and 2.2. More important, so few cases fall

TABLE 2.3

Grouped Frequency Distribution of Anxiety Scores for 100 Mental Patients and 100 Normals where $i = 3$

PATIENTS		NORMALS	
Class Interval	f	Class Interval	f
48-50	3		
45-47	10		
42-44	8		
39-41	10		
36-38	13	36-38	2
33-35	12	33-35	3
30-32	9	30-32	2
27-29	5	27-29	6
24-26	5	24-26	5
21-23	8	21-23	5
18-20	5	18-20	5
15-17	3	15-17	14
12-14	3	12-14	10
9-11	4	9-11	17
6-8	1	6-8	15
3-5	1	3-5	14
	$N = 100$	0-2	2
			$N = 100$

at each score value that the group pattern is not too clear. We can, however, simultaneously make our distribution more compact and obtain a better idea of the over-all pattern of scores by bringing together the single measures into a number of groups, each containing an equal number of score units. This has been done on the left in Table 2.3 with the anxiety scores of the psychotic patients. In this table the test results have been grouped into blocks of 3 score values each. *Each block is called a class interval and is identified by putting down the "class limits."* These limits are the highest and lowest score in the interval. Thus the top interval shown in the first column of Table 2.3 includes score values of 48, 49, and 50 and is identified as class 48-50.

We can describe these intervals by saying that each has a width of 3, since 3 score values are included in each. The symbol we will be using to indicate the width of the interval in any grouped frequency distribution is i. The second column again contains frequencies (f) but these are now the number of individuals falling into each class interval rather than the number receiving each separate score (as was the case of Table 2.2). The data from the normal subjects on the anxiety test have also been arranged into a grouped frequency distribution, as shown on the right in Table 2.3, each class again consisting of 3 score units ($i = 3$).

The resulting distributions can be seen to be an improvement over the previous ones in determining group trends. We can now see quite dramatically that the scores for the patients tend to pile up at the high anxiety end of the scale and trail off in number towards the low end. The normals, in marked contrast, tend to cluster at the lower end, only a few (fugitives from a psychiatrist perhaps) receiving high scores.

The degree of condensation obtained by grouping data is determined by the number of score units included in each class interval, since increasing the size of i decreases the number of class intervals. In Table 2.4 the patients' data are again represented but i has been increased from 3 to 5 units, thus decreasing the number of intervals and shortening the length of the table. In Table 2.5, i is 10 units, making the resulting grouped frequency distribution even more compact. A comparison of these frequency distributions, all derived from the same raw data, reveals an interesting fact. As the width of the class interval, i, increases, the group pattern formed by the scores at first emerges and then later it disappears again as the number of classes becomes smaller and more and more scores are lumped together. We see that as far as obtaining information about group trends is concerned, condensing a frequency distribution by grouping scores can be overdone.

A further point to be noted about grouping data is that in the process the identity of the individual score is lost. For example, in Table 2.5 the uppermost interval contains 22 people, but we do not know exactly what score each received; we know only that

TABLE 2.4

Grouped Frequency Distribution of Anxiety Scores for 100 Mental Patients where $i = 5$

CLASS INTERVAL	f
46–50	9
41–45	13
36–40	22
31–35	16
26–30	11
21–25	12
16–20	6
11–15	7
6–10	3
1–5	1
	N = 100

each person falls somewhere within the interval. As i becomes larger, the numerical value of the individual score becomes more and more obscured. As we will see in subsequent chapters, the loss of the individual score value as a result of grouping has a practical implication when we compute certain statistics from grouped frequency distributions.

TABLE 2.5

Grouped Frequency Distribution of Anxiety Scores for 100 Mental Patients where $i = 10$

CLASS INTERVAL	f
41–50	22
31–40	38
21–30	23
11–20	13
1–10	4
	N = 100

How Many Intervals?

Before a set of data can be converted into a grouped frequency distribution we must first decide upon the number of class intervals to employ. This is largely an arbitrary matter, depending on such factors as the number of cases, the range of the measures and the purpose for which the distribution is intended. As a general principle we might say that the number of classes should be small enough so that the resulting distribution reveals the group pattern, but not so few in number as to obscure the group pattern and cause great loss in the precision with which we can identify the individual score. A rule of thumb often given is that between 10 and 20 intervals should be employed since most data can be adequately handled within these limits.

TABLE 2.6

Frequency Distribution of Number of Errors Made by 12 Animals in Maze Learning

SCORE (ERRORS)	f
5	1
4	1
3	4
2	3
1	2
0	1
	N = 12

Note that 10-20 intervals are appropriate for use in most, but not all, distributions. A frequent mistake made at the beginning is to apply such suggestions blindly, sometimes with ridiculous results. In Table 2.6 there are 12 numbers, each standing for the total number of errors made by animals in a maze experiment.[3] Such numbers would rarely be grouped at all. If they were grouped in order to present a very compact summary of the results the number of intervals would probably be 2 or 3, not 10 or 20. With respect to choosing the number of class intervals, or indeed in deciding whether the range of measures is so small that scores

[3] Thacker, L. A. An investigation of non-instrumental learning. *J. comp. physiol. Psychol.*, 1950, 43, 86-98.

should not be grouped at all, each set of data must be examined individually to determine the most adequate procedure to follow.

How Many Units for the Class Interval?

Once the *approximate* number of class intervals has been chosen, the width of the class interval necessary to produce the desired number of intervals must be determined. A rough estimate of the needed i can be found by dividing the range of the scores (the highest minus the lowest score) by the number of intervals wanted. Thus if a set of scores ran from 90 to 143 and about 15 intervals were to be employed, the approximate width would be 3.5 score units since:

$$\frac{143 - 90}{15} = 3.5$$

Since whole numbers are more convenient than fractions for widths of intervals, especially when the original measures are themselves integers, we have a choice of selecting either 3 or 4 units for our i. In most situations there will be a similar choice, since dividing the range by the number of intervals wanted usually results in a fractional value.

On the basis of practical considerations certain widths are preferable to others. When the choice is among widths smaller than 10, odd-sized widths (3, 5, 7, 9) are more convenient than even widths. In the example above, therefore, we would select 3 as our i instead of 4. For interval sizes of 10 and above, multiples of 5 (10, 15, 20, and so forth) are usually selected.

Nothing is sacred about any of these widths; they just turn out to have certain practical advantages. As for the larger widths, we are a "ten-minded" people and are happier when dealing with multiples of 10 or 5 than with other numbers. Employment of odd numbers for smaller widths is dictated by a different reason. We will frequently be using and referring to "midpoints" of class intervals, the middle score value in any interval. Taking a few made-up intervals at random as an illustration, 11 is the midpoint of the interval 10-12, 105 is the midpoint of the interval 103-107, 47.5 is the midpoint of 46-49. Note that in the first two examples i is an odd number (3 and 5 score units respectively) and the midpoints are whole numbers (11 and 105); in the third case i is an even number (4 units) and the midpoint, 47.5, involves a fraction. These results are not coincidental: when i is an odd number, the midpoint is an integer, but when it is an even number, the midpoint of each interval is a fractional value. Odd-numbered widths are employed, then, so that the midpoints will be whole numbers. Since most individuals are frightened by fractions the rule of using odd-sized i's should win easy acceptance.

In the frequency distributions used as illustrations up to this point, the raw measures have been whole numbers, i.e., no score has a fractional value. When such data are grouped we note that there are gaps between the upper and lower limits of adjacent classes. Thus, if we had classes 10-12 and 13-15, the first class goes up to include (has an upper limit of) 12.0 and the next starts

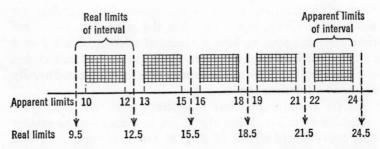

Fig. 2.1. An illustration of the relationship between real and apparent class limits

at (has a lower limit of) 13.0. Such values as 12.1 or 12.9, had they occurred, could not have been assigned to either class since they fall in the gap between 12.0 and 13.0. These class limits with gaps in between, which we will call "apparent limits," are to be contrasted with "real limits." Real limits extend the upper and lower apparent limits of adjacent classes equally until they meet at the point midway between them and the gap is closed. The real limits of class 10-12, used as an illustration above, are 9.5-12.5 and for the adjacent class 13-15, the real limits are 12.5-15.5. The process of forming real limits from apparent limits is illustrated further in Figure 2.1.

It would be possible to go off into a long discussion of the why's and wherefores of real vs. apparent limits. For our purposes, however, it will be sufficient to remember the distinction between real and apparent limits and to know how the former are obtained. The necessity for making the distinction at all will become obvious in later chapters in which it will be seen that real rather than apparent limits are used in certain statistical operations.

3

Graphic Representations

Most of us have seen graphs appearing in newspapers and magazine articles representing various types of statistical information: infant mortality rate in different countries, popularity of political candidates, the distribution of incomes, and so forth. Such graphs are used by popular writers in preference to tables of numbers because they are both more interesting and more easily interpreted than columns of figures. The graphic method is also employed extensively in technical articles since the outstanding features of group performance are most readily grasped in this form.

GRAPHIC REPRESENTATIONS OF FREQUENCY DISTRIBUTIONS

We will confine ourselves here to a discussion of three graphic methods of presenting frequency distributions: the histogram, the frequency polygon, and the cumulative frequency curve. Certain common-sense rules and ways of graphing data apply to all three methods. These will be outlined after a brief description of each specific type is given.

Histogram

The histogram or bar diagram is probably the graphic method best known to you. Two sample histograms, along with the frequency distributions from which they were derived, are shown in Figure 3.1.

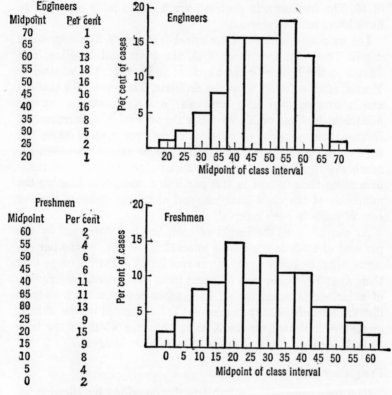

FIG. 3.1. Histograms showing engineer interest scores for adult engineers and college freshmen and the grouped frequency distributions from which they were drawn

The frequency distributions in Figure 3.1 give the scores made by a group of adult engineers and a group of college freshmen on a test of engineering interest.[1] The frequency in each class interval is expressed in percentage. These distributions contain all the necessary information about the scores for the two groups, but we can see how much easier and faster it is to obtain this information by inspecting the histograms. We see first that the scores of the engineers are relatively concentrated around a score

[1] Strong, E. K. Jr. Nineteen-year followup of engineer interests. *J. appl. Psychol.*, 1952, 36, 65-74.

of 50. The freshmen, in contrast, are more variable and tend to have lower interest scores.

Let us now examine the technical features of a histogram in detail. There are two axes: first, the horizontal baseline, also known as the X axis or the abscissa, and second, the vertical or Y axis, often referred to as the ordinate. The scores (in this example grouped into class intervals) are represented along the horizontal baseline or X axis while the vertical Y axis represents frequency or per cent of cases. Although per cent of cases has been chosen for illustration, it could just as easily have been the number or frequency. Each axis is appropriately labeled, the numbers along the abscissa in this particular example indicating the midpoints of the class intervals, and along the ordinate the per cent of cases in each interval.

As can be seen, the height of each bar is determined by the per cent of cases in each class interval. The width of the bar extends from the lower to the upper *real* limits of each class so that there are no gaps between adjacent bars. This general description of a histogram holds for all histograms representing frequency distributions: frequency or per cent is represented on the Y axis, scores are indicated on the X axis, while the width of the bars extends between the real limits of each class interval.

Frequency Polygon

The frequency polygon can best be described by showing its relationship to the histogram. In Figure 3.2 the same histogram for adult engineers drawn in Figure 3.1 has been reproduced with a frequency polygon superimposed upon it. The polygon has been formed by drawing straight lines between the successive midpoints of class intervals. The polygon has been completed by dropping the line to the baseline at both ends, at points representing the midpoints of the next interval above and the next interval below.

A frequency polygon can, of course, be drawn directly from a frequency distribution without the intervening step of forming a histogram. This is done by plotting points over the *midpoints* of each interval, the height of each point being determined by the appropriate frequency or per cent. The polygon is completed by connecting adjacent points with a straight line and dropping the lines to the baseline at either end.

We are sometimes interested in comparing the frequency distribution of *two* groups. In this case the distributions can be rep-

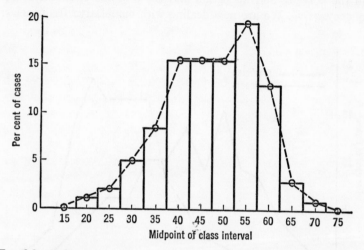

Fig. 3.2. A frequency polygon superimposed on the histogram plotted from the engineer interest scores of adult engineers

resented in a single figure. This process is illustrated in Figure 3.3, in which the polygons for both adult engineers and freshmen are drawn in the same graph.

Cumulative Frequency Curve

The cumulative frequency curve is used less often than the other two methods outlined above, but as we will see in subsequent discussions it is often preferable for certain purposes. Before describing the construction of such a graph, let us first examine a specific example of a cumulative frequency curve.

Earlier a distribution was presented showing the scores obtained by 100 normal individuals on a test of anxiety (see Table 2.2). The distribution of these scores is reproduced in Figure 3.4 along with the cumulative frequency curve derived from it. This curve, incidentally, has been "smoothed," i.e., a continuous line has been drawn so that it comes as close as possible to all points. As in histograms and polygons, scores (here class intervals) are indicated along the baseline of the graph and frequency along the Y axis. But there is a difference between the frequencies plotted in the polygon and histogram and those of the cumulative frequency curve. We are now dealing with cumulative frequencies:

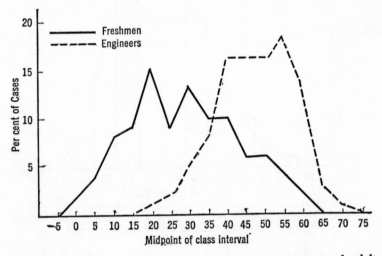

Fig. 3.3. Frequency polygons of the engineer interest scores of adult engineers and freshmen plotted on the same graph

the total number of cases earning a certain score or below. As a demonstration, find the score 11.5 (an upper real class limit) along the baseline of Figure 3.4. Going up to the curve and across to the vertical axis, you discover that 48 people have scores of 11.5 or less. (Conversely, 52 have scores of 11.5 or more.) On the other hand, you will note that 95 individuals received a score of 32.5 or less (the upper real limit of class 30-32), indicating that an anxiety score higher than this was a relatively rare occurrence.

In order to plot a cumulative frequency curve, we must first derive the cumulative frequencies themselves from the distribution. In the case of Figure 3.4, there are two individuals falling in the bottom interval and 14 in the second from the bottom. Thus

$2 + 14$ cases have scores of 5.5 or below. This sum, 16, is entered in the cumulative frequency column. To determine the next entry we find by adding that 31 individuals have scores of 8.5 or below $(2 + 14 + 15$ or $16 + 15)$. By successive addition, from bottom

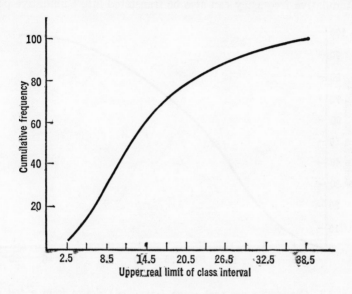

Class interval	f	$Cum.f$
36-38	2	100
33-35	3	98
30-32	2	95
27-29	6	93
24-26	5	87
21-23	5	82
18-20	5	77
15-17	14	72
12-14	10	58
9-11	17	48
6-8	15	31
3-5	14	16
0-2	2	2
	$N = 100$	

FIG. 3.4. A cumulative frequency curve of anxiety scores for 100 normal individuals and the frequency distribution from which it was derived

to top, of the entries in the frequency column we are able to get the cumulative frequencies. The entry in the topmost interval will be equal to the total number of cases since all individuals have a score equal to or less than the upper limit of this class. Cumulative frequency can also be translated into cumulative per

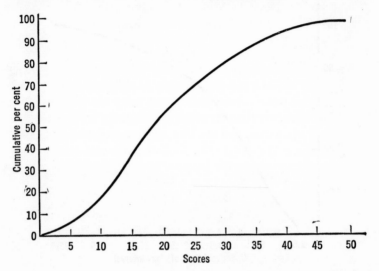

FIG. 3.5. Cumulative per cent curve (smoothed) drawn from a test of mechanical aptitude

cent, as is shown in Figure 3.5, representing scores on a test of mechanical knowledge.[2] Here the cumulative per cents of the total group earning scores of a certain value or below have been computed.

A cumulative frequency curve represents the graphing of a cumulative distribution and is carried out in a manner similar to the frequency polygon. In this method, however, the points are plotted directly above the upper real limit of each interval rather than the midpoint. The upper limits are used because of the fact that cumulative frequency represents the number or per cent of cases that have scores equal to or below the value at the particular upper limit. The height of each point above the abscissa is, of

[2] Boyd, J. Unpublished data.

course, determined by the appropriate cumulative frequency or per cent.

Cumulative frequency curves are utilized in preference to the polygon or histogram when we are primarily interested in determining the position of an individual in a group, rather than the general form of group performance. Let us take the case of Archie who scored 7 points on the test of mechanical knowledge referred to in Figure 3.5. Can Archie be trusted to build the new shelves his wife wants, or should he leave them to a carpenter? Looking at Figure 3.5 we quickly see that only about 10 per cent of the group tested scored lower than Archie. If the test results are any indication, we would advise him to put away his tools.

We find therefore that the results from many tests of abilities, personality attributes, and the like are reported with cumulative frequencies and graphed in this fashion, since test scores of this type are often used for the purpose of individual diagnosis and evaluation.

GENERAL PROCEDURES IN GRAPHING
FREQUENCY DISTRIBUTIONS

With the brief descriptions of the three types of graphic representations before us, we can now go on to a discussion of certain procedures applicable to graphing in general.

Selection of Axes

As was demonstrated in the previous illustrations, the custom in graphing frequency distributions is always to let the horizontal baseline represent scores or measures and the vertical axis frequencies (or per cent of cases). This convention should always be followed since reversal would only cause confusion for those used to the customary method.

Size of Units Selected

The physical distance selected to represent a score unit or frequency unit is purely arbitrary, except for convenience, since a graph can be drawn large enough to cover the wall of a room or small enough to require a microscope to be seen. Whatever the size of the graph, however, the general rule for histograms and frequency polygons has been to choose the units in such a way that the length of the vertical axis is 60-75 per cent of the length of the baseline. This rule may seem picayune but there are reasons for it. Not only does the uniformity produce esthetically pleasing results but there are practical implications as well. The latter become clearer if you examine the polygons in Figure 3.6. Each graph gives a different impression at first glance even though each represents the same frequency distribution. These differences have been produced by manipulating the physical distances chosen to represent scores and frequency units, or more accurately, by changing the relationship between the length of the two axes. Since the reader's impression of a frequency distribution can be so easily influenced by such an arbitrary factor, the adoption of an approximately standardized relationship between the two axes facilitates the interpretation of histograms and frequency polygons.

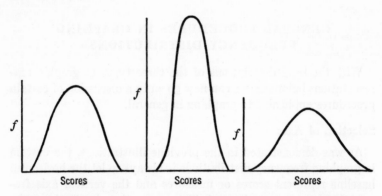

FIG. 3.6. Three curves drawn from the same frequency distribution

Because the highest frequency appearing in a cumulative frequency curve is greater than that in the polygon or histogram of the same data, the same rigid rule does not apply to this type of graphic representation. Most investigators, however, seem to make the baseline equal to or slightly longer than the vertical (cumulative frequency) axis and it might be well for you to follow this custom whenever convenient.

Labels of Graphs

Graphs should always be completely labeled. These labels include what each axis represents (e.g., scores, frequencies, per cents) and the numerical values of each. The lowest values for both frequencies and scores should start at the intersection of the two axes, at the lower left of the graph. It is not necessary to indicate or number the position of every possible score along the baseline, but only certain representative ones at regular intervals. Specifically, it is usually sufficient to have class limits (real or apparent) or midpoints of intervals labeled. In histograms and frequency polygons, for example, it is most often convenient to indicate the midpoints of intervals, and for cumulative curves the upper real limits.

There is no general rule for the frequency scale; as long as enough points are identified to make interpretation easy and these are placed an equal number of units apart, labeling will be considered adequate.

Titles of Graphs

Every graph should have a concise title containing sufficient information to allow a reader to identify relevant aspects of the data, such as exactly what they measure, their source, and so forth. If several graphs are to be presented, each graph or figure should in addition be given its own number for further identification (e.g., Figure 17).

Beginning students readily agree that a title is necessary for a graph but too often neglect to add them to their own productions. Every person who has dealt with data knows how easy it is to forget where his own graph came from or even what it represents, let alone how nearly impossible it is to figure out someone else's unidentified figures. A graph without labels and a title, then, is often next to being meaningless. You are, therefore, strongly urged to make "titling" second nature to you, even on statistical exercises.

FORM OF A FREQUENCY DISTRIBUTION

Frequency polygons (or histograms) can occur in an unlimited number of shapes and forms. Since form is often an important bit of information about a distribution, it is necessary for us to know some of the descriptive terms used to indicate various types.

Some frequency distributions, and consequently the frequency polygons derived from them, are bi-laterally symmetrical. That is, if the polygon is folded in half, perpendicular to the baseline, the two sides are identical in shape. A variety of symmetrical distributions is shown in Figure 3.7.

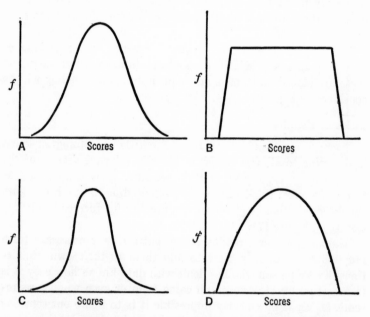

FIG. 3.7. Illustrations of symmetrical frequency distributions

Any distribution that is not symmetrical is said to be skewed. Such distributions can be more exactly described in terms of degree and direction of skewness. Degree refers to the amount that a distribution departs from symmetry. Thus distribution *a* in Figure 3.8 is more highly skewed than *c*. Direction of skewness takes account of the fact that in some asymmetrical distributions the measures tend to pile up at the lower end of the scale and to trail off, in terms of frequency, towards the upper end, while in other cases the situation is reversed. Curves *a* and *b* in Figure 3.8 are illustrations of these two possibilities. Differences in the

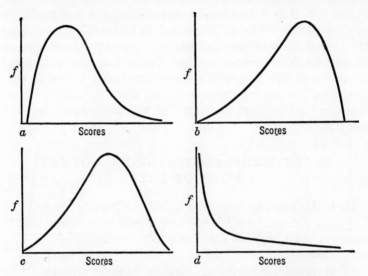

Fɪɢ. 3.8. Illustrations of skewed frequency distributions

direction of skewness are indicated by saying that the distributions are positively or negatively skewed. Both as a way of explaining which is positive and which negative and as a device for remembering the difference between the two, the following is offered: the lower or left end of the baseline can be pictured as the negative end (values are low) and the upper or right end as positive (values are high). If the "tail" of a distribution (where scores are relatively infrequent in number) lies in the negative end of the scale, the distribution is negatively skewed. If the tail extends out towards the upper or positive end, the distribution is positively skewed. Curve *b* in Figure 3.8 is therefore negatively skewed while *a* is positively skewed.

Certain distinctive forms of distributions that occur with some frequency are given special names. Curve *d* in Figure 3.8 is called a *J curve*. This type is found primarily with certain types of socially conditioned behavior as, for example, a distribution of the number of major crimes committed by members of a large group of individuals. The vast majority have none to their credit, whereas a few members of the group are multiple offenders. In Figure 3.7, B is a *rectangular distribution*, the frequencies in every class interval being the same. A in Figure 3.7 approximates *the normal curve*, a specific form of a symmetrical bell-shaped distribution. Many phenomena, including such psychological characteristics as IQ's and certain personality traits, appear to take this form. The normal curve is of such great theoretical importance in statistics that its properties will be discussed in some detail in Chapter 7.

GRAPHIC REPRESENTATIONS OF OTHER TYPES OF DATA

Up to this point we have been considering methods of graphing frequency distributions. We will now discuss very briefly how to represent other types of data commonly encountered in psychological investigations.

Often research in psychology involves obtaining repeated measures from the same individuals in order to study changes in their performance. Experiments in learning are perhaps the most common of this type, subjects being given repeated presentations (trials) of an unfamiliar task so that their rate of progress towards mastery can be studied.

In other kinds of research we are concerned with comparing different groups, objects, or conditions with respect to some characteristic. We might for example be interested in the effects different degrees of hunger have on performance and thus compare the average scores made by groups operating under different hours of food deprivation.

Illustrations of graphic representations of such data are shown in Figures 3.9, 3.10, and 3.11. A line graph of typical learning data is shown in Figure 3.9. The learning consisted of the acquisition of a conditioned eyelid response (blinking to a light in an-

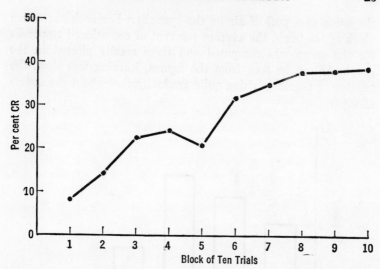

FIG. 3.9. A line graph representing the acquisition of a conditioned eyelid response

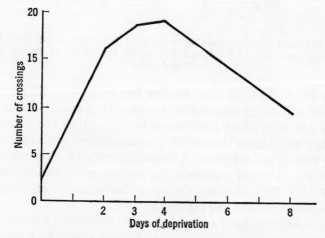

FIG. 3.10. Line graph of the average number of crossings made by groups of rats with different periods of food deprivation

ticipation of a puff of air on the eyeball).[3] For each successive block of ten trials, the average per cent of conditioned responses for the group was computed and these results plotted in the graph. As can be seen from the figures, learning was slow, the number of responses rising quite gradually throughout the course of the trials.

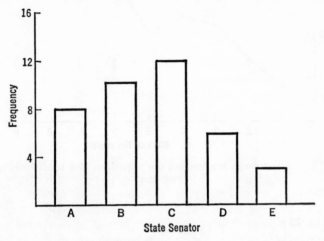

FIG. 3.11. Bar diagram showing number of times the voting record of five state senators (A,B,C,D,and E) on 16 key measures agreed with editorial policy

In Figure 3.10, we have another line graph, this time representing data taken from different groups. Here groups of animals were deprived of food for different lengths of time and tested to see how many times they would cross an electrically charged runway leading to food during a ten-minute period.[4] Although each point on the graph represents the average number of crossings made by a different group, the graph gives a picture of changing responsiveness as hunger becomes greater.

Often different groups or objects do not vary along a continuum

[3] Spence, K. W., and Norris, E. B. Eyelid conditioning as a function of inter-trial interval. *J. exp. Psychol.*, 1950, 40, 716-720.

[4] Warner, L. H. A study of hunger behavior in the white rat by means of the obstruction method. A comparison of sex and hunger behavior. *J. comp. Psychol.*, 1928, 8, 273-299.

with respect to the characteristic differentiating them (e.g., groups varying in hours of deprivation of food or degree of intelligence) but are a collection of discrete objects (e.g., types of animals, a series of different personality tests, different countries of the world). The data from such groups are usually presented in the form of a bar graph or histogram to emphasize the discreteness of the groups. An illustration is found in Figure 3.11, showing the number of times five Illinois State Senators voted on 16 important bills in accord with the editorial policy of a Chicago newspaper.[5]

In graphs of the type shown in the illustrations, it will be noted that in each case the response measure (average number of conditioned responses, number of crossings) is always indicated on the Y axis. Trials, groups, or conditions are plotted along the baseline. This arrangement is, in a sense, comparable to the one followed in graphing frequency distributions: frequency or per cent of the cases plotted along the ordinate in frequency distributions, frequency or per cent of response also along the Y axis (ordinate) in data involving repeated measures or different groups; scores are plotted along the X axis (abscissa) in frequency distributions and so are groups or trials with other types of data.

A further similarity to graphic representations of frequency distributions is found in the general relationship of the axes, the ordinate being approximately 75 per cent of the length of the baseline. Needless to say, the requirements for labeling and identifying the graph are just the same with all kinds of methods of graphing.

[5] Data adapted from the Chicago *Sun-Times,* July 5, 1953.

4

Percentiles

THE PROBLEM OF INTERPRETING A RAW SCORE

Probably you all have had instructors put frequency distributions on the board after an examination. But what interests you primarily is not how well the class as a whole was able to do but where you placed in the group: how many students (or what per cent of the class) scored above you, or, perhaps more consolingly, how many were below you. Or a vocational counselor may find that a client receives a certain score on a test of clerical aptitude; he is less concerned with the score itself than with how that score compares with those earned by successful clerks. Shifting the emphasis slightly, there are other occasions on which we are interested in the position of a particular *score* (rather than the relative status of an individual who happens to get a given score). In World War II, for example, there was a minimum score on the Army General Classification Test necessary for admission to Officer Candidate School. Determination of the percentage of inductees who exceeded this score would not only be a matter of scientific interest but might also be of military importance in helping to estimate the number of potential officer candidates available for the future.

There are, in other words, many situations in which our primary concern is the relative position of an individual (or of a specific score) in a group rather than the performance of the group as a whole. Implicit in this statement is not only the fact that our concern is in an individual rather than a group, but also that a score, a numerical representation of some characteristic, is seldom meaningful in and of itself. In order to interpret a particular measure we must know something about the scores of other objects or individuals. What if we were told that Johnny Jones had scored 120 on an arithmetic test? Taken alone, this bit of information would be completely useless. The statement would take on more significance, however, if we knew something about the scores of others taking the test (and, it should be added, the composition of the group as well). Thus, for any measurement, particularly one of a psychological characteristic (e.g., an intelligence test score, personality rating, or learning score) that has no meaning by itself, our interpretation of the measure or score depends wholly or partially on a knowledge of its relative position in a group.

PERCENTILE RANKS AND PERCENTILES

The need for designating the particular position a specific score occupies in the group from which it is drawn in order to interpret its significance should now be quite obvious. The next step is to find a method that will enable us to state with numerical precision the relative position of any specific measure. The simplest procedure would be to count up the number of individuals above (or below) a given score and express that score in terms of numerical rank, e.g., a score of 40 ranks 102nd out of 200. And if you read the example carefully, you may have made it more meaningful to yourself by thinking: just about 50% of the group scored below 40. This process of translating a numerical rank into percentage terms is one of the most common ways of expressing relative position. The result of such a conversion is known as a percentile rank.

The percentile rank of any specific score is a value indicating the per cent of cases in a distribution falling at or below this score. A percentile rank therefore defines, in percentage terms, the position of that score in its distribution. If, for example, 83% of a group score 101 or lower, the score 101 would have a percentile rank of 83. If only 8% of the group obtained a score of 26 or lower, then 26 has a percentile rank of 8. Conversely, if a given score has a percentile rank of 54, we would know that 46% of the group fall *above* it.

When we are obtaining a percentile rank, we are given or start out with a score and find the per cent of cases falling at or below it. But we can also reverse the procedure, starting out with a given per cent in mind and finding the score corresponding to it. To illustrate, a college registrar might be forced to reject 30% of the applicants for the freshman class and decide to make use of a scholastic aptitude test as the selective device. His problem is to find the *score* on this test below which 30% of the applicants fall. This score would be called the 30th percentile. A percentile, then, is the score at or below which a given per cent of the cases lie.

The percentile scale, derived from percentages, is one that contains 100 units. A number of points along this scale are given special names. The most commonly used of these are the quartiles. The first quartile (known as Q_1) is a special name for the 25th percentile, the second quartile (Q_2, also called the median) is equal to the 50th percentile, and the third quartile (Q_3) to the 75th percentile. Occasionally certain percentiles are referred to as deciles: the first decile (or 10th percentile), the second decile (20th percentile), and so forth up to the tenth decile (100th percentile).

At or In? Students occasionally say something like this: "This score is in the second quartile" (or "in the 71st percentile"). These statements are inaccurate because as we have already pointed out, a quartile, (or decile, or percentile) *is* a score, a specific point, and therefore no other score can fall "within" that point. A score, then, is, or falls *at*, a percentile, quartile, or decile, not "in." We could, however, make a statement of this sort: X falls *between* the 2nd and 3rd quartiles (or between two percentiles) since this would indicate a position somewhere between two points.

OBTAINING PERCENTILE RANKS

We anticipated the topic of percentile ranks to some extent when we discussed cumulative curves. We saw then that we could determine the per cent of cases falling below each score (or below an upper real limit) in a frequency distribution and graph these results. Inspection of such a cumulative percentage curve is the simplest way to approximate the percentile rank of any score. To recall how this is done we can refer to the cumulative curve in Figure 4.1, derived from the results of a scholastic aptitude test given to college students.[1] We first find along the baseline the

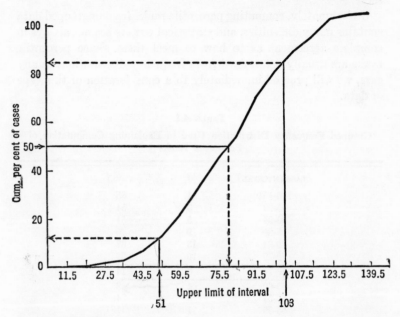

Fig. 4.1. Cumulative percentage curve of scores from a scholastic aptitude test

score in which we are interested, let us say 51, go up to the curve and then across to the Y axis. The value we read there, about 12, tells us the percentile rank of the score. Individuals with scores as low or lower, then, are relatively lacking in scholastic aptitude as determined by the test scores of other students. Similarly, a score of 103 can be seen to have a percentile rank of about 85, 85% of the cases falling at or below it.

While inspection of a cumulative frequency curve is a painless,

[1] Clark, E. L. Unpublished data.

quick method of determining percentile ranks, exclusive use of this procedure has a drawback. If we are interested in the percentile ranks of only one or two scores, obtaining and graphing an entire cumulative distribution involves much needless effort. For this reason it is desirable to have a method of computing a relatively precise estimate of the percentile rank for any single score.

Unfortunately, computing percentile ranks from ungrouped data contains many difficulties, and statistical writers are not always in complete agreement as to how to meet them. Since percentile ranks are usually determined from frequency distributions in any case, we will proceed immediately to a consideration of this type of data.

TABLE 4.1

Grouped Frequency Distribution Used in Explaining Computation of Percentile Ranks

CLASS INTERVAL	f	$cum.f$
100-104	1	55
95-99	3	54
90-94	5	51
85-89	9	46
80-84	13	37
75-79	10	24
70-74	6	14
65-69	4	8
60-64	3	4
55-59	1	1
	$N = 55$	

In order to explain the method of computation of a percentile rank from a frequency distribution, we will take a concrete example. Suppose we are interested in determining the percentile rank of the score 72 found in the distribution shown in Table 4.1. What we want to determine is the *number* of cases below the score, and from there, the *per cent* of cases. Looking at the table we discover first that 72 falls in the interval 70-74 and secondly, from the *cum.f* column, that a total of 8 cases fall below that interval. This entry tells us the number of cases (8) up to the lower real limit (69.5) of the interval in which our score is contained. But we also need to add to this the number of cases between 69.5 and 72. However, as is schematically represented in Figure 4.2, this number of cases cannot be determined because the identity of the individual score is lost; we know that 6 indi-

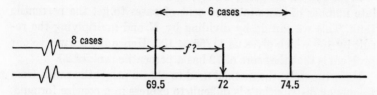

Fig. 4.2. Schematic representation showing why it is impossible to obtain the exact number of cases between a lower real limit and a given score when scores are grouped

viduals fall within the interval but not how many are between 69.5 and 72. We can, however, estimate the needed number by assuming that the cases in the interval are evenly distributed, i.e., the same number of cases fall at each score value so that the

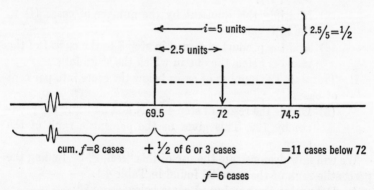

Fig. 4.3. Schematic representation showing method of estimating the needed number of cases when computing percentile ranks

intra-interval distribution of cases is rectangular. Let us now examine Figure 4.3 to see the implication of this assumption. First, our score of 72 lies half way up the interval. This is true because 72 is 2.5 score units away from the lower real limit, 69.5, and i, the total number of units in the interval, is 5. Secondly, it follows that if the scores are evenly distributed, then one-half of the 6 cases fall between 69.5 and 72. Thus 3 is the number of cases we need. Add 3 to 8 (the *cum.f* in the interval below) and we have the total number of cases (11) below our score.

From now on the going is easy, for all we have to do is to translate number of cases into per cent of cases to get the percentile rank. This we can do by dividing by N and multiplying the result by 100 which gives us $11/55 \times 100$. Hence the answer to our problem is that the score of 72 has a percentile rank of 20.

Unfortunately, the method used to obtain percentile ranks from frequency distributions is difficult to express in a concise formula. In lieu of this, we recommend a sort of "cookbook recipe" that can be followed step by step.

A. Determine the number of cases falling below the given score:
   (1) Subtract from the score the lower real limit of the interval in which it is contained.
   (2) Divide the result of step 1 by the width of the interval (i).
   (3) Multiply this quotient by the number of cases (f) in the interval.
   (4) Add the product obtained in step 3 to the *cum. f* of the interval *below* the one in which the score falls.

B. Translate the number of cases below the score into per cent of cases:
   (5) Divide the result of step 4 by N and multiply the product by 100. This gives us the percentile rank of the score.

We will now demonstrate the use of this "recipe" by finding the percentile rank of the score 86 found in Table 4.1.

A. Determine the number of cases below score 86:
   (1) $86 - 84.5 = 1.5$ (Score minus lower real limit)
   (2) $1.5/5 = .3$ (Result divided by i)
   (3) $.3 \times 9 = 2.7$ (Quotient multiplied by f of the interval)
   (4) $2.7 + 37 = 39.7$ (Result plus *cum.f* in interval below)

B. Translate number of cases into per cent of cases:
   (5) $39.7/55 \times 100\% = 72.2\%$. Thus 72.2 is the percentile rank of score 86.

COMPUTATION OF PERCENTILES

A percentile, you will remember, is a score at or below which a given per cent of the cases fall. As in the case of percentile ranks, the simplest method of determining any percentile is by inspection of a cumulative percentage curve. Again we can refer to Figure 4.1 as an illustration. Since we start with a given percentage value, we first locate this value on the Y axis, go across to the curve, then drop down to the score scale. Following this procedure, we find that a score of about 79 is the 50th percentile or median. In like manner, examination of Figure 4.1 shows us that 92 is the 70th percentile and 63 the first quartile (Q_1).

TABLE 4.2

Grouped Frequency Distribution Used in Demonstrating Computation of Percentiles

CLASS INTERVAL	f	cum.f
150-159	1	60
140-149	2	59
130-139	5	57
120-129	8	52
110-119	14	44
100-109	10	30
90-99	7	20
80-89	6	13
70-79	4	7
60-69	3	3
	$N = 60$	

A computational procedure for determining percentiles is convenient for the same reason as discussed in connection with percentile ranks. To demonstrate the method, let us find the 25th percentile (or the first quartile, Q_1) from the grouped frequency distribution in Table 4.2. Our first step is to determine how many of the total number of cases constitute the given per cent. Here we must take 25% of N, which gives us 15 cases ($60 \times .25$). The score we want, then, is 15th from the bottom of the distribution. Going up the *cum.f* column we find that the 15th case lies someplace in the interval 90-99, since there is a total of 13 cases up to the lower real limit of this interval (too few) and 20 individuals up to the upper real limit of the interval 90-99 (too many). Now we have a similar problem as in computing percentile ranks: we know that there are 13 cases below the score 89.5 and that we therefore need to go up to the 2nd of the 7 individuals in the interval to make up our needed 15 (13 + 2). But how can we find out the score of the second case in the interval when we don't know the placement or distribution of the 7 scores in the interval? If we again assume that the scores are equally distributed throughout the interval, we can take 2/7 of the score units (i) in the interval. Taking 2/7 of 10, we get 2.9 score units, the "score distance" the 2nd case is from the lower real limit. Adding 2.9 to 89.5, we find that the score 92.4 is the 15th case from the bottom of the complete distribution or the 25th percentile. This process is pictorially represented in Figure 4.4.

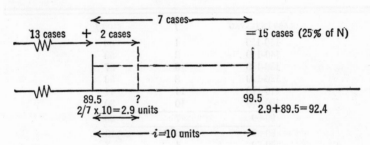

FIG. 4.4. Graphic representation of obtaining a given percentile

We can again offer, step by step, a "recipe" for computing a percentile.

A. Translate the given per cent of cases into number of cases (the nth case).

B. Find the score corresponding to the nth case:

(1) Locate by inspection of the *cum.f* column the class interval in which the nth case lies. This is the interval containing the percentile.

(2) Subtract from the nth case the *cum.f* of the interval *below* the one in which the nth case is contained. This tells us the number of cases we need from the interval.

(3) Divide the value found in step 2 by the number of cases (f) in the interval containing the given percentile.

(4) Multiply the quotient obtained in step 3 by i.

(5) Add the number from step 4 to the lower real limit of the class in which the percentile (the nth case) is contained. This score is equal to the desired percentile.

These steps can be summarized in the following formula which should be easy to apply after a few practice trials have made the terms in it familiar.

$$\text{Score} = \text{lower real limit of int.} + i \left(\frac{[n\text{th case}] - [cum.f \text{ in int. below}]}{\text{no. of cases in int.}} \right)$$

where: nth case = the number of cases corresponding to given per cent (e.g., for 37th percentile when N = 40, nth case = 37% of 40)

int. = class interval in which nth case is contained (determined by inspection of $cum.f$ column)

int. below = class interval immediately below the one in which the nth case is contained

The use of both of these methods can be demonstrated by applying them to a concrete example. Let us find the 80th percentile (or 8th decile) of the distribution in Table 4.2.

A. nth case = 80% of N = 48

B. Find the score corresponding to the nth case:

(1) The 48th case is located in interval 120-129

(2) A $cum.f$ of 44 is found in the interval below class 120-129 : 48 − 44 = 4 cases

(3) $\frac{4}{8} = \frac{1}{2}$, where 8 is the number of cases (f) in interval containing the 48th case

(4) $\frac{1}{2} \times 10 = 5$ where $10 = i$

(5) $119.5 + 5 = 124.5$. This is the score equal to the 80th percentile

OR

$$\text{lower real limit} + i \left(\frac{[n\text{th case}] - [cum.f \text{ in int. below}]}{\text{no. of cases in int.}} \right)$$

thus: $119.5 + (10) \left(\dfrac{48 - 44}{8} \right) = 124.5$

Occasionally when computing percentiles from frequency distributions we encounter some special situations that are not covered by the computational procedures just discussed. The first of these is one in which the given percentile falls between intervals. Suppose we were finding the median or 50th percentile from the data in Table 4.3. Since there are 20 cases in all, the nth case is 10 (50% of 20). Looking at the *cum.f* column, we find that to get 10 cases, we have to take all of the individuals falling in the interval 25-29, since 10 is the *cum.f* entry for this interval. Conversely, the top 10 cases would include all the individuals in interval 30-34. The 50th percentile or median, then, is the upper real limit of class 25-29 (or the lower real limit of 30-34) which is 29.5. Fifty per cent of the cases then fall below this score and 50% above it.

TABLE 4.3

A Frequency Distribution Illustrating Some Special Situations in Computing Percentiles

CLASS INTERVAL	f	*cum.f*
45-49	1	20
40-44	2	19
35-39	3	17
30-34	4	14
25-29	5	10
20-24	0	5
15-19	3	5
10-14	2	2
	N = 20	

Median (50th percentile) = 29.5
25th percentile = 22

The second situation is one in which the percentile falls into an interval with no cases (zero frequency). This is really the same situation as the one above but with an added wrinkle. As an illustration, let us find Q_1 or the 25th percentile of the distribution in Table 4.3. What we are asked to find is the score below which 25% of the individuals fall and above which 75% fall. But examination of the *cum.f* column shows us that due to the zero frequency in interval 20-24, exactly 5 cases (25%) are below 19.5 and 15 cases (75%) above 24.5. Since a percentile is a point, one score value, we must choose some specific value for

Q_1, some score between these two points (19.5 and 24.5). We can best solve our problem by compromising, giving the percentile the value midway between 19.5 and 24.5. This turns out to be the *midpoint* of the interval with no cases, 22. This general method of solution holds, of course, for all similar situations in other distributions.

Before leaving the topic of percentiles it should be reëmphasized that a raw score seldom has meaning by itself but must be interpreted in terms of its position in the distribution from which it was drawn. Translation of scores into percentile ranks is one of the most frequently used methods of expressing relative position. We will take up other methods in later chapters.

5

Measures of Central Tendency

Everyday observation shows us that all the individual members of a group rarely have the same amount of some common characteristic. Instead they vary among themselves. We have already seen how such group patterns can be made clearer by sorting raw data to form frequency distributions and how to represent such distributions by graphing them. But there are many instances in which we are not interested in group patterns but instead want to characterize a group as a whole. We might have such questions as: What is the average running speed of a Kentucky Derby entry? How many dates a week does the typical coed have? What is the average income of male college graduates?

Each of these questions requires a single number that will represent a whole distribution of measurements. While it may be true that there is no such person as "the common man," it is nevertheless true that on many occasions we want to know what characteristic (or amount of a characteristic) is most common, or best represents a group of differing individuals. This representative number will usually be near the center of a distribution where the measures tend to be concentrated rather than at either extreme where, typically, only a few measures fall. From this fact comes the term "measure of central tendency."

Although a number of measures of central tendency have been devised, we will be studying only three of them: the arithmetic mean (M), the mode (Mo.), and the median (Mdn.). There is nothing magical about any of these measures of central tendency; each is simply a different method of determining a single representative number. As we shall see, the numbers resulting

44

from each method usually do not agree exactly with each other. The particular measure we compute in any instance depends on which one yields the number that best represents the fact we wish to convey. The specific situations in which each method is most appropriate will be discussed in a later section.

ARITHMETIC MEAN

Definitions of the Mean

The arithmetic mean (M) is a measure with which most of you are already familiar and is popularly known as the "average." The arithmetic mean, or simply "the mean" for short, is the result of the well-known procedure of adding up all the measures and dividing by the number of measures. Defining the term more formally, *the mean is equal to the sum of the measures divided by their number.* A much more compact way to express this verbal definition is by using symbols, a kind of mathematical shorthand, as shown in the formula below:

$$M = \frac{\Sigma X}{N}$$

where M = arithmetic mean
Σ = Greek capital letter Sigma, meaning the "sum of" a series of measures
X = a raw score in a series of measures
ΣX = the sum of all the measures
N = number of measures

Before proceeding with a discussion of the mean (M), we will take time out to explain in more detail the meaning of the Greek capital letter Sigma (Σ), one of the most frequently used symbols in statistics. The presence of Σ in any formula indicates that a group of numbers is to be added or summed. Since for convenience we usually refer to any raw score in a frequency distribution as X, ΣX indicates the total obtained by adding together all the scores belonging to a distribution. Sometimes we deal with two frequency distributions (e.g., scores made by a group of high school boys and scores made by a group of high school girls on a test of clerical aptitude). To distinguish between the two distributions we might call one set X's (let us say the boys) and the other Y's (the girls' scores). If we wrote the symbols ΣY, we would mean the sum of all the girls' scores (the Y's). In like manner, Σf stands for the sum of all the frequencies in a distribution; or we might arbitrarily choose the symbol A and then ΣA is the sum of all of the A scores, whatever they happened to be, and so forth. The expression $\frac{\Sigma X}{N}$, then, is shorthand for the sum of all the raw scores (X's), divided by N (their number).

There is another definition or characteristic of M that is important for us to state since it contributes to an understanding both of M and of the concept of variability, a topic to be considered in Chapter 6. *M may be described as that point in a distribution of scores at which the algebraic sum of the deviations from it (the sum of the differences of each score from M) is zero.*

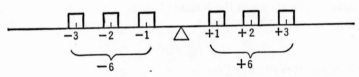

Fig. 5.1. Representation of a balanced teeter-totter with "children" of equal weight placed at the distance indicated

Or, expressed differently, M is a kind of "point of balance," where the sum of the deviations of the scores above M is equal in absolute value (i.e., without regard to plus or minus sign) to the sum of the deviations below M. In order to clarify these statements, we will first introduce a kind of analogy. Imagine that the horizontal line shown in Figure 5.1 is an old-fashioned teeter-totter. Suppose further that each square drawn in Figure 5.1 represents a child, each of equal weight, seated at the place indicated. We can see that the fulcrum has been placed at a point where the board balances. But why does the board balance at this particular point? First observe that we can give each child a "value" in terms of his distance from the fulcrum (-1, -2, -3, $+1$, $+2$, $+3$). These distances from the fulcrum we will call deviations from it. The absolute sum (that is, ignoring signs) of the deviations of the three children to the right of the fulcrum is the same as the absolute sum of the deviations for the children to its left, namely, 6 units. From painful experience, you know that the balance of the teeter would be destroyed if a child were moved from one position to another, even on the same side (e.g., from −1 to −3). When we disturb the values of the deviations so that their sums are not equal on both sides of the fulcrum, the balance is destroyed and the fulcrum must be moved to restore it.

Let us now relate this analogy to M, which we have already said is a kind of point of balance. First, let us find M by the method of adding up the scores and dividing by N, as in the example given in Figure 5.2. Since there are 9 scores in Figure

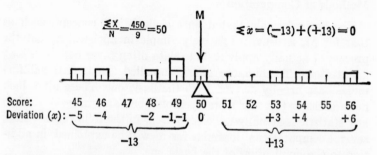

Fig. 5.2. A distribution of raw scores and deviations of these scores from M showing that the algebraic sum of the deviations is zero

5.2 and their sum is 450, M is 50. Next, let us find the deviation or distance each score is from M. Each deviation is designated by the symbol x and is obtained by subtracting M from each score $(x = X - M)$. Obviously, scores with values greater than M will be plus deviations, those with lesser values minus deviations. If we now add the plus deviations (those above M) and the minus deviations (those below it), as was done in Figure 5.2, we find that the absolute value of the two sums is equal; retaining signs, the two sums cancel each other so that the sum of the *total* deviations is zero $(\Sigma x = 0)$. Take as another example the numbers 5, 9, and 16. M of these numbers is 10, the sum of deviations below it is $-6[(-5) + (-1)]$ and above it $+6$; the algebraic sum of the deviations equals 0. Thus, in any distribution of scores, M is a "point of balance," comparable to the fulcrum in the teeter-totter example, in that the algebraic sum of the deviations of the scores above and below it equals zero.

Some of you, encountering this demonstration for the first time, may be incredulous, insisting that the relationship ($\Sigma x = 0$) may hold for *some* cases, such as in the examples given where the maximum frequency in any class is one, but certainly not in *all* cases. If you are skeptical you can only be urged to demonstrate the phenomenon for yourself, with any set of numbers you choose, and you will see that the sum of the deviations from M is *always* zero.

Methods of Computation

The basic formula that defines a statistical concept, such as that for M, is usually relatively simple in appearance, but the process of actually applying it to data often turns out to be long and tedious. To minimize effort, so-called "computational formulas" are usually derived from the basic one. These often look more difficult (involve more symbols) but are timesavers when any statistic is actually to be computed. In the following sections, several computational formulas for M will be explained, in addition to the application of the basic one.

Computing M from ungrouped data. When M of ungrouped data is to be calculated, the basic definitional formula should be followed: the scores added and the results divided by the number of scores. An application of the basic formula is demonstrated in Table 5.1, which shows the number of trials taken by each of a group of 8 rats to make 10 successive correct runs in a maze.[1] This process is simple and should be followed if only a few scores are involved. If the number of measures is large, however, the method is prohibitively time-consuming. The use of frequency distributions, already found to be convenient for other purposes, will reduce our labor considerably in such instances.

[1] Tolman, E. C., Ritchie, B. F., and Kalish, D. Studies in spatial learning II. Place learning versus response learning. *J. exp. Psychol.*, 1946, 36, 221-229.

Computing M from a frequency distribution. A group of 124 college students was given a list of words to learn. The simple frequency distribution in Table 5.2 gives the number of trials these students took to reach one perfect recitation of the list. To obtain the mean number of trials required by the group to learn the list, we could add up all the individual scores and divide by 124. But note that most of the scores occur more than once. For example, two students learned in 5 trials and eight in 19 trials. Instead of summing all the individual scores, duplicates and all (e.g., adding eight 19's, two 5's), we could save time if we first multiplied each score by the number of individuals re-

TABLE 5.1

Calculation of M from Ungrouped Data. The scores represent trials to a learning criterion taken from eight experimental animals.

X
12
12
11
16
17
18
12
12
$\Sigma X = \overline{110}$

$$M = \frac{\Sigma X}{N} = \frac{110}{8} = 13.75$$

ceiving it. Thus 8×19 will result in the same answer as adding 19 eight times and give it to us quicker. If we then add all of the products (each the result, you remember, of multiplying every X by its corresponding frequency, f), we will have the sum of all the X's with far less labor than if we had summed each raw score separately. The remaining step needed to obtain M is the usual one: dividing the sum of the scores by N.

We can express these operations symbolically by amending the basic formula for M to take account of the fact that we are now dealing with a frequency distribution. The amended formula is reproduced below and a demonstration of its application is shown in Table 5.2.

$$M = \frac{\Sigma(fX)}{N}$$

where: Σ = the sum of the quantity that follows (here, all the fX's)
  X = the midpoint of a class interval
  (fX) = a midpoint multiplied by its corresponding frequency (f), i.e., by the number of cases within a class interval
  N = total number of cases, equal to the sum of the frequencies (Σf)

The formula can also be applied to a *grouped* frequency distribution, one in which the width of the class interval, i, is greater than one. This has been done in Table 5.3 using the same data as were utilized in the previous table, now grouped into class intervals with a width of 3. In applying the formula to grouped distributions, it should first be noted that the symbol X is now the *midpoint* of a class interval. Actually, X in the formula for M of a frequency distribution is always a midpoint, even when $i = 1$ as in Table 5.2. In the latter instance, we can think of a series of class intervals, each with a width of 1 (e.g., class 5, 6, and 7). Thus, each raw score, X, is in a sense its own midpoint.

Going back to Table 5.3, multiplication of each midpoint by its corresponding frequency (fX), as was done in Col. 3 of the table, gives the (approximate) total of the scores in each interval. By adding all of the entries in the fX column, we get $\Sigma(fX)$. This is equivalent to the ΣX that would have been obtained if ungrouped scores had been added together. M is determined, of course, simply by dividing $\Sigma(fX)$ by the total number of *cases*, N (*not* the number of class intervals).

While the foregoing method is convenient, the use of grouped frequency distributions introduces a source of error into the computation of M. Underlying its use is the assumption that all scores in a particular interval fall at the midpoint of the interval or, more accurately, that M of the scores in a specific interval is the same as the midpoint of the interval. If this is true, we can get the total of the scores in the interval by multiplying the

TABLE 5.2

Calculation of M from a Simple Frequency Distribution where $i = 1$.*
The data show number of trials to one perfect recitation of a serial
list of words.

X	f	fX
35	2	70
34	1	34
33	2	66
32	0	0
31	0	0
30	1	30
29	3	87
28	1	28
27	2	54
26	1	26
25	2	50
24	0	0
23	4	92
22	6	132
21	7	147
20	8	160
19	8	152
18	6	108
17	4	68
16	8	128
15	6	90
14	6	84
13	5	65
12	7	84
11	6	66
10	11	110
9	7	63
8	2	16
7	3	21
6	3	18
5	2	10
	$\Sigma f = 124$	$\Sigma fX = 2059$

$$M = \Sigma fX/N = 16.60$$

* Data taken from Elkin, A. *Personality as a variable in serial verbal learning.*
Ph.D. Dissertation, Northwestern University, 1950.

number of measures (f) by the midpoint (X).[2] This assumption is rarely fulfilled exactly. Take from Table 5.3, for example, the 4 scores in interval 29-31. Here we have assumed that M of these 4 scores is the midpoint 30 and that the sum of the scores therefore is 30×4 or 120. The actual raw scores happen to be 29, 29, 29, and 30. Thus, their actual M is 29.25, not the midpoint

TABLE 5.3

Calculation of M from a Grouped Frequency Distribution. The data are derived from Table 5.2.

CLASS INTERVAL	X	f	fX
35-37	36	2	72
32-34	33	3	99
29-31	30	4	120
26-28	27	4	108
23-25	24	6	144
20-22	21	21	441
17-19	18	18	324
14-16	15	20	300
11-13	12	18	216
8-10	9	20	180
5-7	6	8	48
		$\Sigma f = 124$	$\Sigma fX = 2052$

$$M = \frac{\Sigma fX}{N} = 16.55$$

30, and their total 117 rather than 120. Subtracting their true total of 117 from the estimated total of 120 shows us that our entry in the fX column is 3 units in error. The net effect of such errors on M of the total distribution is not great, however, when the following facts are considered. As can be seen from Figure 5.3, in the intervals below M the errors tend to be in the direction of underestimation, since scores usually pile up at the upper end of the interval, thus making the true M of the scores in the interval higher than the midpoint. For intervals above M, the opposite error more frequently occurs as scores tend to concen-

---

[2] Since $M = \Sigma X/N$, by rearrangement of terms, $\Sigma X = M(N)$. Thus, if M of the scores in a particular interval is equal to the value of the midpoint, the total of the scores in the interval (ΣX) can be found by multiplying the midpoint by the frequency [$\Sigma X = M(N)$].

trate at the lower part of the interval. Thus, when all intervals are considered together, the errors in one direction tend to cancel the errors in the other so that M for the total distribution is fairly close to the more accurate figure that would have been obtained had ungrouped data been used. A concrete illustration of this fact can be seen by comparing Tables 5.2 and 5.3. In the

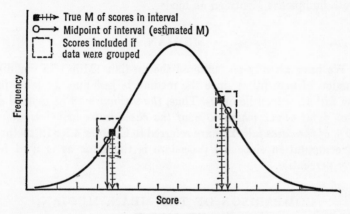

FIG. 5.3. A hypothetical simple frequency distribution showing the relationship of the true M of the scores within a class interval to the midpoint of that interval had the scores been grouped. The discrepancies have been exaggerated for the purpose of illustration.

former table M was obtained from a simple frequency distribution and found to be 16.60; in the second table, showing the same data in the form of a grouped distribution, M had a value of 16.55, an error of only .05.

MODE

The mode (Mo.) may either be computed or estimated roughly from inspection of the data. Estimation of the mode by inspection is the only method that we will be considering here.

In ungrouped data, the mode is defined as that score which occurs most frequently. For data grouped into class intervals, Mo. is the midpoint of the interval with the greatest frequency. Thus, in Table 5.1, showing ungrouped data, Mo. is 12, since this score occurs four times and all others only once. In Table

5.3 Mo. is 21, this score being the midpoint of the interval with the greatest frequency.

Occasionally a frequency distribution will have, like camels, not one hump, but two, thus indicating two points of maximum frequency rather than one. This type of curve is called bi-modal in contrast to the more usual uni-modal or single-peaked curve. Both humps are identified as modes.

MEDIAN

We have already encountered the median (Mdn.) in our discussion of percentiles since the median is just another label for the fiftieth percentile or Q_2. Thus, *the median may be defined as that point above which 50% of the cases fall and below which 50% of the cases fall.* You are referred to Chapter 4 for its method of computation since the procedure is the same as is used for any percentile.

COMPARISON OF THE MEAN, MEDIAN, AND MODE

In any uni-modal symmetrical distribution, the values of M, Mdn., and Mo. are the same. This is true because the same point on the baseline occurs most frequently (Mo.), divides the number of cases into the upper and lower 50% (Mdn.), and is the point of balance (M). As a curve departs from symmetry and becomes skewed, however, the values of the three measures of central tendency show differences. The relative positions of the three measures, however, will be the same for all single-peaked nonsymmetrical distributions, as shown in Figure 5.4. Mo. in any skewed distribution occurs, of course, at the highest point of the curve. M falls someplace toward the "tail" of the distribution. This can be understood if you remember that M is a "point of balance" and is therefore very sensitive to the extreme deviations contained in the tail. Mdn. in a skewed distribution lies between the M and Mo. Thus, the order of the three measures, when we start at the hump and proceed towards the tail, is always (1) Mo., (2) Mdn., and (3) M.

Because there is this relationship among the values of the three measures, we are ordinarily able to tell whether a distribution is skewed, and if so, the direction, merely by being told the values of any two measures of central tendency. If we read that M of a distribution was 26 and that Mdn. was also 26, we would infer that the distribution was symmetrical in shape since this

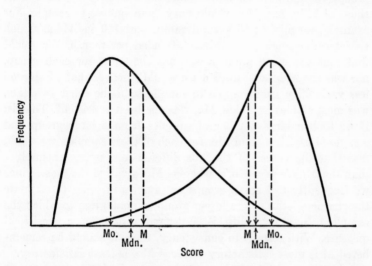

FIG. 5.4. The relationship between M, Mdn., and Mo. in skewed distributions

is the only case in which the measures coincide. But if we were told that M was 109 and Mo. from the same distribution 102, we would know that the distribution was positively skewed. That is, since M always lies closest to the "tail" in a skewed distribution and in this case is greater than Mo., the tail must be in the upper, positive, end of the scale. The value of Mdn. in this example could be roughly estimated—greater than 102 and less than 109 —since Mdn. always falls between M and Mo.

When to Use the M, Mdn., or Mo.

In deciding which measure of central tendency to compute, there are a number of factors to consider, including how much time is available, the characteristics of the particular set of data involved, and the purpose for which the measure is intended. Some of these considerations are discussed below.

Stability of the measures. The three measures of central tendency differ with respect to their consistency or stability from sample to sample. That is, if we tested a number of successive groups (or samples) of individuals, the values of M, as well as those of Mdn. and Mo., would vary from sample to sample. For example, we might poll several samples of 100 individuals each to determine number of movies attended per month. We would find that the mean number was not the same for each group, nor was the Mdn. or Mo. But we would discover that M showed less variability from sample to sample than the other two (i.e., was most stable) and that Mo. was the least consistent. That is, if we took a large number of samples from a large group and computed M, Mdn., and Mo. for each of these samples, we would find that the values of the M's differed less among themselves than the Mdn.'s and Mo.'s, whereas Mo.'s varied the most. Since we frequently test small groups or samples in order to estimate the characteristics of the larger group or population to which the sample belongs, stability is a desired virtue for a statistical measure. With respect to consistency, then, it should be remembered M is most satisfactory whereas Mo. is least satisfactory.

Subsequent manipulations of the data. In later chapters, we will discover that M may be used in further statistical operations that have not yet been discussed, thus yielding additional kinds of information about data. Mdn. and Mo., in contrast to M, are "terminal statistics"; once they are obtained, little more can be done with them. If more information is to be obtained from data than a measure of central tendency, computation of M becomes almost obligatory.

Time factors. A trivial but often practical consideration is the time taken to compute each measure. If a measure of central tendency is needed in a hurry, the Mo. can be rapidly obtained by inspection and would therefore be preferred over the other measures.

Characteristics of the data. 1. *Skewed distributions.* When a distribution is markedly nonsymmetrical, it is possible to give a distorted impression of the data when reporting central tendency. Take, for example, a frequency distribution of incomes in the United States. Such a distribution is extremely skewed in a positive direction, incomes trailing off, in terms of frequency, from the modest modal point to fabulous incomes of several million dollars each. The modal and median incomes will be much lower sums than M which is drawn far out towards the tail. It might be good anti-Communist propaganda to give M as the "average income in the U.S.," but it would give an uninformed reader, who is likely to assume that this figure ⌐epresents the most frequent income, or the income of the common man, a very inflated view of our personal wealth. A Communist, on the other hand, would be more likely to select Mo. to represent us since this measure would have the smallest value. Neither way is completely honest, of course, and what is usually done in the case of extremely skewed distributions is to report all three measures. From these, the direction and amount of skewness can be inferred by the reader and proper interpretation of the data made.

2. *Some special cases.* In some instances, unusual characteristics of the data, other than skewness, dictate the measure of central tendency to use. One peculiarity that sometimes occurs is that one extreme of a distribution is not available for testing. For example, if we gave an intelligence test to a sample of school children in order to estimate the central tendency of IQ's of *all* children of similar age, the lower extremes (feeble-minded) would not be represented in our sample, as these children are not in school.

In such a situation computation of M would yield a very distorted estimate of M for children in general since this measure is highly sensitive to extreme deviations and these are missing at the lower end. Mo. or Mdn. would be more appropriate, since each would give a closer estimate of the value of central tendency that would have been obtained if the lower extremes had been available.

Occasionally representative cases are available for testing but exact scores cannot be obtained from cases falling in one or both extremes of the distribution. An illustration of this can be drawn from learning experiments involving animals in which running-time from one end of a path to the other is used as a response measure. Often a few animals refuse to run and after sitting at the starting point for a period of time (e.g., 5 minutes) are removed from the apparatus. Their exact running-times are therefore unknown, since they might have run had they been left a second longer or they might have stayed there until the end of time. Since M requires the exact value of every measure, it should not be computed. Mdn. could be used, however, since an approximate score (5 minutes plus) for the extreme cases is sufficient.

Many further examples of very special situations in which one measure is appropriate (or inappropriate) could be given. Instead, you will merely be reminded that every set of data should be examined to determine whether any specific problems exist and which measure of central tendency would be most appropriate.

Specific purpose for which measure is intended. There are times when a measure of central tendency is to be put to some special use rather than intended to be a purely scientific description of data. Such a purpose will often determine the measure to be employed, especially when a distribution is skewed so that the values of the M, Mdn., and Mo. disagree markedly. Occasionally, the "typical case" is wanted, thus calling for Mo. A furniture manufacturer, hoping to make money on volume of sales might want to know the size of the typical living room, the modal dimensions, so that he could design furniture scaled to suit the largest single consumer market. At other times, the "middle case" is desired, the median individual. Test grades are sometimes given on this basis, Mdn. being the dividing line between B's and C's.

In summary, M is the most generally preferable measure of central tendency, particularly in a nearly symmetrical distribution, since it has the greatest stability and lends itself to further statistical manipulations. Mdn. is the middle case and is usually considered most appropriate when the distribution shows peculiarities: marked skewness, missing cases, and the like. Finally, Mo. is utilized in situations in which a quick, rough estimate of central tendency is sufficient or the typical case is wanted. While these are good general rules, remember that they are not exhaustive and that each set of data should be examined to see exactly which measure or measures are best in a specific situation or for a particular need.

6

Variability

NEED FOR AN INDEX OF VARIABILITY

Assume that two friends spent many hours on a golf driving range together. These men, Mac and Joe, decided to keep a record of the distances they each hit 500 balls. Markers on the range allowed them to make estimates of distances of their drives to the nearest 20 yards. Grouping the 500 drives into class intervals gave the two distributions as shown in Figure 6.1.

Now note that for the two hypothetical distributions, M's are equal; average length of drives for the two men is the same. Yet, it is obvious from looking at the two distributions that the two men differed in their shots. How do they differ? Before presenting the rather apparent answer to this question as shown by the graphs, let us look at another illustration.

Assume that a group of students in a public school was given an intelligence test. Assume further that the same test was given to a comparable age group in a private school. The two hypothetical distributions are shown in Figure 6.2. Again it can be seen that the two M's are the same. Like the golf drives for the two men, giving only M would leave the description incomplete for the IQ's.

Let us look first at what the differences in the distributions indicate about the two golfers. Mac is inconsistent; he sometimes hits the ball a mile and sometimes he barely rolls it off of the tee. Joe, on the other hand, is more predictable; he rarely dubs one badly but he never gets the tremendous distance that Mac sometimes does. And look at the two distributions of IQ's. In

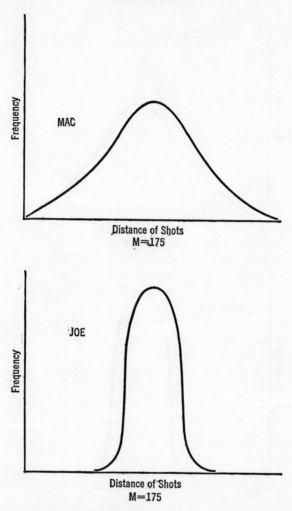

FIG. 6.1. Hypothetical distributions of 500 tee shots for two golfers

the public school there are a few children that might be classed as potential geniuses but there are also a few at the other extreme that are well on their way toward being first-class morons. In the private school there are no such extreme cases; all of the students are much more alike in regard to IQ than are those of

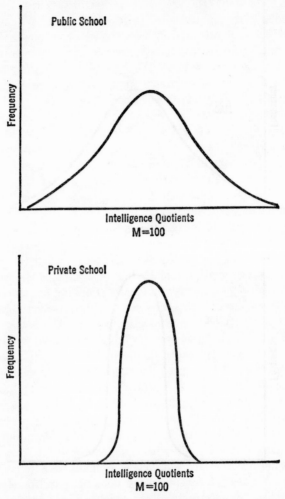

FIG. 6.2. Hypothetical distributions of IQ's for students in a public school and in a private school

the public school. The private-school students are said to be more *homogeneous* than the public-school group. Or, the latter group is said to be more *heterogeneous* than the private-school students.

What terms might be used to describe further the differences in the pairs of distributions in Figures 6.1 and 6.2? We might say that one has a greater spread than the other; a greater scatter, or dispersion, or, most commonly, greater *variability*. In the first illustration (the two golfers) the variability is *within* an individual, or the curves may be said to represent differences in *intra-individual variability*. That is, repeated measures of the same activity were taken on the same person and each curve indicates how much that person varies from moment to moment on the same task. In the case of the second set of distributions (IQ's) the values represent differences *among* individuals or *inter-individual variability*, since only one measure was obtained on each person. For most statistical purposes the differences between inter- and intra-individual variability are not important; they are important only in interpreting what those differences in variability indicate.

As statisticians we cannot be concerned primarily with the cause and effect relationships in the data with which we work. Inter-individual and intra-individual variability are so commonplace that we usually do not pause to ask ourselves the "why" of this variability. As psychologists we find that when we do ask such questions the answers we give are not very satisfying. Why is Mac so inconsistent in his tee shots? Why doesn't he always hit the ball 175 yards? Two shots, made 30 seconds apart, are quite different. Yet it is the same man, same club, same weather; many, many conditions seem to have remained the same. When we get right down to the bottom of the problem, all we can say is that there seems to be a basic variability of a single living organism for which we cannot, with our limited methods of observation, completely account. We must simply accept it. We do not consider it as uncaused; we merely admit our ignorance for specifying all the exact factors which caused it.

Causes of inter-individual variability are likewise difficult to specify in detail, but that they exist is apparent in all nature. Out of thousands of leaves on a tree, no two can be found that are identical; slight differences can be observed in the simple one-celled organisms, such as the amoeba; identical twins are really not identical or they could not be distinguished. The fact that an individual differs from moment to moment and that individual organisms differ from one another is a fundamental fact of nature and, of course, if such variability did not exist there would be little need for the statistics you will learn in this book. So, always keep in mind that such variability is to be expected and that most of our statistical concepts are intended to aid us in interpreting measures which demonstrate this fundamental fact of variability.

If we agree that differences in variability represent important differences that must be fully recognized if we are to describe distributions adequately, what statistics can be used? We shall discuss two, the *range* and the *standard deviation*.

RANGE (R)

As we have seen in Chapter 2, *the range* (R) *is simply the "distance" from the lowest to the highest score in a distribution.* Or, highest score minus lowest score is R. If the lowest IQ in a distribution is 65 and the highest 140, R is 75 (140 — 65 = 75). If the shortest drive in Mac's 500 shots is 40 yards and his longest 290, his golf range is 250 yards.

As a measure of variability R has much the same status as Mo. does as a measure of central tendency. It is useful only as a gross descriptive statistic, although, as we shall see later, it can form the basis for a quick and easy estimate of another statistic which requires considerable computation.

The most obvious difficulty with R as a measure of variability is that its value is wholly dependent upon the two extreme scores, and since these scores may be capricious, R will be equally capricious. This becomes quite evident when we are working with a small number of measures. In dealing with psychological data it is common to have no more than 20 or 30 cases in a group and by no means rare to have as few as 10 cases. Suppose we had 10 measures as follows: 11, 14, 14, 16, 19, 20, 21, 24, 26, 42. R is 42 — 11, or 31. Now if we eliminate the 10th case, R becomes 26 — 11, or 15. The elimination of one score halved the range. Of course, any measure of variability must represent changes in variability when these occur, but an ideal measure would not fluctuate so much as R does when a single score is eliminated as in the above case. As can be seen, R depends only upon two cases. These two cases, or perhaps only one of the two, may not be representative of the individual's performance. He may have been measured when he had a bad cold or a hangover. Since the size of R depends so heavily upon the performance of just one or two individuals within a group, we can see also why R would not be satisfactory if we wish precise comparisons of variability among groups. All things considered, therefore, we shall think of R as only a rough index of variability.

STANDARD DEVIATION (SD OR σ)

This is the first statistic we have met which requires several computational steps and which is, at the same time, a difficult statistic to visualize or picture. Therefore, we shall work into it gradually.

In the previous chapter we discussed the deviation of raw scores from M. For each score a deviation score, $X - M$ (raw score minus mean), can be calculated. The sum of these deviation scores above M is equal to the sum below M, signs disregarded. Furthermore, each of these deviations is symbolized by x, so that $X - M = x$. A little consideration will show you that these deviation scores could be used to reflect differences in variability. For illustration, let us take two distributions, A and B, of five scores each, which clearly differ in variability as indexed by R.

Dist. A		Dist. B	
X	x	X	x
23	−2	15	−10
24	−1	20	− 5
25	0	25	0
26	1	30	5
27	2	35	10
M = 25		M = 25	
R = 4		R = 20	

You will remember from the previous chapter that Σx (sum of the deviations from M) equals zero when added algebraically. For the moment, however, disregard the signs in the x columns and sum each for the two distributions. The sum for Dist. A is 6, for B, 30. Thus, the arithmetic sum of the x values reflects a difference in variability. We might divide each of these sums by N to get an *average* deviation, giving us an average deviation of 1.2 for A and 6 for B. Hence, the greater the variability the greater the average or mean deviation. Yet, for various reasons, the average deviation is rarely used as a measure of variability.

TABLE 6.1

Basic Steps in Calculating a Standard Deviation

X	x	x^2
16	5.5	30.25
14	3.5	12.25
12	1.5	2.25
11	.5	.25
10	— .5	.25
10	— .5	.25
9	—1.5	2.25
9	—1.5	2.25
8	—2.5	6.25
6	—4.5	20.25
$\Sigma X = \overline{105}$	$\Sigma x = \overline{0.0}$	$\Sigma x^2 = \overline{76.50}$

$$M = \frac{\Sigma X}{N} = \frac{105}{10} = 10.5$$

$$\sigma = \sqrt{\frac{\Sigma x^2}{N}} = \sqrt{\frac{76.50}{10}} = \sqrt{7.65} = 2.77$$

However, a few additional steps beyond the average deviation lead us to the *standard deviation*. The standard deviation is symbolized by the small Greek sigma, σ; or simply by the letters SD.

To obtain SD each deviation is first squared (a step which will make all signs positive). Then, all of the squared deviations are summed. Following this we divide the sum by N to obtain the mean of the squared deviations. Finally, to get the SD, the square root of this mean square deviation is obtained. This is the verbal description of SD; it is simply an average of certain deviation scores. To put the steps into symbolic form we have:

$$\sigma = \sqrt{\frac{\Sigma x^2}{N}}$$

To repeat: a deviation-from-the-mean score for each raw score is obtained. Each of these is squared and then all are summed—they are *not* summed and then squared. This sum-of-the-deviations-squared is divided by the number of cases and then the square root is taken. In total, SD is the root mean square deviation. Thus it is clearly a kind of average wherein each score is represented just as in the case of M.

It may be useful at this point to run through a complete computational procedure. The data in Table 6.1 were obtained from 10 subjects, each of whom learned a vocabulary list of 8 items. A complete presentation of all words was considered a trial; the number of trials required for each person to learn to perfection is the raw score (X). These raw scores have been ranked—although they need not be—and the basic computational steps shown.

Let us summarize the steps in the above calculations:
   (1)   Find M by summing the raw scores and dividing by N.
   (2)   Subtract M from each raw score to obtain each x. (The algebraic sum of these x's must equal zero or there is an error in calculating M or in subtracting.)
   (3)   Square each x value.
   (4)   Sum the x^2, and then substitute directly into the formula.

Meaning of SD

Before continuing with additional computational procedures, we need to discuss the meaning of SD. We know that SD is to be used as a statistic for describing variability within a distribution and also differences in variability among distributions. But, supposing we calculate SD for a distribution of scores and get a value of 5. What does this number mean? Five what? Is there any way to visualize this SD of a distribution? Let us see if there are satisfactory answers to these questions.

The SD may be thought of as a unit of measurement along the baseline of a frequency polygon. To see what this statement means, let us first remember that moving from left to right along the baseline of a polygon we plot scores in ascending order of size, from smallest to largest. If our class interval is only one, our steps along this scale are each one unit in width. We already know that R is a measure of width, the width being the total baseline between the highest and lowest scores. R, therefore, as a measure of variability, may certainly be thought of as a width measure. Now, it is this characteristic of width which also provides a method for visualizing SD and making its usefulness clear. The SD represents a width measurement which is neither as large as R nor as small as the width between two adjacent scores along the baseline. How wide, then, *is* SD? It is, of course, as wide as it is calculated to be for a given distribution, and it is expressed in raw-score units. If SD is 12, this means a width of 12 raw-score units. If SD is 5, this means a width of 5 raw-score units. Let us see how the width feature can be visualized.

In Figure 6.3 we have assumed M of 25 and SD of 5. We want to "lay off" the baseline in SD units. To do this we start at M and add one SD to the value of M. Since M is 25 and SD is 5, we add 25 and 5 to get 30. The *distance* between 25 and 30 is one SD; it has a width of 5 raw-score units. Most commonly this distance is called $+1\sigma$ ("plus one sigma"). It is "plus" because, we remember, all deviations above M are positive and those below, negative. The raw score of 30, therefore, is located at a point that is exactly one SD above M. Next, we add the value of SD to 30, obtaining 35, and the raw score 35 is said to be located at a point two SD's above M. And, the distance from M (25) to 35 is a width of $+2\sigma$'s. Adding one more SD to 35 makes 40 which is at a point three SD's above M and the total distance between M and 40 represents the width of $+3\sigma$'s. It will be noted in Figure 6.3 that a width of three SD's above M includes all or nearly all the cases in the distribution which lie above M. Therefore, in such an ideal, symmetrical distribution as the one in Figure 6.3, approximately three SD's will "cover the distance" between M and the highest score in the distribution.

To continue the above procedure we repeat our "laying down" of a succession of SD widths below M. Since the distribution is symmetrical we may expect that three SD's below M will approximately cover the distance. The actual points are obtained by subtracting 5 from 25, 5 from 20, and 5 from 15. These successive

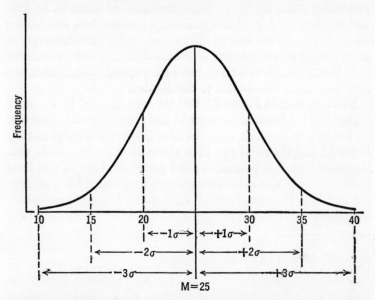

FIG. 6.3. Visualization of SD as a unit laid out along the baseline of a distribution in which M is 25 and SD is 5. The diagram shows that from 25 to 30 is plus 1 SD; from 25 to 35, plus 2 SD's; and so on.

widths are spoken of as -1σ ("minus one sigma"), -2σ's, and -3σ's.

We have seen that in a typical, symmetrical distribution, there are just about three SD's above M and three below. This must mean, of course, that R is made up of six SD's; or, SD is one-sixth of R. In any case, regardless of whether the distribution is symmetrical or skewed, SD may be visualized as a width measure and may be "laid off" as in Figure 6.3. It is apparent, however, that if the distribution is skewed we will not find three SD's above M and three below.

We are now aware that SD is a unit of width which is some

multiple of the raw-score width. For any given distribution the size of SD is a calculable value of fixed size. But clearly, SD may vary in absolute size from distribution to distribution. If R in one distribution is 24 and in another 48, we would not expect SD to be the same size for both. Now we are accustomed to think of our measuring scales for linear dimensions such as width to be fixed and unalterable. A yard is a yard and a foot is a foot, and neither varies in size. In the case of SD as a width measure, however, we must change this conception of the absolute value of a measuring unit. To repeat, SD is a given value for a specific distribution, but may vary from distribution to distribution.

You may note in Figure 6.3 that the area enclosed by the curve on top and the baseline between M and a point one SD above M on the bottom is larger than the area between the point one SD above M and the point two SD's above M. Also, this latter area is greater than that between a point two SD's above M and three SD's above M. The same relationships hold below M. This fact, the fact that the area "above" SD's differ, has certain implications for use of SD, but discussion of this will be postponed until the next chapter.

A Check on Gross Calculation Errors

A check on computational errors is an important asset when figuring SD's. Such a check is provided by the fact that SD is about one-sixth of R. Beginning statisticians often make such horrendous arithmetical errors in calculating SD that it is worth while exploring the relationship between R and SD as a means of avoiding such gross errors. The check is provided by examining your calculated SD to see if it is approximately one-sixth of R. After you have calculated several SD's you will begin to get the "feel" of them in relationship to the distribution of scores from which they have been calculated. You will quickly find out that if R of your distribution is 24 and your calculated SD is 25, something is wrong with your calculations since SD is larger than R. Or, if you have R of 24 and you obtain SD of 1, something has also gone wrong with your calculations. But we must stress now, and stress emphatically, that we don't calculate SD by taking one-sixth of R; rather, *after* we have calculated SD we check to see if its value is approximately one-sixth of R. Of course this provides only a very crude check, unless the number of measures is very large and the distribution quite symmetrical and shaped like Figure 6.3. However, so many sets of data are distributed like those of Figure 6.3 that we will find our check has considerable usefulness. The number of measures involved provides a special problem to which we will now turn.

The ratio of 6:1 between SD and R holds only when N is large. When N is small there will be less than six SD's in R. Why should this be? The reason is simply that the greater the number of cases we draw the more likely we are to get the extreme scores—those at the tails of the distributions. Clearly, then, R should increase as N increases. What happens to SD as N increases? Many students quickly answer that SD decreases as N increases. This isn't so, as you will realize if you examine the basic components of the formula, namely, $\frac{\Sigma x^2}{N}$. As N increases, both the numerator and the denominator, Σx^2 and N, also increase. For, as we add another case we also have its x^2 to add to the Σx^2. Of course, if these two components increase proportionately, SD should remain constant. As a matter of fact, that pretty nearly describes the situation, but not quite. As N increases from a very small value, there will be some increase in the size of SD. This occurs for the following reason. As we increase N from a very small value, we are more likely to pick up those extreme cases (as discussed above). And, these extreme cases add more to the Σx^2 than they do to N, simply because their deviations are bigger than those we have gotten for those cases near the middle of the distribution. So, we may expect some increase in SD with increases in N, but overall, when N is fairly large to start with, say 20 to 30, we will expect little further increase with increasing N.

If we accept the general principle that R increases fairly sharply as N increases, and SD increases less sharply, it means that the ratio between R and SD must increase as N increases. That is, R/SD increases with increases in N. As mentioned above, with large N's, this ratio is about six and is a useful rough check on our computational accuracy. We may also have such checks when N is not large. Figure 6.4 gives the number of SD's in R

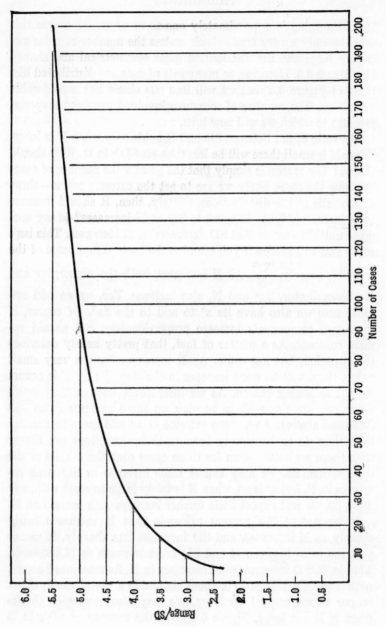

FIG. 6.4. Curve for making a rough check on accuracy of calculation of SD. For complete explanation see text.

(R/SD) for N from 5 to 200.[1] Actually, of course, only certain points are plotted but the smoothed curve will give an approximate check on SD for any size distributions from 5 to 200.

This is the way to use Figure 6.4. Suppose we calculated SD for a fairly symmetrical distribution of 30 cases and get SD of 5. We note that R is 20. Hence R/SD is 4. Now, we look on the abscissa (horizontal axis) at 30, look directly above until we hit the curve, then cross over to the ordinate where we see that 4 is about the proper ratio for this N. Take another illustration. With 90 cases, and R of 40, we get SD of 3. Something is wrong; the ratio should be approximately 5, whereas from our calculations it is about 13.

We must add a final word of caution about estimating SD from R. The check on correctness of SD provided by Figure 6.4 is crude; if the calculated SD is 14 and Figure 6.4 indicates that it should be 15 or 16, we should not get upset. The difference between our calculated SD and estimated SD would have to be greater than this before we would suspect an error in arithmetic. There is, of course, no way to tell exactly how much difference there must be between calculated and estimated SD before we should suspect a computational error. But the use of Figure 6.4 will help to avoid gross errors, and that is all it is intended to do.

FURTHER COMPUTATIONAL TECHNIQUES

SD from Frequency Distribution

In the one illustration we have given of the computation of SD (Table 6.1), we used ungrouped data. Just as in computing M we may group the data and add a frequency (f) column. Such a problem is worked out in Table 6.2. The first three columns are those we use customarily to obtain M. The fourth column, x, is the deviation of each raw score from M, and the fifth column gives the squares of these deviation scores. The final column is the frequency of each raw score multiplied by the square of the deviation of each raw score from M, or, fx^2. The sum of this column gives the total of all fx^2 values.

[1] Tippet, L. H. C. On the extreme individuals and the range of samples taken from a normal population. *Biometrika*, 1925, 17, 364-387.

Raw-Score Method

In many sets of data obtained from psychological experiments, the number of cases is too few to warrant grouping. Furthermore, the use of deviation scores (x) is fairly tedious, and because

TABLE 6.2

Calculation of SD with Grouped Data and Deviation Scores

X	f	fX	x	x^2	fx^2
11	3	33	4.37	19.10	57.30
10	3	30	3.37	11.36	34.08
9	12	108	2.37	5.62	67.44
8	15	120	1.37	1.88	28.20
7	23	161	.37	.14	3.22
6	24	144	$-$ .63	.40	9.60
5	13	65	-1.63	2.66	34.58
4	10	40	-2.63	6.92	69.20
3	5	15	-3.63	13.18	65.90

$$N = \overline{108} \; \Sigma fX = \overline{716} \qquad \Sigma fx^2 = \overline{369.52}$$

$$M = \frac{\Sigma fX}{N} = \frac{716}{108} = 6.63$$

$$\sigma = \sqrt{\frac{\Sigma fx^2}{N}} = \sqrt{\frac{369.52}{108}} = \sqrt{3.42} = 1.85$$

decimals usually result in subtracting M from X (to obtain x), many opportunities for errors are present. It is often more convenient to use what is commonly called a raw-score formula for calculating SD. This formula is as follows:

$$\sigma = \sqrt{\frac{\Sigma X^2}{N} - \left(\frac{\Sigma X}{N}\right)^2} \text{ and, since } \frac{\Sigma X}{N} = M, \; \sigma = \sqrt{\frac{\Sigma X^2}{N} - M^2}$$

Origin of raw-score formula. It will be worth while to see just how this formula came about. Knowing this, you will have at least one formula that need not be taken on faith and you will get a little understanding of the derivation of formulas. We start, of course, with the basic formula for SD:

$$\sigma = \sqrt{\frac{\Sigma x^2}{N}}$$

The first step is to square both sides of the equation, obtaining $\sigma^2 = \dfrac{\Sigma x^2}{N}$. Incidentally, the quantity represented by the symbol, σ^2, is called the *variance*, a statistic which has a great deal of use in more advanced statistical techniques and which will be discussed in Chapter 12. But, let us get back to the derivation. We know that $x = X - M$, so we substitute this to get:

$$\sigma^2 = \frac{\Sigma(X - M)^2}{N}$$

Now, to expand the term, by squaring $X - M$:

$$\sigma^2 = \frac{\Sigma(X^2 - 2MX + M^2)}{N}$$

And, placing the summation sign and N with each term gives:

$$\sigma^2 = \frac{\Sigma X^2}{N} - \frac{2M\Sigma X}{N} + \frac{\Sigma M^2}{N}$$

Looking at the second term on the right hand side, we can see that a portion of it is $\dfrac{\Sigma X}{N}$, which we know equals M. So, substituting M for $\dfrac{\Sigma X}{N}$, gives us:

$$\sigma^2 = \frac{\Sigma X^2}{N} - 2(M)(M) + \frac{\Sigma M^2}{N}$$

which reduces to:

$$\sigma^2 = \frac{\Sigma X^2}{N} - 2M^2 + \frac{\Sigma M^2}{N}$$

Now, look at the last term, $\dfrac{\Sigma M^2}{N}$. We know that Σ means summation from the first to the last score in a distribution, so that in effect, $\Sigma = N$. Therefore the last term could be $\dfrac{NM^2}{N}$. If these N's are cancelled, we have:

$$\sigma^2 = \frac{\Sigma X^2}{N} - 2M^2 + M^2$$

and then, $-2M^2 + M^2 = -M^2$, so:

$$\sigma^2 = \frac{\Sigma X^2}{N} - M^2$$

Taking the square root of both sides produces the formula for raw score calculation of SD, namely: $\sigma = \sqrt{\dfrac{\Sigma X^2}{N} - M^2}$

The final step shall be to give concrete proof that this formula is equivalent to the basic formula for SD, $\sqrt{\dfrac{\Sigma x^2}{N}}$. We will use the data in Table 6.1, for which we have already worked the SD by the deviation method. The SD (2.77) in Table 6.3 is exactly the same value obtained in Table 6.1 by the deviation method.

TABLE 6.3

Calculation of SD by the Raw-Score Method

X	X²
16	256
14	196
12	144
11	121
10	100
10	100
9	81
9	81
8	64
6	36
$\Sigma X = \overline{105}$	$\Sigma X^2 = \overline{1179}$

$$M = \frac{105}{10} = 10.5$$

$$\sigma = \sqrt{\frac{\Sigma X^2}{N} - M^2} = \sqrt{\frac{1179}{10} - (10.5)^2} = \sqrt{117.9 - 110.25} = \sqrt{7.65} = 2.77$$

This raw-score formula is very useful especially when the raw scores are not so large that the squares become unmanageable. For calculational purposes in order to reduce the size of the raw scores (hence reduce the size of the scores squared), investigators often subtract a constant (that is, the same number) from all scores. For example, suppose the lowest score in a distribution is 103 and the highest, 194. R for this distribution is 91. Now, let us subtract a constant from all scores. A nice round number would be 100. If we subtracted 100 from all scores, the range will now be from 3 to 94, still a range of 91. As you may suspect, if R doesn't change in this situation we won't expect SD to change; by subtracting a constant from all scores we simply move the whole distribution "down the scale" by the amount of the constant. Thus we may calculate SD from these smaller numbers and come out with the same value as would be obtained with the large scores. You will probably be most satisfied on this point if you set up a sample problem in which you calculate SD with and without a constant subtracted.

TABLE 6.4

Calculation of SD by Raw-Score Method with Grouped Data *

CLASS INTERVAL	f	X	fX	fX^2
62-64	1	63	63	3969
59-61	4	60	240	14400
56-58	23	57	1311	74727
53-55	47	54	2538	137052
50-52	47	51	2397	122247
47-49	30	48	1440	69120
44-46	14	45	630	28350
41-43	5	42	210	8820
	$N = 171$		$\Sigma fX = 8829$	$\Sigma fX^2 = 458685$

$$M = \frac{\Sigma fX}{N} = \frac{8829}{171} = 51.63$$

$$\sigma = \sqrt{\frac{\Sigma fX^2}{N} - M^2} = \sqrt{\frac{458685}{171} - (51.63)^2} = \sqrt{2682.37 - 2665.66} =$$

$$\sqrt{16.71} = 4.09$$

* Data from Rothe, H. F. Output rates among butter wrappers: II. Frequency distributions and an hypothesis regarding the "restriction of output." *J. appl. Psychol.*, 1946, 30, 320-327.

Grouped data. The raw-score formula may also be used with grouped data. All we do is add a frequency column to the work sheet. An illustration is worked out in detail in Table 6.4. These data show the varying number of pounds of butter wrapped in wax paper by a single operator during 15-minute work periods. The data are for 171 such work periods. In this table we have placed the f column before the X column so that our multiplica-

tion is always for adjacent columns. The main job is to get the
ΣX^2. To do this we first multiply each f by X and so obtain the
ΣfX's, from which we get M. Then we multiply each value in the
X column by the corresponding value in the fX column. The result of this multiplication gives fX^2, the sum of which we substitute directly into the formula.

z-SCORES

Thus far we have discussed three different width measurements of a frequency distribution. These are R, SD, and the raw-
score unit, the latter which is used directly in constructing a frequency polygon. And, we have seen how we can roughly translate
from R to SD, and SD to R, because of the 6:1 ratio between these
two measures.

We now ask about translating from the SD scale to the raw-
score scale, and from the raw-score scale to the SD scale. Take the
simplest example: If we want to translate feet into yards we
divide the number of feet by three. If we want to change ounces
to pounds we divide the number of ounces by 16. In the same
fashion exactly, if we want to change a raw-score distance into
SD units, we divide the distance by SD. Of course, we have to
have a reference or zero point. This reference point is M, for we
know that we always "lay off" SD units by starting at M. Now
then, suppose we have a raw score of 62 in a distribution in
which M is 50 and SD is 8. This raw score is 12 raw-score units
above M, i.e., $62 - 50 = 12$. To translate this distance into SD
units we simply divide by SD, or, $12/8 = 1.5$. So, a raw score
of 62 is 1.5 SD's above M. This value, that is, *a value which
indicates how far a raw score deviates from M in SD units, is
called a z-score*. If we put the steps in equation form we have:

$$z = \frac{X - M}{\sigma}$$

But, since $X - M$ is also x, we can write the formula as:

$$z = \frac{x}{\sigma}$$

In the sample we worked out above, the steps were $62 - 50/8 =$ $+1.5$. For a raw score of 56 in this same distribution:

$$z = \frac{56 - 50}{8} = \frac{+6}{8} = +.75$$

If a raw score is below M, the z-score is given a minus value. For example, in this same distribution, what is the z-score of a raw score of 42?

$$z = \frac{42 - 50}{8} = \frac{-8}{8} = -1.00$$

Thus, for this distribution, a raw score of 42 lies at a point that is exactly the distance of one SD below M.

We can see that in the typical distribution where there are three SD's above M and three below, the largest z-score we can obtain will be 3.0, either plus or minus. And, if a raw score lies exactly at M, $z = 0$. Therefore, z-scores will normally range from -3.0 through zero to $+3.0$.

Changing raw-score distances into SD distances is not done merely to give practice in arithmetic. These z-scores have very definite uses. The need sometimes arises to compare the same person with himself in two different distributions of scores. If a class takes a test of intelligence and a test of mechanical aptitude, we might want to know the relative standing of an individual on both tests. If both tests have the same M and SD, and neither is badly skewed, the raw scores can be compared directly. This would be a rare case. More likely, the two distributions would have different M's and SD's. A raw score of 60 on one test will probably mean quite a different thing from a raw score of 60 on another.

One quite satisfactory way of making the above comparison is by the rank of the individual on each test. This, in effect, is what a percentile rank is. If on one test a student has a percentile rank of 78 and on the other 62, we know that he has done better on the first test than on the second. We may use z-scores for this same purpose of comparing two scores in distributions in which SD's are different. Suppose that a class is given the mechanical aptitude test and the intelligence test as suggested above, and suppose we get the following:

	M	SD
Mechanical Apt.	100	10
Intelligence	60	6

A student gets a raw score of 69 on the intelligence test and 75 on the mechanical test. His z-score for the former is:

$$z = \frac{x}{\sigma} = \frac{9}{6} = +1.5$$

and for the latter:

$$z = \frac{-25}{10} = -2.5$$

He is much worse on the mechanical aptitude test than on the intelligence test even though the raw score is higher for the mechanical test. For, his z-score on the mechanical test is nearly at the bottom of the distribution, being 2.5 SD's below M, while considerably above M on the intelligence test. The pattern of aptitude shown by this student would recommend that he go to college rather than try doing something useful.

Table 6.5 shows two distributions of test grades obtained from the same 18 graduate students in psychology. One test was an examination in advanced statistics and the other was concerned pretty much with principles of psychology. The range and SD are about the same for the two tests but the M's are quite different. Comparing raw scores doesn't mean very much. For example, the first student got about the same raw score on both tests, while on the principles test he is about one-half SD below M and on the statistics test he is above M. Student number six got quite different raw scores but about the same z-scores. In brief, by translating raw scores to z-scores, direct comparisons of position in the group can be made easily.

We have seen how to translate a raw score, expressed in a raw-score unit, into a z-score, expressed in an SD unit. Now, we can reverse this procedure so that if we know a z-score we can obtain the raw score. It is the simple case of solving for an

TABLE 6.5

Calculation of z-Scores on Two Tests given to 18 Graduate Students. One Test Measured Knowledge of Principles of Psychology, the other, Advanced Statistical Knowledge.

STUDENT NUMBER	PRINCIPLES X	X-M	z	STATISTICS X	X-M	z
1	66	− 6.17	− .55	65	3.67	.29
2	79	6.83	.61	71	9.67	.76
3	86	13.83	1.23	72	10.67	.84
4	58	−14.17	−1.26	44	−17.33	−1.36
5	75	2.83	.25	63	1.67	.13
6	69	− 3.17	− .28	57	− 4.33	− .34
7	100	27.83	2.47	82	20.67	1.62
8	66	− 6.17	− .55	71	9.67	.76
9	64	− 8.17	− .72	45	−16.33	−1.28
10	65	− 7.17	− .64	46	−15.33	−1.20
11	73	.83	.07	61	− .33	− .03
12	54	−18.17	−1.61	73	11.67	.92
13	62	−10.17	− .90	35	−26.33	−2.07
14	80	7.83	.69	64	2.67	.21
15	81	8.83	.78	62	.67	.05
16	60	−12.17	−1.08	50	−11.33	− .89
17	80	7.83	.69	62	.67	.05
18	81	8.83	.78	81	19.67	1.54

$M = 72.17$
$R = 46$
$SD = 11.27$

$M = 61.33$
$R = 47$
$SD = 12.73$

unknown. Let's illustrate this with the very poor score made by the student on the mechanical aptitude test. His z-score was −2.5, and we solve as follows:

$$z = -2.5 = \frac{X - M}{\sigma}$$

$$-2.5 = \frac{X - 100}{10}$$

Multiplying both sides of the equation by 10: $-25 = X - 100$
$$X = 100 - 25$$
$$X = 75$$

For those who don't like to go through even these simple algebraic equations, we can give a simple, straightforward, and pat formula for obtaining a raw score from a z-score. This formula is:

$$X = z\sigma + M$$

If we apply this to the above illustration again we get:

$$X = (-2.5)(10) + 100$$
$$X = -25 + 100$$
$$X = 75$$

Finally, we should look ahead and point out that the idea of z-scores has great importance for other statistical operations with which we will deal in subsequent chapters. By the "idea" of z-scores we mean the expression of a deviation of a given value from M in terms of SD units.

7

The Normal Distribution Curve

THE PROBLEM

So far we have learned methods that may be used to *describe* distributions of data. In trying to make a set of scores meaningful to someone else, usually the first thing we do is present the *descriptive statistics*, that is, a measure of central tendency and a measure of variability. But often this is not enough; we almost always want more information from a distribution than can be obtained from descriptive statistics alone. We can illustrate what we mean by the following example.

In a study [1] dealing with various athletic skills, 203 men students at the University of California were measured as to how far they threw a baseball. The M was 164.1 feet and SD was 22.8 feet. With only this information we could answer some questions immediately, e.g., we know that the average (mean) student should have no trouble throwing from third base to home plate (90 feet). But consider the following questions: How many men in this group could throw to home plate from a spot 200 feet away in center field? What proportion of the men could not throw farther than 130 feet? Anyone who qualifies among the top 10 per cent of the men must be able to throw at least how far? What distances are so extreme that they are thrown by only 1 per cent of the men? What is the probability that someone picked at random from this group could throw 225 feet or more? We can readily see that such questions cannot be answered, knowing only

[1] Cozens, F. W. The measurement of general athletic ability in college men. *Physical Education Series*, 1, No. 3, Univ. of Oregon Press, 1929.

83

M and SD. To answer such questions we need to know the properties of a particular distribution called the *normal distribution*, one of the most important tools in statistics. We shall find that this distribution, commonly called *the normal curve*, is basic to nearly everything to be studied throughout the rest of this book.

Let us anticipate an objection you may raise. You could say, "If I had the raw data in the baseball-throwing distribution, I could answer all those questions without using further statistical techniques," and you would be correct. But suppose we asked you to assume that the 203 men who were measured are representative of the total group of several thousand men at the University of California, and then asked you to answer all those questions for that total group. Then, as will be more fully explained in the next chapter, knowledge about the normal curve is essential. Since we shall be concerned in this chapter only with explaining the normal curve and its properties, we shall, for convenience, deal mostly with groups that have been measured, like the 203 men.

THE NORMAL CURVE

The normal curve is shown in Figure 7.1. Let us examine the curve and note some of its characteristics. The most obvious thing about the normal distribution is its *shape*, somewhat like a bell, rising to a rounded peak in the middle and tapering off

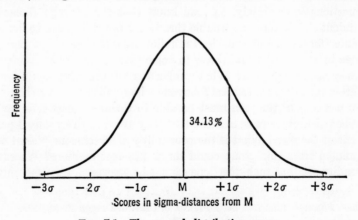

FIG. 7.1. The normal distribution curve

symmetrically at both tails. *The normal curve is a frequency distribution curve;* therefore, as we learned in Chapter 3, the ordinate or Y axis indicates frequency and the abscissa or X axis indicates units of measurement or scores. (As will be seen later, in the normal curve the units along the baseline are SD units, *z*-scores.) We can see that in the normal curve *both* low scores and high scores (extreme left and right on the X axis) are infrequent. Scores near the middle of the X axis, those close to M, occur frequently. Suppose, for example, height of adult men is normally distributed. If this is true, few men are either very short or very tall; most men are of medium height. No matter whether the trait is athletic ability, height, intelligence, the ability to tolerate frustration, or any other measurable characteristic, if the trait is distributed normally, there will be more people with an average amount of the trait than any other amount, and the further a score deviates from M the fewer the people making that score.

The normal curve is not a distribution of actual data because it was not obtained by measuring something. It is a theoretical distribution, a mathematical equation. Figure 7.1 is the curve plotted from the equation. But there is an infinite variety of curve shapes and we could plot any shape we wished by choosing the appropriate equation. The normal curve is symmetrical but there are many symmetrical distributions—U-shaped, rectangular-shaped, and so forth. It is clear that we are giving special emphasis to the normal curve, so a question is in order: Since the scientist deals mostly with *empirical* distributions, that is, *distributions obtained by actually measuring something,* why is the normal curve so important? *The answer is that many empirical distributions are distributed like the normal curve.* The research worker often finds that the frequency polygon plotted from his data is bell-shaped, especially if he has measured a fairly large number of cases. Figure 7.2 will serve as one example. The figure shows the distribution of scores made by 1000 college students (713 men, 287 women from five colleges in New York City) on a cancellation task.[2] The students cancelled the letter A

[2] Anastasi, A. Practice and variability: A study in psychological method. *Psychol. Monogr.,* 1933-34, 45, No. 5.

each time it appeared printed among other letters. The score for each student was the number of A's cancelled in four minutes. Note that the curve is approximately normal; it looks a good deal like the true normal curve in Figure 7.1.

Although Figure 7.2 is only one example of an empirical distribution that is roughly normal, many other characteristics in both the biological and social sciences, when measured, are found to be approximately normally distributed. Whenever a set of data *is* distributed approximately normally, the normal curve is very useful because we can use it to help us get a good deal of infor-

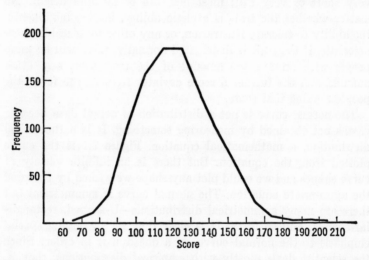

Fig. 7.2. Distribution of scores of 1000 college students on a cancellation task

mation from the data. As we shall soon see, by applying the properties of the normal curve to empirical distributions, we shall not only be able to answer questions of the type asked earlier with reference to the baseball-throwing distribution, but many other questions as well.

Characteristics of the Normal Curve

Look at Figure 7.1 again. The total *area* under the curve, that is, the area between the curve and the baseline, is taken as 100%.

If we draw two lines from the baseline up to the curve (as is shown in the figure), one line at M and the other at the point that is one SD above M, we have enclosed a portion of the total area. Now in *any* curve, normal or any other shape, the portion of the total area under the curve between M and the point that is one SD above M is always the same for that particular curve. In other words, for any single curve, regardless of its shape, there is a fixed relationship between distance along the baseline, measured in SD units, and area under the curve. In the *normal* curve the area under the curve between M and + 1SD turns out to be 34.13% of the total area. *Now the percent area is the same as the percent frequency;* therefore, we know immediately that in the normal curve 34.13% of the total frequency is included between M and the point that is one SD above M. *When distance along the baseline is measured in SD units, percent area under the normal curve between M and any other point is the same as percent frequency.* Recall that SD units are z-scores; the score that is one SD above M is the score where $z = +1.00$. Thus we can restate what we have just said in z-score terms; in the normal curve the percent frequency between M and the point where $z = +1.00$ is 34.13.

Since the normal curve is symmetrical, another 34.13% of the frequency lies between M and the point one SD below M, between M and $z = -1.00$. Therefore 68.26% of the cases falls between $z = -1.00$ and $z = +1.00$. From M to the point two SD's above M is 47.72% of the frequency, so 95.44% falls between $z = -2.00$ and $z = +2.00$. Three SD's above and below M, 6 SD's in all, include 99.74%, or almost all, of the total frequency.

Let us illustrate what we have said. If the weight distribution for 10,000 men were exactly normal, 3,413 men (34.13% of N) would fall between the mean weight and the weight that was one SD above M. Take as another example the distribution of cancellation scores shown in Figure 7.2, where N = 1000, M = 120.90 and SD = 20.40. If that distribution were exactly normal, 34.13%, or 341 students, should score between 120.90 and 141.30 (120.90 + 20.40, the score where $z = +1.00$). The actual number scoring between the two values was about 330, not too different from the frequency of 341 predicted from the normal curve.

Since 68.26% of the frequency in the normal curve falls between $z = -1.00$ and $z = +1.00$, we should find, if the cancellation distribution is normal, that 682.6 or 683 students got cancellation scores between 100.50 and 141.30 (the raw scores that are, respectively, one SD below and one SD above M). The actual number is about 680.

As a final illustration, consider the distribution of measurements of chest circumference of American women. Since all women have not been measured, the actual M and SD are not known. But the results of several studies [3] permit us to estimate that M of this distribution is about 35 inches, with $SD = 3$ inches. Probably the distribution is sufficiently normal to permit us to predict that about 95% of American women would achieve, naturally, scores between 29 and 41 inches (M $-$ 2 SD's and M $+$ 2 SD's). Almost all women would score between 26 inches $(35 - 9)$ and 44 inches $(35 + 9)$; i.e., between $z = -3.00$ and $z = +3.00$.

The Normal Curve Table

The percent area under the normal curve, and therefore the percent frequency, between M and various SD-distances from M is shown in Table B at the back of the book. This table will be used repeatedly from now on. Let us examine the table and determine how to read it. The left-hand column, labeled x/σ, *gives deviations from M in SD units.* Remember that x stands for the deviation of a score from M of the distribution containing the score: $x = X - M$. Dividing the deviation, x, by SD of the given distribution, σ, tells us how far the score deviates from M in SD units. But $(X - M)/\sigma$ is the definition of z, therefore *the values in the left-hand column in Table B are z-scores.* An x/σ value, or z-score, of 1.00 indicates a raw score that deviates one SD from its M; an x/σ value of 2.58 indicates a raw score that deviates 2.58 SD's from M, and so forth.

The values in the x/σ column in Table B are given to one decimal place; the second decimal place is shown in the top row

[3] *Handbook of Human Engineering Data for Design Engineers.* Tufts College Institute for Applied Experimental Psychology. Special Devices Center, Technical Report No. SDC 199-1-1, 1949.

of the table. The values in the body of the table are the *percent area* or *percent frequency* between M and the point x/σ distant from M. For example, if we wished to determine the percentage of the total frequency between M and the point 1.96 SD's above M, we would first find the value of 1.9 in the x/σ column, then go along that row to the column headed .06 and read off the percent frequency, which in this case is 47.50%.

Note that the table gives percentages only on *one* side of the M, that is, for only one-half of the normal curve, so none of the values in the table is larger than 50%. Because the normal curve is symmetrical it is not necessary to print another table of the percentages for the other half of the curve; the percent frequency between M and any x/σ value is the same whether the x/σ value is above or below M, whether the z-score is plus or minus.

Using the Normal Curve Table to Solve Problems

Let us now take up some problems involving real data and show how the normal curve table can be used to solve them. It may be helpful to state our general procedure first. On the assumption that our empirical distribution is normal, or approximately so, the relation shown in Table B between percent frequency and z-score in the normal curve also holds for the empirical distribution. But the raw scores in an empirical distribution may be in any kind of units, such as feet, seconds, letters cancelled per four minutes, and the like. In the normal curve the units are z-scores, x/σ values. Therefore, we shall have to convert the raw score from the empirical distribution, given us in the problem, into a z-score or x/σ value, and then immediately Table B becomes applicable. Let us see how this works.

Consider the distribution of distances a baseball was thrown, given early in this chapter, where N = 203, M = 164.1 ft. and SD = 22.8 ft. Since it will not affect the method we are illustrating, we shall make the data more convenient to handle by rounding off M to 164 ft. and SD to 23 ft., although we would not do this in actual practice. *The first question* we asked concerning this distribution was: How many men in this group could throw to home plate from a spot 200 ft. away in center field? This problem simply asks how many men (a frequency)

could throw 200 ft. *or more* (because anyone who can throw
farther than 200 ft. can also throw 200 ft.). This problem is
shown graphically in Figure 7.3; it will help to study this figure
in connection with the following. The raw score of 200 ft. must
first be converted to an x/σ value: $x/\sigma = (200 - 164)/23 =$
$+1.57$. (We use the $+$ sign to indicate that the raw score with
which we are dealing is above M.) From Table B, 44.18% of
the frequency are included *between* M and the x/σ value $+1.57$,
therefore 5.82% $(50 - 44.18)$ remain *beyond* $+1.57$. We now
have the answer to the problem in percent frequency but we
were asked for the actual number of men, the raw frequency.

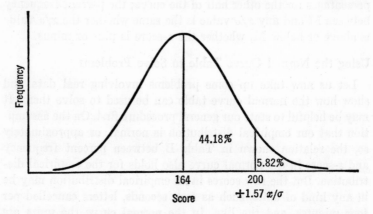

Fig. 7.3. Per cent frequency above a score of 200 ft. in the baseball-
throwing data, assuming normality of distribution

Since there were 203 men, 5.82%, or about 11 men, can throw
200 ft. or more.

The second question asked was: What proportion of the men
could not throw farther than 130 ft.? Again, note carefully what
this question asks for: the proportion of men whose longest
throw was 130 ft. or *less,* in other words, all those who cannot
throw more than 130 ft. Converting the raw score to a z-score,
$(130 - 164)/23$, we get $x/\sigma = -1.48$. From Table B we find that
between M and $x/\sigma = -1.48$ are 43.06%, so 6.94% remain beyond this x/σ value. This is the answer in percentage; to convert
to proportion move the decimal point two places to the left, thus

.0694 is the proportion of men who could not throw farther than 130 ft.

The third question was: Anyone who qualifies among the top 10% of the men must be able to throw at least how far? Note the difference between this question and the previous ones. Instead of being given a raw score and ending up with a percent frequency or a raw frequency as we did in the two previous problems, here we are given a percent frequency (10%) and are asked for a raw score. Thus we shall go through the same steps as before but in the opposite direction. We must first find, from Table B, the z-score, or x/σ value, *beyond* which 10% of the cases fall, because the problem asks for the top 10%. Remember that Table B gives frequencies *from* M *to* a particular x/σ; therefore we must find in the body of the table the value 40%; this will give us the z-score beyond which 10% remain. The closest value to 40% we can find in Table B is 39.97%, which corresponds to $x/\sigma = +1.28$. We now know that the top 10% of the men deviate at least 1.28 SD's above M but the problem asks for a raw score, so we must convert the z-score of 1.28 into a raw score. Recall that we can transpose terms in the z-score formula $(z = (X - M)/\sigma)$ to get $X = z\sigma + M$. Since SD is 23 ft., these men deviate 29 ft. from M $(1.28 \times 23 = 29.44)$. Adding this value to M (164 ft.), we find that the top 10% of the men can throw at least 193 ft. You should note again that the steps in this problem are the same as in the previous two problems but we went through them in reverse order.

The fourth question, What distances are so extreme that they are thrown by only 1% of the men, also gives us a percent frequency and asks us to find a score. But unlike the previous questions, this problem does *not* tell us whether it is high scores or low scores that are desired. We will therefore assume that the 1% means the top ½% plus the bottom ½%. Note that in the previous three problems the direction of the deviation from M was implied in the question. For example, we asked how many men could throw 200 ft. or more. We therefore asked *only* for those who deviated at least 1.57 SD's *above* M. Perhaps all this will be clearer if we restate the problem we are working on as follows: what scores (distances of throw) deviate from M to

such an extent that the *total* frequency of scores remaining beyond the deviation is 1%. Stated this way we can more easily
see that we are asking for the top ½% and the bottom ½% of
the scores. The problem is shown graphically in Figure 7.4. The
raw score values given in the figure as the answer to the problem

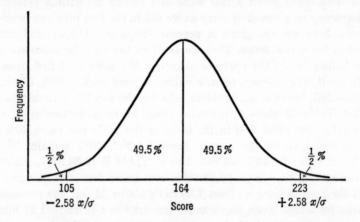

FIG. 7.4. **Scores in the baseball-throwing data that occur 1% of the time
or less, assuming normality of distribution**

are found by our usual procedure. First find in Table B the x/σ
value beyond which only ½% of the frequency remain, the
x/σ value that includes 49.5% between it and M. In the table
the value 49.5% falls halfway between the x/σ values 2.57 and
2.58, so we can choose either one. We shall arbitrarily decide
on 2.58 and we now have the answer to the problem in z-score
terms: scores that occur 1% of the time are all those that deviate
at least 2.58 SD's from M, including both directions from M.
However, we were asked for the raw scores so we must convert
the z-score of 2.58 to raw score units. Since SD of the distribution is 23 ft., 2.58 SD's are 59 ft., $(2.58 \times 23 = 59.34)$. Now we
have the answer as a deviation in raw score units: distances in
the baseball-throwing data that occur 1% of the time are all
those that deviate at least 59 ft. from M in either direction.
Since M is 164 ft., these are distances of 105 ft. or less and 223 ft.
or more.

The problem we have just solved was chosen because it illustrates something which we shall now emphasize. The problem asked for the deviation beyond which a certain percent frequency occurs without specifying the direction of the deviation. As we shall find in later chapters, this type of problem occurs often. We may state as a general rule that whenever the direction is *not* specified in a problem, you always assume the deviation in both directions is meant. In other words, when you are given a percent frequency and have to find the deviation corresponding to it, *unless it specifically states otherwise* the problem means that the deviation be such that half the percent frequency remains beyond it at each end of the curve.

One more reason why the above problem was chosen is that in a later chapter when we take up the important problem of testing the significance of a difference between M's, we shall find that the frequency of 1%, ½% under each tail of the curve, has special significance. You should memorize the x/σ value corresponding to the 1% frequency. *Remember* that scores that deviate at least 2.58 SD's from M, considering both directions from M, occur 1% of the time.

We are going to put off the last question we asked concerning the baseball-throwing data (What is the probability that someone picked at random from the group could throw 225 ft. or more?) until we take up the concept of probability and show how it relates to the normal curve later in the chapter. We want first to illustrate a few more problems that can be solved by means of the normal curve. To do this we shall use the distribution of cancellation scores shown in Figure 7.2, where N = 1000, M = 120.90, and SD = 20.40. Again we shall simplify computation by rounding off M to 121 and SD to 20.

In the cancellation data, how many students scored between 95 and 135? The score 95 corresponds to a z-score of -1.30: $(95 - 121)/20 = -1.30$. The score 135 corresponds to a z-score of $+.70$: $(135 - 121)/20 = +.70$. The algebraic signs are used to indicate that one of the scores is below M, the other above (see Figure 7.5). From Table B, 40.32% are between M and $x/\sigma = -1.30$, and 25.80% between M and $x/\sigma = +.70$, so the total frequency between the two points is 40.32% plus 25.80%, or 66.12%. Since $N = 1000$, about 661 students got cancellation scores between 95 and 135.

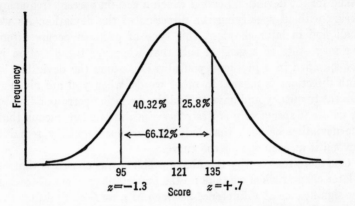

FIG. 7.5. Per cent frequency between the scores 95 and 135 in the cancellation data, assuming normality of distribution

Let us take a problem where both scores are on the same side of M. In the cancellation distribution, what proportion of the students scored between 110 and 115? The problem is shown graphically in Figure 7.6. The x/σ value corresponding to 110 is —.55 and for 115 the x/σ value is —.30. From Table B, 20.88%

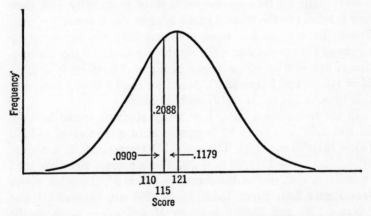

FIG. 7.6. Proportion of the frequency between the scores 110 and 115 in the cancellation data, assuming normality of distribution

score between M and $z = -.55$, and 11.79% between M and $z = -.30$. Since the 11.79% is part of the 20.88%, we must subtract: $20.88\% - 11.79\% = 9.09\%$. Thus as a proportion the answer is .0909.

Remember that we asked you to memorize the fact that in the normal curve the x/σ value 2.58 is the deviation beyond which 1% of the frequency remains. There is one other value that will also be used so frequently in later work that you should learn it now: beyond $x/\sigma = 1.96$ there remain 5% of the frequency,

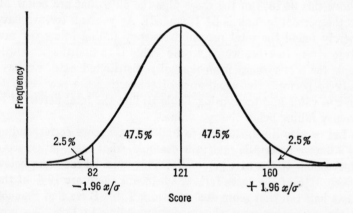

Fig. 7.7. Scores in the cancellation data that occur 5% of the time, assuming normality of distribution

i.e., 2.5% at each tail of the curve. To take an example, in the cancellation data what scores occur only 5% of the time? Since 2.5% remain beyond the deviation, we must look in Table B for the deviation that includes 47.50% between it and M, and doing so we find the x/σ value is 1.96. The SD of the cancellation data is 20, so 1.96 SD's equal about 39 raw-score units. Since M is 121, scores that occur 5% of the time are all those of 82 or lower and those of 160 or above. Figure 7.7 shows this problem graphically.

Percentiles from the Normal Curve

Table B is also useful for determining percentile ranks for raw scores from normally distributed data. It must be emphasized, however, that percentile ranks determined from Table B will not be accurate unless the raw scores are distributed normally or very nearly so. Recall that the percentile rank of a given score is the percentage of the total number of cases, the percent frequency, lying *below* that score. To illustrate from the cancellation data, what is the percentile rank of the raw score 141? As usual, we have to get the z-score corresponding to the raw score; in this case $z = +1.00$. From Table B, 34.13% fall between this x/σ value and M. Therefore, the raw score 141 is above this 34.13% of the cases plus the 50% that are below M, so the percentile rank is 84 (rounded). As you can see, we have merely found the total percent frequency falling below the raw score given. In other words, to use Table B to find the percentile rank for a raw score from normally distributed data, we have only to perform the usual step of converting the raw score to an x/σ value and then, using Table B, find the total percent frequency falling below the x/σ value.

Let us also illustrate how to find the raw score corresponding to a known percentile rank; for example, what cancellation score corresponds to the 31st percentile? This must be the score below which 31% of the cases fall, which means there are 19% of the cases between that score and M. From Table B we find that .50 is the x/σ value most closely corresponding to 19%. We now know that the cancellation raw score we are looking for is ½ SD below M, therefore the 31st percentile is a cancellation score of 111.

We have now considered a variety of normal curve problems and before going further it may be helpful to point out how similar all these problems are. We should find the solution of normal curve problems easier if we keep in mind that all problems will give us some information expressed in one kind of unit, and that to answer the problem the given information will have to be translated into some other kind of unit. Specifically, the problem will give us at least one of the following units: a raw score, a z-score or x/σ value, a percent frequency, or a raw frequency. Answering the problem will require translating from one to another of these units. Perhaps the diagram below will make this clearer. The top row of the diagram shows the general procedure

$$X \longleftrightarrow z \longleftrightarrow \% f \longleftrightarrow f$$

$$\frac{X - M}{\sigma} = z \longrightarrow \text{Table B} \longrightarrow \frac{\% f \ (N)}{100} = f$$

$$X = z\sigma + M \longleftarrow \text{Table B} \longleftarrow \% f = \frac{f}{N} \ (100)$$

in all problems: we are given one kind of unit and we translate into another kind of unit. The two-headed arrows indicate that we can translate in either direction. Note, however, that whether we are translating from left to right or right to left, *we cannot skip a step*. To get from X to $\% f$ we have to go from X to z, then from z to $\% f$; to get from f to X, we must first convert f to $\% f$, then $\% f$ to z, then z to X.

The other two rows of the diagram show the specific steps to take. Thus, suppose a problem gives a raw score (X) and asks for the percent frequency $(\% f)$, or raw frequency (f), above or below that score. For example, how many men scored below 150 ft. in the baseball-throwing distribution? We would proceed from *left to right* in the top row of the diagram and we would go through the steps shown in the *second* row.

On the other hand, suppose the problem gives a percent frequency or raw frequency and asks either for a z-score or raw score. As an example, the top 300 students are above what score in the cancellation distribution? In this case we would go from *right to left* in the top row of the diagram and would go through the steps shown in the *bottom* row.

The point we want to make is that there are really not several different kinds of normal curve problems. All normal curve problems are essentially the same; they only look different because they can be stated in so many different ways. One more thing: we strongly advise drawing a graph for each problem, as we did for some of our problems in Figures 7.3, 7.4, 7.5, 7.6, and 7.7. You will often find that if you express graphically the information given in a problem, it will help you get started answering it.

PROBABILITY

Let us now recall that a fifth question was asked about the baseball-throwing data: What is the probability that someone picked at random from this group could throw 225 ft. or more? Before the question can be answered we must introduce the concept of *probability* and indicate its relationship to the normal curve. For our purposes *the probability of an event will be defined as the number of times out of 100 that the event would occur*.

Probability questions are concerned with the *frequency* (or infrequency) *of occurrence* of some event. For example, what is the probability of drawing the ace of spades from a well-shuffled deck of cards in a single draw? Since the ace of spades is only one card in a deck of 52, each one of which has an equal chance of being drawn, the probability is 1 in 52, or 1.92 in 100. Note that the probability of drawing the ace of spades would be the same if we had, say, 6 decks of cards all shuffled together; the probability in this case would be 6 in 312, still 1.92 in 100. We can see that *a more general definition of the probability of any specific event is the ratio of the number of times the specified event can occur to the total possible number of events*. In the deck of cards illustration the ace of spades was one event out of 52 equally-possible events.

To see how probability is related to the normal curve, remember that the normal curve is a theoretical distribution of *frequency of occurrence*. It was actually developed in connection with the mathematics of probability and is often called the normal probability curve. The curve's bell-shape indicates that the *greater* the deviation of an event from M of all events, the *less* the frequency of occurrence. In other words, as deviation from M increases, probability decreases. In the example we used earlier in which we asked what scores in the baseball-throwing distribution occurred 1% of the time or less, we were asking about scores that have a probability of 1 in 100. The *percent frequency* of occurrence, determined from Table B, is the same as the *probability* of occurrence.

In addition to expressing probability as the number of chances in 100, two other ways of expressing probability are used. One can give the *odds against* the occurrence of an event, or one can state the probability as a *proportion*. The letter P is the symbol used when probability is expressed as a proportion. To illustrate: in a normal distribution events that deviate 2.58 SD's from M occur 1% of the time; the chances of such events are 1 in 100. The same probability can be expressed by saying that the odds are 99 to 1 against the events, or that $P = .01, \left(\frac{1}{100}\right)$. Similarly, in a normal distribution 5% of the cases deviate more than 1.96 SD's from M. The chances of such events are 5 in 100 (or 1 in 20), the odds against them are 19 to 1, $P = .05$.

Now let us return to our empirical distribution of the distances that a baseball was thrown and answer the question: What is the probability that someone chosen at random from the group of men could throw 225 ft. or more? This is exactly the same as asking how frequently do scores of 225 ft. or more occur. The raw score must first, as always, be converted into a z-score before Table B can be used: $(225 - 164)/23 = +2.65$, the x/σ value. Note that this problem asks for the probability of a score at least 2.65 SD's *above* M, that is, the direction of the deviation is specified. By means of Table B we determine that 49.6% of the cases are between M and $x/\sigma = 2.65$, therefore .40% deviate more than 2.65 SD's. Thus the probability that someone could throw 225 ft. or more is .4 in 100, 4 in 1000, 1 in 250. The odds against a throw of 225 ft. or more are 249 to 1, $P = .004$.

Further Problems

Probability problems involving the use of the normal curve can, like our earlier illustrations, be stated in a variety of ways without basic change in the method of solution. With this in mind, let us solve some more problems.

Recall that we said earlier that the mean chest circumference of American women is about 35 inches, with SD of about 3 inches. For our purposes let us simply say $M = 35$ in. and $SD = 3$ in. We shall assume the distribution is normal. Consider the following problem: the odds are 19 to 1 against meeting a girl whose chest measurement deviates how far from M? Since the odds are 19 to 1, we are talking about measurements that occur only 5% of the time (5 in 100 or 1 in 20). You should be able to remember without having to look it up that, in a normal distribution, cases that occur only 5% of the time are those that deviate at least 1.96 SD's from M. Thus we have the answer to our question, the deviation we want, in z-scores; since we were asked for the deviation in raw scores we convert by multiplying the SD of 3 in. by 1.96, obtaining 5.88 in. The odds are 19 to 1 against meeting a girl whose chest measurement deviates 5.88 in. from M, a circumference of either less than 29.12 in. or more than 40.88 in.

We shall continue our illustrations of probability problems by referring to another distribution, namely, the height of American men. Of course, the actual M and SD of height are not known, since all men have not been measured. However, several independent investigators have measured the heights of different groups of men, groups with N's ranging from a few hundred to several thousand. All report M's around 68-69 inches, and SD's of 2-3 inches.[4] For convenience let us assume the mean height of American men is 69 in. with an SD of 2.5 in. It can be assumed that the distribution is normal.

Modern fighter planes are so crowded with equipment that there is not much room left for the pilot. Assume the Air Force specifies that no one taller than 6 ft. 2 in. will be accepted for training as a fighter pilot. You bet a friend of yours five cents that the next man you see walking along the street would be rejected by the Air Force because he is taller than 6 ft. 2 in. How much money should you make your friend bet against your nickel, so the bet won't favor either of you? To answer this you have to figure out the odds against choosing a man at random and finding him taller than 6 ft. 2 in., or 74 in., tall. Such a man deviates at least 5 in., or 2 SD's, above M. Referring to Table B we find that 2.28% of the cases deviate more than 2 SD's above

[4] *Handbook of Human Engineering Data for Design Engineers.* Tufts College Institute for Applied Experimental Psychology. Special Devices Center, Technical Report No. SDC 199-1-1, 1949.

M; therefore there are 2.28 chances in 100 ($P = .0228$) that a man selected at random will be taller than 6 ft. 2 in. The odds against you are roughly 43 to 1 (actually 42.86 to 1), so you should not make the bet unless your friend puts up 43 times as much as you do, $2.15 to your five cents.

Two doctors are doing physical examinations, including measurement of height, on men being drafted. Each time they measure a man's height Doctor A offers to bet Doctor B a dime against a nickel that the man's height will fall between 5 ft. 6½ in. and 5 ft. 11½ in. Over a long period of time; that is, after they have measured many thousands of men, will Doctor A win a lot, lose a lot, or about break even? The answer is he will about break even because he has given 2 to 1 odds (10 cents to five cents) that any man will fall within one SD, 2.5 in., of M. We know that 68% of the cases deviate less than one SD. Thus the odds are 68 to 32, or roughly 2 to 1, that any man's height is between 66.5 and 71.5 in. Actually, Doctor A will win slightly more than he will lose because he is giving odds of 66⅔ to 33⅓, exactly 2 to 1, instead of 68 to 32.

Suppose a girl insists she will never marry a man as short as or shorter than she is. After studying this chapter, she says she is not worried because she knows there is only 1 such man in 400. How tall is the girl? To answer this problem note that you are given the probability or percent frequency and you have to get back from it to a raw score. Men with heights so short that they occur only once in 400 times make up the bottom .25% of the cases, because 1 in 400 is .25 in 100. We must find in Table B the deviation below which .25% of the cases fall, the deviation that includes 49.75% of the cases between it and M. According to the table this is the x/σ value -2.81. Multiplying this z-score by 2.5 in., the SD of the men's height distribution, gives us 7.025 in., or 7 in. Subtracting from the M of 69 in., we get 62 in., or 5 ft. 2 in. This is the height of the girl; 1 man in 400 is 5 ft. 2 in. or shorter.

In summary, it may be worthwhile to emphasize in general terms the relation between the normal curve, which is a theoretical distribution, and sets of data, or empirical distributions. In one sense we can consider the normal curve as a model, a model about which we know a good deal. We have available on the one hand an unvarying model, the normal curve, and on the other hand we obtain distributions of scores by measuring a great variety of characteristics expressed in many kinds of units. Many of these sets of data will be distributed approximately normally, in which case we can, by converting the raw-score units into SD-units, z-scores, apply the model, the normal curve, to the data. Some of the advantages gained in dealing with empirical distributions by use of the normal curve have been illustrated in the present chapter and we will find that even more important applications of the normal curve will be demonstrated in later chapters.

Let us repeat something we said earlier. We said you might think that applying the normal curve to the baseball-throwing distribution in order to answer questions about it was a waste of effort. If we wanted to know, say, how many men could throw 200 ft. or more, why didn't we just go to the raw data and count up how many men had scores of 200 ft. or more? The reason we didn't do this is that we wanted you to learn *how* to apply the normal curve; we did not bother to explain fully *why* you were applying the normal curve. Even now we shall not go very thoroughly into the reason why we apply the normal curve to a set of data because it is better to take this up in later chapters when we are better prepared for it. The present chapter is largely groundwork. We may, however, briefly anticipate our future work by noting that what we often want to do in research is predict what we would get if we measured a large group of people, predicting from the data we obtained by measuring only a small part of the large group. This is where the normal curve comes in. If we can assume that the trait measured is normally distributed, we can use the normal curve with the data we have in order to make estimates about people we have not measured. Although you may not have realized it, we did this for some of our distributions, such as the chest circumference of women and the height of men. For those distributions we knew only M and SD, obtained by measuring a few thousand cases, and from that information we made estimates, by means of the normal curve, of frequencies and scores for the huge groups defined as all U.S. women or all U.S. men. Thus, the normal curve has one of its most important uses in making estimates and predictions about groups so large that we lack both the time and money to measure them.

8

Sampling Error

THE PROBLEM

Let us recall from the discussion in the first chapter that a major purpose of psychological statistics is to determine the significance of the difference between means. The phrase, "significance of the difference," doesn't have much meaning to you now but it is the intent of this chapter and the one to follow to develop your thinking so that it will have meaning. The concept of significance of differences between means, the understanding of its implications, and the computational techniques involved, are probably the most important set of ideas which statistical thinking has contributed to psychological research. Of course, M, SD, z-scores, and so forth, all have descriptive importance in their own right, but it is upon these concepts that we build the critical step of determining the significance of the difference between means. Indeed, as far as the mere statistics of the matter is concerned, if you understand how to assess the meaning of a difference between means you are in a position to report acceptable psychological research. The content of this chapter provides the initial step in this understanding.

Let us set up a problem to refresh your memory as to what we intend to do by studying the significance of a difference between two M's. By now you realize that in its simplest form a psychological experiment usually consists in treating one group of subjects in one way, a second group in a different way, and seeing if the two different treatments result in different behavior. For example, suppose we did a study to determine if cramming is better or worse than not cramming for an examination. One group of students is allowed to spend five hours studying for the exam but all five hours of study come the night before the exam. Another group of students studies one hour a night for the five nights preceding the examination. As we can see, both groups have five hours of study but the treatment of each group is different in terms of how the study time is distributed, one treatment being what is commonly called cramming, the other non-cramming. On the single examination, which both groups take, the cram group has M of 52, and the non-cram, M of 55. Are we going to conclude from this that cramming results in poorer test scores than non-cramming? You may answer: "Of course cramming results in poorer test scores; the cram group got only 52 and the other 55." You are undeniably correct in the second, the numerical, part of your statement, but the critical consideration is this: would you be willing to conclude that if we repeated the experiment with other groups a non-cram group would again be better?

We see, then, that in the simplest sort of an experiment we have two groups which are treated differently. For each group we calculate M. Since these two M's will rarely be identical, we need some technique by which we can decide whether or not we would predict that if this experiment were repeated over and over again with different groups, we would find that one M is systematically larger than the other. It is the intent of these two chapters to discuss the techniques used to cope with this problem. Several steps are involved in attaining the final goal; we must discuss what is meant by samples and populations, sampling error, variability of sample M's, variability of differences between M's, and finally, the assessment of the significance of the difference between any two sample M's.

SAMPLE AND POPULATION

Illustrations

Voting intentions of the American people are often determined by public-opinion polls. There are about 75 million eligible voters in the United States. Now, the investigators conducting the polls do not ask all 75 million people how they are going to vote; rather, they ask a very small proportion of the 75 million, say 25 thousand voters. In this case the 75 million voters is the population; 25 thousand is the sample from this population.

An investigator wished to determine the mechanical aptitude of boys living on farms as compared with the aptitudes of those living in cities. His two populations are all city boys and all country boys in the United States. He doesn't try to test all of these boys; he takes two samples of, say, 1000 each, one from among city boys and the other from among farm boys.

Definitions

If we generalize from these illustrations it can be said that *a population is any group of people who are alike on at least one specified characteristic.* (We could also make use of populations of lower animals, or plants, or stones, but for illustrative purposes we will most commonly refer to people.) A population has no upper or lower limit on the number of cases except those imposed by nature, e.g., we couldn't have a population of 100 million American bachelors for there simply aren't that many fortunate American males. A population might be specified as all men in the world or as all men yet unborn, as all senior college students in Big-Ten schools, or as all red-headed freshmen women who made straight A's during their first term. The population, then, is specified by the investigator and he confines his work to finding out something about this population. He may, of course, work with more than one population in a single study, as was the case when the mechanical aptitude of city and farm boys was tested.

A sample is any number of cases less than the total number of cases in the population from which it is drawn. If we have a population of 50 thousand, a sample might consist of five cases or 49 thousand. Normally, however, samples consist of only a small or a very small proportion of the population being investigated.

Generalizing from Sample to Population

The relationship between samples and population is very important when we consider what an investigator tries to do in a psychological experiment. He is interested in the behavior of people in certain situations. That is, he is interested in responses to a test; he is interested in rate of learning; he is interested in the hallucinations of hospital patients, and so forth. The population in whose behavior the investigator is interested is usually so large that it is impractical to test or measure the whole population. Therefore, the investigator must take a sample from this population and use the behavior of this sample as representative of that of the entire population. If we ask 25 thousand people how they are going to vote in the national election, we will use the replies of these 25 thousand voters to infer how the entire population is going to vote and place our bets accordingly. The investigator is interested in behavior in general. Therefore he is going to use the behavior of the sample to predict or infer the behavior of the population.

It has probably already occurred to you that there are certain dangers in this procedure of generalizing from a sample to a population. If the 25 thousand people we ask about voting are all from the Gold Coast of Chicago, the investigator would be slightly balmy if he then proceeded to say that all the rest of the people in the country would vote in the same way that these 25 thousand Chicago citizens say they are going to vote. In other words, we would like to be sure that a sample is a miniature picture of the population from which it is taken. We say that a sample ought to be *representative* of the total population from which it is drawn.

Most commonly we try to obtain a sample that is representative by drawing (measuring) a random sample. *By a random sample we mean that every individual in the population has had the same chance or opportunity of being chosen for the sample as has every other individual.* The theory is that by drawing such a sample all aspects of the population should be represented in our sample and we should have a miniature picture of that population. Because obtaining a random sample is not so easy as it sounds, we will defer the discussion of these difficulties to a later chapter. It is sufficient for us to know at the moment that to be representative a sample should be random. We now must turn to problems associated with studying samples in order to estimate characteristics of the population.

VARIABILITY OF MEANS

Let us repeat that the purpose of measuring or testing a sample from a population is to get data which mirror the characteristics of that population. The data for our sample will be treated as we have treated previous distributions of scores. First, we will calculate M. Since we wish our sample to reflect the population's characteristics, we ask how closely the sample M approximates the true M (the M of the population; the M we would get if we measured everyone in the population). This, you will think at first, is a rather stupid question for we can't tell what the true M is without measuring the entire population and if we did measure the entire population we wouldn't have to worry about a sample M. But, we might still ask whether it is likely that the sample M is *exactly* the same as the true M even though we don't know what the true M is. To this question we will answer "no." The reason for this is that our random sample will rarely mirror the population exactly. Therefore, we may expect that the M of the sample will not be exactly the same as the true or population M. As a matter of fact, as we will show you later, if we took a series of samples from a population whose M was known we would discover that very few, if any, of these sample M's would be exactly the same as the population M. In short, *we may expect that M of a random sample will not be arithmetically identical with M of the population.* This fact is known as *sampling error* of M's.

If the sample M is not expected to be the same as the population M, how can we use the sample M as indicative of the population M? The best answer that can be given to this question is that if we draw a truly random sample from a population it is known that the sample M will rarely deviate far from the true M. We go on now with further elaboration of this important problem.

Means of Successive Random Samples

Strictly speaking, the steps in reasoning we are going through now are based upon the assumption that we are drawing an infinite number of samples from an infinite population. However, since such a procedure is infinitely difficult to write about, and since it is quite satisfactory to go through the steps with a finite population and a finite number of samples, we shall leave the infinite to the less diffident.

Suppose, however, we take successive random samples from a large, known population. We draw one sample of subjects and measure them on some aspect of behavior; we then draw another sample of the same size, measure it, and so on. Let us say we draw 500 samples, calculate M for each sample, and make a frequency distribution of these M's. Such a distribution is called the *sampling distribution* of M. What is the nature of the distribution formed by these M's? If we group the M's and place them along the baseline (X axis) with frequency along the ordinate (Y axis), we will find that these M's fall into a normal distribution. Furthermore, the M of all these sample M's would be our best estimate of the true (population) M.

But again, we probably wouldn't say that M of these 500 M's would be exactly the same as the true M. However, we would have a great deal of confidence in saying that the true M lies somewhere within the range established by the 500 M's. Moreover, we could take the SD of these 500 M's and make statements of probability about where any subsequently drawn sample M's would fall in this distribution.

In the previous chapter we made certain statements of probability about where a raw score would fall in a distribution. Thus, if you had SD for a distribution of test scores and you measured a new individual you could say that the chances were 68 (approximately) out of 100 that this new case would fall between the points established by $+1\sigma$ and -1σ. We can do exactly the same thing in the case of any sample M if we know SD of a distribution of random sample M's. The chances are 68 out of 100 that any randomly drawn sample M lies within the range of values between $+1\sigma$ and -1σ of this distribution. Or, the chances are 95 out of 100 that any sample M will fall between $+1.96\sigma$ and -1.96σ.

It becomes apparent that our SD of a large number of sample M's is a critical statistic in making statements of probability about where any sample M will fall. We shall also see that it is important for estimating the range in which the true M lies. But, it might seem that if we are going to take a lot of samples in order to get a measure of variability of M's, we might just as well measure the entire population, thereby giving us the true M and avoiding all the problems of sampling error. Fortunately, we do not have to measure a lot of samples to get a measure of variability of such sample M's; statisticians have provided us with a technique for making a good estimate of the SD of a series of sample M's. *This estimate is based upon a single sample.* This statistic, called the *standard error* of the mean, is symbolized σ_M, and literally is *an estimate of the SD of a distribution of randomly drawn sample M's.* In other words, it is the variability of the sampling distribution of M's. The word "error" is used in this statistic because each sample M may incorporate a sampling error in the sense that it will usually differ from the true M.

STANDARD ERROR OF THE MEAN

The formula for estimating the standard error of a mean from a single sample is relatively simple:

$$\sigma_M = \frac{\sigma}{\sqrt{N-1}}$$

All we have to do is find the SD of the raw scores of our sample and divide this by the square root of one less than the number of cases in the sample.

In Table 6.1 (Chapter 6) we gave a distribution of scores for 10 students representing number of trials required to learn a vocabulary list. The SD for this distribution was 2.77. To find the σ_M we simply substitute in the formula:

$$\sigma_M = \frac{\sigma}{\sqrt{N-1}} = \frac{2.77}{\sqrt{10-1}} = \frac{2.77}{3} = .92$$

Let us take another illustration. Two investigators developed a short personality questionnaire and got what they called emotionality scores. The scores ranged from 0 to 13, with a high score indicating high emotionality. The test was given to 100 mental patients and the distribution of scores is shown in Table 8.1. We first calculate SD and find it to be 2.63. Then, substituting in the formula, we find the σ_M to be .26.

TABLE 8.1

Illustration of Calculation of σ_M from Raw Scores *

EMOTIONALITY SCORE (X)	f	fX	fX^2
13	2	26	338
12	6	72	864
11	7	77	847
10	14	140	1400
9	14	126	1134
8	18	144	1152
7	11	77	539
6	8	48	288
5	9	45	225
4	5	20	80
3	2	6	18
2	3	6	12
1	1	1	1
0	0	0	0
	$\Sigma f = \overline{100}$	$\Sigma fX = \overline{788}$	$\Sigma fX^2 = \overline{6898}$

$$M = \frac{\Sigma fX}{N} = \frac{788}{100} = 7.88$$

$$\sigma = \sqrt{\frac{\Sigma X^2}{N} - M^2} = \sqrt{\frac{6898}{100} - (7.88)^2} = \sqrt{68.98 - 62.09} = \sqrt{6.89} = 2.63$$

$$\sigma_M = \frac{\sigma}{\sqrt{N-1}} = \frac{2.63}{\sqrt{100-1}} = \frac{2.63}{9.95} = .26$$

* From Mitchell, M. B., and Rothe, H. F. Validity of an emotional key on a short industrial personality questionnaire. *J. appl. Psychol.*, 1950, 34, 329-332.

Interpretation of σ_M

What does this statistic imply? How are we to interpret it? What do we do with it? As we have already said, σ_M, based on a single sample, gives us an estimate of SD of a very large number of M's taken from successive samples of the same size (same N) as our single sample. This in turn allows us to make statements of probability about where the true M (the population M) lies. Now, there is a little trick to the language used in expressing these matters. What we do is set up hypotheses about where the true M lies. We may then test any one of these hypotheses by asking ourselves: "If the true M is (some value), is it likely that

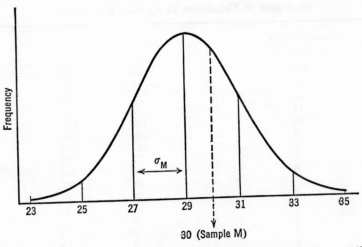

FIG. 8.1. Visual test of the hypothesis that the true M (population M) is 29 when the obtained sample M is 30

we would get the M we got in our single random sample?" We are in the position of having an estimate of the SD of a distribution of M's, but not of the M of this distribution. Our sample M is only one point on this distribution. But we can use these facts to make statements about values that might be the true M. Let us say we have a sample M of 30 and σ_M of 2.0. Remember that this value, 2.0, is an estimate, based on a given sample N, of the SD of a very large number of M's. We know that in a normal distribution of raw scores we have about 6 SD's. Likewise, if we have a normal distribution made up of M's of many random samples we also would have 6 SD's. Now, again, our σ_M is an estimate of this SD of a large number of M's. Therefore, our interpretation is the same as in the case of SD for raw scores.

With a sample M of 30 and σ_M of 2.0, suppose we set up the hypothesis that the true M is 29. The question we ask in order to test the hypothesis is: "If the true M is 29, is it likely that we would get (as we *did* get) a sample M of 30?" To answer this, let's use initially a visual aid as in Figure 8.1. We draw a normal distribution curve with assumed M_t (true M) at 29 and SD (σ_M) of 2.0. You will probably agree from inspecting the graph that if the true M is 29, we could very easily obtain a sample M of 30.

To make statements of probability, more information than that given by the visual aid is needed. To obtain data for a statement of probability we must find out how far our sample M (30) deviates in σ_M units from the hypothesized true M. Such data are obtained by the formula:

$$\frac{M_s - M_t}{\sigma_M}$$

where M_s is the sample M and M_t is the hypothetical true M. This formula, you will note, is just another z-score formula; it is basically the same as that used in obtaining z-scores for individual raw scores. Substituting our values in the formula, we have: $\dfrac{30 - 29}{2.0} = .5$. Thus, the sample M deviates $.5\sigma_M$ units from the hypothesized true M. Referring to Table B we see that a deviation of $.5\sigma_M$ units in a given direction includes 19% of the total frequency in the distribution.

In interpreting this value (19%) it is necessary to remind ourselves that we are dealing with sampling errors, and that a distribution of sample M's will be symmetrical around the unknown true M. Therefore, the question we must finally ask is: "If the true M is 29, how frequently are we likely to get a deviation (due to sampling error) as *large* or *larger* than that of our single sample M?" This question does not indicate a direction of deviation. In our illustration the sample M deviates one score unit (30 − 29) from the hypothetical true M. So, what we need is a statement of probability about a deviation of one score unit independent of direction. Since a deviation of one score unit in this example includes 19% of the frequency on each side of M, on both sides it will include 38%. Thus, due to sampling error, we may expect a deviation that is this *big* or *bigger* in 62% (i.e., 100% — 38%) of the cases if the true M is 29. It is quite apparent, therefore, that the true M could be 29.

Let's try another one. We will test the hypothesis that the true M is 35. If the true M is 35, would we expect to get a deviation due to sampling error that is as big or bigger than that indicated by the sample M? Since our sample M is 30, we see that the deviation due to sampling error would be five score units if the true M is 35. Now, five score units is:

$$\frac{30 - 35}{\sigma_M}, \text{ or } -2.5\sigma_M$$

Referring to Table B we find that the portion of the distribution between M and a deviation as large as this includes 49% of the cases in each half of the distribution, or 98% of the total. Therefore, if the true M is 35, we would expect (as a consequence of sampling error) a deviation of five score units or more in only two cases in 100. It doesn't seem very likely that our one sample is one of these two rather rare cases; the odds are 49 to 1 against its being one of these cases. We will conclude, therefore, that the true M is not 35. We may conceivably be wrong but we would conclude this because with a true M of 35 it is a very remote possibility that we would get the sample M we got. We reject the hypothesis that the true M is 35.

From the above illustrations it is apparent that with a single sample M we can test any hypothesis concerning the value of the true M. For each test we either reject the hypothesis or accept it as reasonable. This acceptance or rejection is based upon the level of confidence we have concerning whether or not our sample M could have been obtained if the true M were as hypothesized.

Confidence Intervals

In working with research data we don't usually have hypotheses about specific values of the true M. Rather, we are interested in establishing the range of scores within which we will assert the true M lies. Such an assertion has a certain probability of being correct; we make it with a certain degree of confidence. When we establish such a range *it is commonly spoken of as a confidence interval.* In research reports two confidence intervals are used most frequently. One of these is the 1% confidence interval and the other is the 5% confidence interval.

1% confidence interval. A deviation of $2.58\sigma_M$ units above and below M includes 99% of the cases in a normal distribution. If then we make hypotheses about the true M, we will reject any such hypotheses which would make the sample M lie further away than $2.58\sigma_M$ units. We reject it because it is highly unlikely that by random sampling we would get a sample M which deviates so far; the chances are 1 in 100, and we do not consider this likely for a single sample M. Thus, for any given sample M we can establish the 1% confidence interval for the true M.

Let us establish the 1% confidence interval for the data shown in Table 8.1. The σ_M for these data is .26. Multiplying this value by 2.58 gives us the number of score units by which the sample M can deviate from the hypothesized true M and still allow us to accept hypotheses about the true M while remaining within the 1% confidence interval. The resultant value is .67. The sample M is 7.88. Therefore, we may accept hypotheses about the true M being as high as 8.55 (which we obtain by adding 7.88 and .67) or as low as 7.21 (which we obtain by subtracting .67 from 7.88). If we generalize from these steps we see that the 1% confidence interval can be established for any set of data as:

$$M_s \pm 2.58\sigma_M$$

That is, plus and minus $2.58\sigma_M$ units from the sample M establishes the 1% confidence interval for the true M.

5% confidence interval. A less stringent interval is the 5% confidence interval. What this means is that we will reject any hypotheses about the true M if the sample M is $1.96\sigma_M$ or more units above or below the hypothesized true M. Now, $1.96\sigma_M$ units includes approximately 47.5% of the cases on either side of M or a total of 95% of the cases. If we use this interval we are betting that on this single sample we didn't hit that sample which we would get once in 20 times by sampling error (once in 20 is, of course, the same as 5 in 100). Using the 5% interval one is less sure of including the true M than with the 1% interval, but many research workers are willing to take the chance that true M doesn't lie beyond the limits set up by the 5% criterion. The generalized formula for the 5% confidence interval is:

$$M_s \pm 1.96\sigma_M$$

We may flatly state that the 5% confidence interval represents the minimum probability level that should be used in rejecting hypotheses about the true M. We could, for example, set up a 10% confidence interval. But, if we reject an hypothesis about the true M because our sample M was just barely outside of this 10% interval, we will be in error once in ten times. For, by sampling error alone, we would expect our sample M to deviate from the true M as much as it did once in every 10 samples taken. One may set up confidence intervals at values which fall between the 1% and 5% intervals, e.g., a 3% confidence interval. As a matter of custom, however, the 1% and the 5% intervals are commonly used as reference values. If, for example, our sample M and hypothesized true M differ by $2.3\sigma_M$ units, we would say that we reject the hypothesis about the true M at better than the 5% level but not at the 1% level. Or, we might simply state that we can reject the hypothesis at a confidence level between the 1% and 5% intervals.

The use of confidence intervals (which allow us to reject or accept hypotheses at stated confidence levels) simplifies our writing of research reports considerably. We simply state which one of the two confidence intervals we are using and accept all hypotheses about the true M lying within this interval and reject all others. It is important to note, however, that we must always state which one of the two confidence intervals we are using so there will be no misunderstanding on this matter.

In the strict, absolute, sense of the words "prove" and "disprove," nothing is proved or disproved about the true M by using confidence intervals (or by any other method of stating probabilities). If we accept an hypothesis about the true M using the 1% confidence interval we must realize that the true M could lie outside of these limits; we can't prove that it does or doesn't without measuring the entire population. We simply have a high degree of confidence, based on probabilities, that the true M doesn't lie outside of the interval established as the 1% confidence interval. Nothing is "proved" or "disproved" in the absolute sense whenever we apply probabilities.

σ_M and N

It is useful to consider the components of statistical formulas to see what variations in these components do to the size of the statistic. In the case of σ_M, N is a most critical component. In Chapter 6 we saw that as N increases (beyond a certain minimum), SD remains relatively constant. Now, with SD remaining constant as N increases in our σ_M formula, the numerator doesn't change but the denominator (N — 1) will get bigger and bigger. Therefore, σ_M will get smaller and smaller as N increases. If N gets etxremely large σ_M approaches zero. Of course, if N gets so large that it includes all members of the population the σ_M should be zero since M of the sample will be the true M and the true M ran have no variability due to sampling error.

STANDARD ERROR OF A PROPORTION

Formulas are available to obtain standard errors for several statistics in addition to M. However, except for σ_M, only one other is used with sufficient frequency to warrant discussion here. This is the standard error of a proportion, which we will symbolize as σ_{prop}.

Suppose we are members of a commission assigned to investigate the truthfulness of advertising claims. One claim we are going to investigate is that of a cigarette company which says that 70% of American doctors smoked J cigarettes. Of course in arriving at this figure the company may have made pretty sure that any particular doctor smoked J's before they interviewed him. But, let's assume that the company's survey was really honest. So, we take a random sample of 50 doctors and discovei that only 60% smoke J's, that is, a proportion of .60.

By this time, we hope, we are wise enough not to jump to the conclusion that the advertising is fraudulent because we found that only 60% of the doctors smoke J's whereas the company has been claiming 70%. By this time we recognize that there are sampling errors involved and that the question we really need to ask ourselves is: "If the true proportion is .70, how likely is it that we would obtain a proportion as low as .60 with 50 cases?" If it is likely that we could get such a proportion, then the claim of the makers of J's is not fraudulent; if it is unlikely that we could get a proportion of .60, we have a pretty good case that it is fraudulent or that the sample wasn't random. So, just as in the case of a sample M, we need a technique for determining limits of the sampling error.

If we drew a very large number of random samples of the same size from a single population and for each obtained a proportion, these sample proportions would be distributed normally (a possible exception will be pointed out later). If we calculated SD of this distribution, we could make statements of probability about where any sample would fall. If these statements have a familiar ring it is because we used the same language in discussing the sampling distribution of M. We need to know SD of a large number of sample proportions; an estimate of this statistic can be obtained from a single sample proportion. The standard error of a proportion (σ_{prop}) is given by the following formula:

$$\sigma_{\text{prop}} = \sqrt{\frac{pq}{N}}$$

when: p = any hypothetical true proportion
$q = 1 - p$
N = sample size as usual

It is important to note that p is not the obtained (empirical) proportion; it is the hypothetical true proportion. The reason for this is that we wish to test a hypothesis about the hypothetical true proportion, and the sampling error for this proportion will be different than that for the obtained proportion (unless these two proportions are identical). The general question we ask is: "If the true proportion is (some value), is the sampling error of this true proportion large enough for us to expect the obtained proportion?" In the cigarette problem we want to determine whether or not the proportion .60 could be obtained by random sampling if the true proportion is .70. By substituting in the formula we find:

$$\sigma_{\text{prop}} = \sqrt{\frac{(.7)(.3)}{50}} = \sqrt{\frac{.21}{50}} = .065$$

Now, to visualize this, we set up our hypothesized true proportion as .70, and see how probable it is that we would get a sample proportion of .60. This is shown in Figure 8.2. We can

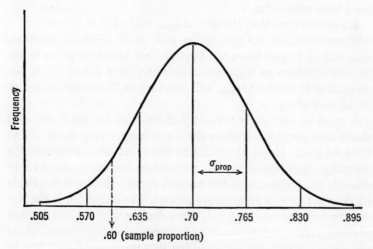

FIG. 8.2. Visual test of the hypothesis that the true proportion is .70 when the obtained sample proportion is .60

see that it is quite feasible that we could get a sample proportion of .60 if the true proportion is .70. Again, as in the case of σ_M, we may figure the amount by which the obtained proportion deviates from the hypothetical proportion and make exact statements of probability. The difference between the two proportions is .10, and σ_{prop} is .065, so that the obtained proportion deviates $1.54\sigma_{\text{prop}}$ units from the hypothetical true proportion:

$$\frac{.10}{.065} = 1.54$$

A deviation of $1.54\sigma_{prop}$ units includes approximately 44% of the cases in each half of the distribution or a total of 88%. Therefore, the chances of getting a sample proportion of .60 or smaller, or .80 or larger if the true proportion is .70, is 12 out of 100.

It can be seen that for any problem in which we obtain a proportion we can test any hypothesis about the true proportion for a given N. In each case we first calculate σ_{prop} for the hypothetical true proportion (using the N of our empirical sample). We then determine how probable it is that our obtained proportion could be drawn from the sampling distribution of the hypothesized true proportion.

We should note that the size of σ_{prop} will vary as a function of the magnitude of the proportion and of N. With N constant, σ_{prop} will be largest when the hypothetical true proportion is .50, decreasing as we go from .50 to zero and from .50 to 1.0. If the proportion is constant, σ_{prop} will decrease as N increases, just as in the case of σ_M.

A word of caution is necessary if we wish to test hypotheses about true proportions when these are large (from about .80 to 1.00) or small (from about .20 to zero). At these extremes the sampling distribution for a proportion becomes considerably skewed; thus, the use of the normal curve relationships (Table B) does not give us an accurate picture. The larger the N the less the effect of the skewness, but, when dealing with a small number of cases, rather serious errors of interpretation may occur. There are certain techniques for handling this problem of skewness in the sampling distribution of extreme proportions but such techniques are reserved for more advanced courses.

9

Significance of Differences between Means

In Chapter 7 we saw that if we want to make statements of probability about a raw score, we need to know SD of this distribution of raw scores. In Chapter 8 we learned that if we want to make statements of probability about M, we need to know SD of the distribution of M's. In the present chapter the reasoning is carried just one step further. We will learn that if we wish to make statements of probability about a difference between two M's, we need to know SD of the distribution of differences between M's. With this step we are able to answer the question which most psychological experiments set out to answer; namely, if we treat one group in one way, and another group in a different way, will there be a difference in their resulting behavior? Will there be a "real" or significant difference in the mean performances of the two groups?

STANDARD ERROR OF A DIFFERENCE

In discussing this concept we have to keep two distributions in mind, not a single distribution as in the previous chapter, but two distributions. At the start of the previous chapter we posed a question: "Do country boys or city boys have better mechanical aptitude?" Suppose we test a large random sample of country boys and one of city boys, the country boys obtaining as a mean score 55, the city boys, 50. Now we know that, due to sampling error, 55 is probably not the true M of the population of country boys, nor is 50 the true M of the population of city boys. In other words, the true M for either population may be higher or lower than their corresponding sample M's. The question we want to answer is whether or not the true M of each population could be the same. As we have said before, we can never know what the true M is unless we measure the entire population. What we need is some technique for determining whether or not the true M's differ, and for efficiency and economy we should be able to determine this from our two randomly drawn samples. Or, in the above illustration, we would hope to be able to determine this by drawing a single pair of samples, one of country boys and one of city boys. Such a technique is available and the key concept to its understanding is the variability of a distribution of differences.

Variability of a Distribution of Differences

We remember from the previous chapter that if we should draw a large number of random samples from a population and find M of each sample, we would expect the distribution of these sample M's to be normal. Furthermore, we saw that SD of this distribution (σ_M) allowed us to make statements of probability about where the true M lies and to make statements of probability about where any subsequently drawn sample M's would fall. Now, let us go one step farther. From a single population we will draw *pairs* of random samples. For each sample in a pair we will get M. Due to sampling error, the two M's of a pair will probably differ. For each pair of samples we take the *difference* between the two M's. We continue drawing pairs of samples until we have a very large number of these differences, say, 500. Each difference would always be obtained in the same way, e.g., we would always subtract M of the first-drawn sample from M of the second-drawn sample in the pair. Since these samples were drawn from the same population we would expect about half of the differences to be positive and about half negative, most falling close to zero. If we plot such a large number of differences (frequency along Y axis and size of difference along X axis) we may expect that this distribution of differences would be normal. This distribution is called a sampling distribution of differences.

Having obtained such a distribution of differences our next

task would be to describe it statistically. We could determine M, and *since the pairs of samples were drawn from the same population, we would expect this M to be approximately zero*. This would be true, for in the long run we would expect the negative and positive values to cancel each other. We could also calculate SD of this distribution of differences. How can we use this SD? The important thing we can do with it is to make statements of probability about where differences between any two sample

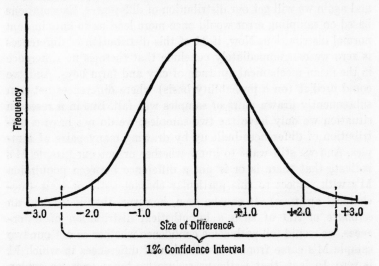

FIG. 9.1. Distribution of a very large number of differences between pairs of sample M's. The distribution is assumed to have an SD of 1.

M's will fall. Or, we could set up confidence intervals limiting the range of scores within which any subsequently determined differences will lie. That is, the 1% confidence interval would set the limits within which we would expect 99 out of 100 differences between two sample M's would fall. Perhaps a visualization of this would be helpful. If we drew a very large number of pairs of samples from the same population, M of the distribution of differences between pairs of sample M's would be zero. Assume that SD of this distribution of differences is 1. In Figure 9.1 we can see that the 1% confidence interval would be from −2.58 to +2.58. Thus, for all subsequent pairs of samples we draw from this population we would expect 99 out of 100 of these differences in pairs of sample M's to fall within this 1% confidence interval.

Thus far in our discussion we have dealt with the drawing of pairs of sample M's from a *single* population. Now, let us consider the situation where we draw two samples, but each from a *different* population. Let us hypothetically draw a large number of pairs of samples from our populations of city and country boys. Each pair will represent one sample from each population and again we will get our distribution of differences. Expectations based on sampling error would once more lead us to anticipate a normal distribution. Now, if M of this distribution of differences is zero we can immediately conclude that there is no difference in the mean mechanical aptitude of city and farm boys. And, we could predict (on a probability basis) where differences between subsequently drawn pairs of samples will fall. But in a research situation we only have the two samples; we do not have a distribution of differences built up by drawing many pairs of samples. And we still want to know whether or not our sample M's indicate that there is or is not a difference between population M's with respect to this particular characteristic or trait (mechanical aptitude). It can be seen, however, that if we had an *estimate* of SD of such a hypothetical distribution of differences, we would tell with some confidence whether or not our two sample M's came from a distribution of differences in which M is zero. In fact, that is the procedure we take: once we get an estimate of SD of this distribution, we test the hypothesis that the true M of the distribution of differences is zero.

The Null Hypothesis

The null hypothesis simply asserts, as we have asserted just above, that M of the sampling distribution of differences is zero. Or, to say it another way, it asserts that the difference between the two population M's is zero. The test of the null hypothesis consists in determining whether or not the difference between the two sample M's ordinarily obtained in such research could, because of sampling error, arise from a sampling distribution of differences in which M is zero. For example, let us assume in our illustration of mechanical aptitude that M of the farm sample is 55, of the city sample, 50. Again, let us assume that SD of the sampling distribution of differences is 1. We can see that a mean difference of 5 would rarely arise due to sampling error if the difference between population M's were zero. With SD of 1, our 1% confidence interval allows a maximum mean difference of 2.58 by sampling error; hence, it is quite unlikely that we would obtain the mean difference we did obtain between our samples if the difference between population M's were zero. Thus we reject the null hypothesis at the 1% level of confidence. *Rejecting the null hypothesis is the same as saying that there is a significant difference between sample M's.*

Estimating SD of sampling distribution of differences. We have seen that if we have an estimate of SD of the sampling distribution of differences we could test the null hypothesis for a pair of sample M's. Remember that we need an estimate of SD of a very large number of differences between sample M's. Such an estimate is given by the formula below. This statistic is called the *standard error of a difference*. It is symbolized as σ_{diff}.

$$\sigma_{\text{diff}} = \sqrt{\sigma_{M_1}^2 + \sigma_{M_2}^2}$$

where: $\sigma_{M_1} = \sigma_M$ of one of the samples
            $\sigma_{M_2} = \sigma_M$ of the other sample

It can be seen that this formula makes an estimate of SD of a distribution of differences between M's by utilizing the σ_M of each of the sample M's (and you will remember that σ_M was an estimate of what SD of a large number of sample M's would be). The σ_{diff} is simply one step further along from σ_M; *it is an estimate of what SD of a large number of differences between sample M's would be.*

Let us take a simple case to show how calculations follow from this formula. Suppose M for country boys is 55, that for city boys, 50. Suppose further that the respective σ_M's are 2.1 and 2.0. Therefore:

$$\sigma_{\text{diff}} = \sqrt{\sigma_{M_1}^2 + \sigma_{M_2}^2}$$
$$= \sqrt{(2.1)^2 + (2.0)^2}$$
$$= \sqrt{8.41} = 2.90$$

We have hypothesized that the true difference between M's is zero. In our illustration the calculated value, 2.90, is to be thought of as SD of a distribution of differences around zero, as shown in Figure 9.2.

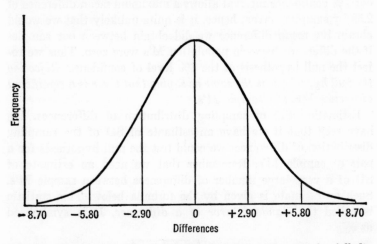

FIG. 9.2. Visualization of σ_{diff} assuming M of zero. See text for full discussion.

In testing the null hypothesis for this example, we ask ourselves: "If the true difference is zero, would we expect to get a mean difference as large as 5 due to random sampling errors?" A difference as large as 5 (in either direction) would fall nearly $2\sigma_{diff}$ units away from M of zero. We would probably say that a difference this big could be expected once in a while; that is, if the true difference is zero, a difference as large as 5 will occasionally occur in sampling. Here again, however, we need something more precise than the inspectional check we get from the drawing of the distribution; we need a more precise statement of probability. Again, to obtain this, we revert to the z-score technique permitting use of the normal curve table. This technique, when applied to test the difference between M's, is to be called the t-ratio.

t-RATIO

To get the t-ratio we divide the difference between the two sample M's by the σ_{diff}:

$$t = \frac{M_1 - M_2}{\sigma_{diff}}$$

We said above that t was just another z-score. This becomes apparent when we remember that we are testing the hypothesis that the true difference between M's is zero. A z-score is X — M divided by SD. In the case of t, X is the difference between M's, i.e., $M_1 - M_2$. Since we are testing whether this difference is significantly different from zero, we should, to make t a z-score, subtract zero from the difference between sample M's. However, most mathematicians would agree that subtracting zero wouldn't change the situation appreciably so it is not done in the t formula.

In the illustration we have been discussing (mechanical aptitude of city and country boys) our M's were 55 and 50, with a σ_{diff} of 2.90. If we substitute these values in the t formula we have:

$$t = \frac{M_1 - M_2}{\sigma_{diff}} = \frac{55 - 50}{2.90} = \frac{5}{2.90} = 1.72$$

Referring to Table B we see that a deviation this big in one direction will include about 45% of the cases, or combining both directions, 90%. Or, to say it another way, a difference this big or bigger would be expected to result from sampling error in 10% of the cases. Thus, it is quite possible that this one difference is an occurrence that could be expected if the true difference were zero; it would be expected once in 10 times and this might be that once. Since we use the 5% confidence level as our minimum level, we have no firm basis for rejecting the null hypothesis, because the true difference between the population M's may well be zero.

Further Illustrations

Three illustrations will show you how the t-ratio is used in actual research problems. An investigator [1] wished to determine

[1] Kausler, D. H. A study of the relationship between ego-involvement and learning. *J. Psychol.*, 1951, 32, 225-230.

what influence ego-involvement would have on performance in a symbol-substitution task. Ego-involvement is a technique for inducing high motivation in subjects. You will probably get the idea from the following instructions which this group of subjects received:

"As a part of the testing program at Washington University you are required to take the Perceptual Intelligence Test. This test measures perceptual intelligence, an important component of total intelligence. Your score on this test will be added to your permanent record at the University" (p. 227).

Actually this symbol-substitution test (so-called Perceptual Intelligence Test) probably has very little relationship to intelligence, so the investigator was in fact lying to the subjects. The purpose, of course, was to motivate the subjects and these kinds of instructions seem to do it, for if the subject doesn't do well he would in effect be admitting he was stupid, an embarrassment which most of us try to avoid.

Another group (non-ego-involved), on the other hand, was told only that the symbol-substitution test was given to them as a demonstration of a learning task. This, as you can probably see, provides quite a different atmosphere for working on the task as compared with the instructions given the experimental group. Therefore, the difference in the treatment of the two groups was in terms of instructions. Both groups were given 10 minutes to complete as many of the substitution problems as possible. The "non-ego" group, consisting of 49 subjects, got a mean of 68.14 substitutions during the 10-minute period. The "ego" group $(N = 44)$ completed an average of 78.09.

The essential question we ask ourselves about these M's is whether or not they represent samples drawn from two populations with the same M. If the difference between M's can indeed be shown to be a likely result of sampling error, then we cannot reject the null hypothesis and can assert that the different treatments accorded the two groups had no appreciable influence on their behavior. If M's can be shown to be significantly different, we may conclude that the treatments very probably produced significant differences in behavior (symbol-substitution performance).

Let us look at the essential steps in the computations to see which conclusion we are going to accept:

Ego: N = 44   Non-Ego: N = 49
M = 78.09   M = 68.14
σ = 17.44 σ = 18.03

$$\sigma_M = \frac{\sigma}{\sqrt{N-1}} = \frac{17.44}{6.56} = 2.66 \qquad \sigma_M = \frac{18.03}{6.93} = 2.60$$

$$\sigma_{diff} = \sqrt{\sigma_{M_1}{}^2 + \sigma_{M_2}{}^2} = \sqrt{(2.60)^2 + (2.66)^2}$$
$$= \sqrt{6.76 + 7.08} = \sqrt{13.84} = 3.72$$

$$t = \frac{M_1 - M_2}{\sigma_{diff}} = \frac{78.09 - 68.14}{3.72} = \frac{9.95}{3.72} = 2.67$$

We now look in Table B to discover what this t means. Remember that a t is essentially a z-score, and shows the number of deviation units from M. In this case the deviation units are those defined by the standard error of the difference (σ_{diff}). The deviation was the difference between the sample M's. If the true difference between M's were zero, i.e., if the population M's were identical, we see that a deviation of 2.67 units would occur only very rarely due to sampling errors. Actually 2.67 units on either side of M includes about 99.6% of the cases. In other words, if the true difference is zero, the difference we found above would occur less than once in 200 times as a consequence of sampling error. Under such slim chances, we are quite justified in rejecting the null hypothesis at the 1% level of confidence and may say that the differential treatment of the two groups produced significant differences in performance.

In discussing some concepts earlier we asked about differences in mechanical aptitude of farm and city boys. Such an investigation was actually carried out. Records were kept at a selection board as applicants for flight training appeared. As a part of the selection process all boys were given a mechanical aptitude test. For 170 city boys M was 49.51, while for 110 farm boys it was 51.28. As before, we shall see if these two M's indicate that both populations could have the same M with respect to mechanical aptitude. The null hypothesis in this case implies that the fact that one group lived on farms and one group lived in cities has no influence on mechanical aptitude. The following values were obtained:

Farm: N = 110   City: N = 170
M = 51.28   M = 49.51
σ = 6.71 σ = 6.47
σ_M = .64 σ_M = .50

σ_{diff} = .81
Difference = 1.77
t = 2.19

Checking in Table B we see that 2.19 sigma units above and below M will include about 97.14 per cent of the cases. That is, if the true difference is zero, we have obtained a difference that would be met or exceeded about one and one-half times out of 100 occurrences by sampling error; we are somewhat short of the 1% confidence interval, but much better than the 5% confidence interval. Strictly on the basis of these statistical results, we are likely to conclude that there is a true difference between the mechanical aptitude of farm and city boys. But a word of caution is in order. Don't take this conclusion too seriously, for we don't actually know that each sample was a random sample of its population. And clearly, if they were not random samples, we have failed to meet one of the assumptions on which t is based. We must remember that statistics only tells us about the differences obtained; it can't tell us whether or not we have a random sample in such a case as this. Whether or not a sample is judged to be random or not depends upon the technique of sampling used by the investigator.

You probably should check the calculations in the above two illustrations to see if you can independently arrive at the values obtained. Note that in each of the two illustrations N's were different for each sample. This is happenstance, and the N's may be the same or different. The procedure and reasoning is the same in both instances.

One final illustration: two groups of 36 college students each were selected and tested on a common task before being introduced to differential treatments. Testing both groups on a common task allows us to find out if the random selection of subjects resulted in two samples which were clearly from the same population. The particular task was learning lists of words. The t value shows that we cannot reject the null hypothesis; both samples could have come from populations with the same M.

Group 1: M = 14.08   Group 2: M = 13.42
$\sigma = 6.03$ $\sigma = 5.09$
$\sigma_M = 1.02$ $\sigma_M = .86$

$$\sigma_{diff} = 1.33$$
Difference = .66
$$t = .50$$

SIGNIFICANCE OF DIFFERENCE BETWEEN MEANS OF SMALL SAMPLES

In our interpretation of t thus far, we have used Table B, the normal-curve table. If we wish to interpret the difference between sample M's based on small samples, we must use a special table. When z-scores are based on large N's, these z-scores are distributed normally and so the normal-curve table is appropriate. When z-scores are based on small samples, they are not normally distributed. Since t is a z-score, we therefore do not expect the sampling distribution of t to be normal when based on small samples. The upshot of this is that we need a special table when evaluating t-ratios based on small samples, this table reflecting accurately the sampling distribution of t for small samples. Such a table is reproduced as Table C in the back of the book. In this table we have indicated the t-ratios which are required for the 5% and the 1% confidence levels. In Table C we also see a column labelled df, which means *degrees of freedom*. This column is necessary for the significance of a t-ratio depends upon df.

The df is based on N and is obtained by either of two formulas:

$$df = N_1 - 1 + N_2 - 1; \text{ or, } N_1 + N_2 - 2$$

If we draw two independent samples where N is 10 each, the df is 18, i.e., $10 + 10 - 2$. If we compare M's of two samples of 7 each, df is 12. As we have previously indicated, we must always indicate the confidence level we are using when testing hypotheses about M, or about difference between M's. In addition, when we are reporting t's based on small samples we must always report df.

Suppose we ran five rats through a maze and fed them a sunflower seed after each trip. Suppose further that another group of five is fed milk after each trip. The question is which kind of reward produces the most rapid learning. Assume that the milk group learns to go through the maze without error in an average of 12 trials and the sunflower group in an average of 9 trials. We calculate SD, σ_M, σ_{diff}, and obtain a t of 2.19. Now we enter the table at 8 df. We see that with 8 df ($N_1 - 1 + N_2 - 1 = 8$) we need a t of 2.31 to be significant at the 5% level of confidence. Therefore, we cannot assert with any confidence that the two rewards produced any difference in rate of learning. In short, we cannot reject the null hypothesis. For comparison purposes, you may note that in our illustration of mechanical aptitude of farm and city boys we obtained the same t (2.19) and we interpreted this as indicating a significant difference. Thus it becomes quite apparent that because of the small N in our groups of rats we must get a larger t if we are to attain the same confidence level we had with large N's.

The calculation of the t-ratio for small samples is exactly the same as for large samples. The only point at which the two methods differ is in the table used in interpreting the ratio. So, let us report only one experimental illustration of the use of small samples.

An investigator [2] wished to determine the influence of electric shock on the learning of a simple discrimination by white rats. The rats were to learn to take a lighted alley to get food and not to take the dark or unlighted alley (no food). The 10 rats in one group were shocked if they took the correct (lighted) alley, and the rats in the second group were shocked if they took the wrong (dark) alley. Each rat was run until it reached the criterion of 18 correct responses in 20 attempts. The data indicate the number of attempts required to reach the criterion.

[2] Wischner, G. J. The effect of punishment on discrimination learning in a non-correction situation. *J. exp. Psychol.*, 1947, 37, 271-284.

Shock Right	Shock Wrong
$N = 10$	$N = 10$
$M = 159.0$	$M = 104.0$
$\sigma_M = 14.3$	$\sigma_M = 6.0$

$$\sigma_{diff} = 15.5$$
$$\text{Difference} = 55.0$$
$$t = 3.55$$

With 10 animals in each group we have 18 df, and we find in Table C that a t of 2.88 is needed for significance at the 1% level of confidence. Since the obtained t is 3.55, far beyond the value required for the 1% level of confidence, we can confidently conclude that the two different treatments produced differences in performance. Somehow it appears that rats don't learn as fast if they are shocked for making the response leading to food as they do if shocked for making the incorrect response. This rat behavior does, of course, square with common human sense.

Additional comments about small-sample t's are needed before we conclude the chapter. The t formula we have used for large samples is not exactly correct for small samples with unequal N's, and strictly speaking should be used with small samples only if the N's are equal. However, if there is a difference of one or two cases no great error will be introduced and we may still feel reasonably confident in the standard formulas as presented here. It is inadvisable, however, to use this formula if the N's are quite different, say, 5 cases in one group and 12 in another.

The question may be asked as to when small samples cease to be small. The table we are using to interpret our small samples stops with 30 df. One should use this table for all interpretations if the df is 30 or less. However, you can see by comparing this table with the normal probability table (Table B) that beyond 30 df there is no appreciable difference in the values needed for stated levels of confidence. That is, there is little difference between 30 df and an infinite number.

Finally, it should be mentioned that the t-ratio for small samples is not appropriate if the populations from which samples are drawn are not normal. It is by no means an easy matter to know whether or not normality exists. In actual practice we seldom know whether or not the assumption of normality is met in our

data. But, knowing about this assumption we may be less inclined
to leap to conclusions based on five cases unless we have some
idea about the way the characteristic measured is distributed in
the populations from which the samples are drawn.

In a later chapter we will return to other techniques for determining the significance of the difference between means. To understand these techniques one needs a knowledge of the coefficient
of correlation, and it is to that statistic that we next turn.

10

Correlation

CORRELATION METHOD VERSUS EXPERIMENTAL METHOD

Scientific problems are usually attacked experimentally if possible. For example, we vary the intensity of light falling on a page, in order to determine whether the amount of light affects reading speed. This is the customary procedure in experimentation; we vary a condition such as intensity of light and note the result of that variation. Another example of the experimental method would be a study in which different groups of students are given different amounts of training in American history in order to find out whether or not such training affects their attitude toward the doctrine of states' rights. Many phenomena, however, are not subject to experimental manipulation. We are unable either to change the movements of the planets or to control the birth rate in the United States to any great degree. To establish scientific laws about either of these phenomena, we must use a correlational approach instead of an experimental one.

Correlation, as the word itself suggests, is an interrelation between two or more sorts of conditions or events. We call these events *variables* because we are studying the way they vary. If families with many children tend to have a higher income than families with few children, we say that there is a *positive correlation* between the two variables of family size and family income. If, however, families with many children tend to have a lower income than families with few children, we would say that a *negative correlation* exists, instead of a positive one. The third possibility, that family income is *the same* regardless of family size, would lead us to say that there is a *zero correlation* between family size and family income.

These three classes of correlation (positive, negative, and zero) are shown graphically in the three parts of Figure 10.1. The three graphs in the figure are each called scatter plots because they show how the points scatter over the range of possible scores. Every point represents two values, an individual's score on one variable (X) and the same individual's score on a second variable (Y). Both variables are plotted on the same graph because we are interested in the relationship between the two variables. In harmony with the practice established in Chapter 4, the X variable is always measured along the horizontal axis and the Y variable along the vertical axis.

Figure 10.1 A shows the relationship between the size of the pupil of a person's eye when he is silent and when he is stuttering, as observed in an experiment designed to indicate some physiological factors related to stuttering.[1] This graph shows that a stutterer whose pupil size is relatively large during silence will also have relatively large pupils when he is stuttering; and vice versa. This, of course, is an example of positive correlation. We notice, however, that this positive correlation between X and Y does not mean that X and Y have the same values: Y, the pupil size during stuttering, is generally about .25 mm. larger in diameter than X. The presence of positive correlation, then, only implies that a person's X and Y scores tend to be of about the same *relative* size, not that they tend to be numerically *identical*. The next figure, Figure 10.1 B, shows the relationship between scores on a personality inventory (X) and an anxiety test (Y). In this scatter plot there is a tendency for persons with high X scores to have low Y scores and vice versa. Therefore, we say that there is a negative correlation between X and Y in this case.

Figure 10.1 C shows a scatter plot of two variables with no relationship between them. Each X score represents the time taken to complete an introductory psychology test, and the Y

[1] Gardner, W. H. The study of the pupillary reflex, with special reference to stuttering. *Psychol. Monogr.*, 1937, 49, No. 1, 1-31.

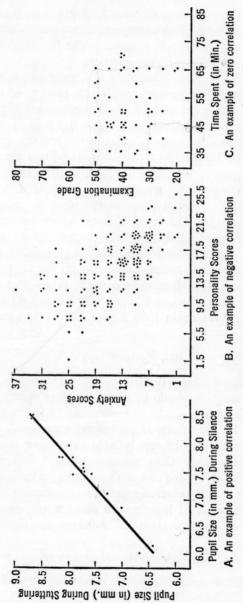

FIG. 10.1. Scatter plots showing three types of correlation between X and Y

A. An example of positive correlation

B. An example of negative correlation

C. An example of zero correlation

score for the same person represents his grade on that test. We say that there is zero correlation here because examination scores do not vary consistently in relation to the length of time spent by the students taking the examination.

We have just seen that the data of Figure 10.1 A and 10.1 B exhibit different *directions* of correlation, positive and negative, respectively. When we look at these figures carefully, we note another difference: each point of Figure 10.1 A lies very close to the straight line drawn through that figure, but any straight line drawn through Figure 10.1 B would lie at quite a distance from several data points. This second way in which scatter plots may differ is with respect to the amount or *degree* of correlation between X and Y. Disregarding the fact that the correlation is positive in one case and negative in the other, we say that the correlation between pupil size during silence and during stuttering is higher than the correlation between personality scores and anxiety scores because the measures of pupil size are more nearly arranged in a straight line. Consequently, Figure 10.1 A shows a *high* positive correlation, and Figure 10.1 B shows a *low* negative correlation. Notice again that Figure 10.1 C represents a *zero* correlation.

What Does a Correlation Study Show?

A good experiment attempts to provide evidence whether changes in one variable do or do not produce changes in some other variable. For example, an experiment by Hovland [2] showed that, under his experimental procedure, nonsense-syllable lists presented at the rate of one syllable every four seconds were learned more quickly than nonsense syllable lists at a two-second rate. Since nothing else was varied, we presume that differences in rate of presentation must have produced the observed differences in speed of learning—in other words, that the first variable, rate of presentation, *did* influence the other variable, learning speed.

Unfortunately, a correlational analysis can seldom produce this

[2] Hovland, C. I. Experimental studies in rote-learning theory. III. Distribution of practice with varying speeds of syllable presentation. *J. exp. Psychol.*, 1938, 23, 172-190.

kind of evidence: that is, evidence that one variable influences another. Consider the possibility that we might find a negative correlation between family size and family income. This may mean that having large families produces low incomes, or that having low incomes produces large families, or that (as is more likely) a third variable is responsible for both low income and large family size. This situation is typical: *a correlational study rarely indicates which variable influences which, or even whether either variable is influencing the other one directly. And in any case a correlation coefficient, as a statistical procedure, can never tell us anything about causality at all.* A ludicrous example of the confusions resulting from an attempt to show a causal relation between two variables by correlational research was once given by Willoughby.[3] In attacking another scholar's argument that a high positive correlation between vocabulary and college grades meant that improvement in vocabulary would produce an improvement in grades, Willoughby stated that by the same reasoning a high positive correlation between the height of boys and the length of their trousers would mean that lengthening trousers would produce taller boys. In neither of these cases have we evidence *proving* that one variable directly controls the other.

Although correlational research seldom shows what factor is responsible for a relationship between two variables, it is nevertheless a valuable method of measuring these relationships. The primary purposes of this chapter are to demonstrate this method of measuring relationships and to show how to make predictions of one variable from another when the correlation between the two is known. The latter technique would enable us to do such things as predicting with some accuracy the intelligence quotients of children from the intelligence quotients of their parents, since there is a sizeable correlation between the IQ's of the parents and their children. Still another use of correlation, a modified *t*-test for use with groups whose scores are correlated, will be described in Chapter 11.

[3] Willoughby, R. R. Cum Hoc Ergo Propter Hoc. *School and Society,* 1940, 51, 485.

THE PEARSON OR PRODUCT-MOMENT
CORRELATION COEFFICIENT (r)

Earlier in this chapter we developed in a general way the meaning of the terms *positive, negative,* and *zero* correlation and of *high* and *low* correlation. These terms are quite serviceable in some situations. For example, if a scatter plot shows that all paired X and Y points lie on a single straight line with large X's and large Y's being paired and small X's and Y's also being paired, there is a high positive correlation. In fact, in this example where all the pairs lie on a straight line, the correlation is as high as it could be, and we call it a perfect positive correlation. In many other cases, however, it is hard to determine at once from a scatter plot alone whether a correlation is positive or negative or whether it is high or low, because we do not employ any exact usage for these terms. Supposedly a positive correlation exists when large X's and Y's tend to be paired and small X's and Y's tend to be paired, but the word "tend" is too vague to help us recognize a positive correlation with certainty. Similarly, we say that a correlation is high if the points on a scatter plot lie close to some straight line drawn through the data, but we don't know the exact meaning of "close."

Such verbal expressions as "tend" or "close" are not precise enough. Therefore, we are forced to introduce a new concept, the *correlation coefficient*. This coefficient will have a specific numerical value for any given set of paired data. Positive values of this coefficient will correspond to what we have called positive correlation, and negative values will correspond to what we termed negative correlation. Furthermore, high values of the coefficient, regardless of whether they are positive or negative, will correspond to what we have called high correlation, and low values of the coefficient will correspond to what we have called low correlation. However, what would be called zero correlation when seen on a scatter plot may not in fact have a correlation coefficient of exactly zero although the value will surely be near zero. This is true, for example, of the data of Figure 10.1 C which actually have a slightly negative correlation coefficient although it is so low that we have called the correlation zero.

In actual practice statisticians use several different correlation coefficients. We will identify the one we will be using most often by its technical name, the *Pearson (product-moment) correlation coefficient,* and its symbol, *r.* This coefficient is named in honor of Karl Pearson, one of the great pioneers of statistics. Because *product-moment correlation coefficient,* an alternative name for the Pearson correlation coefficient, is a highly technical term whose meaning is not essential to the research worker, we will not explain the origin of that term. The three expressions: Pearson correlation coefficient, product-moment correlation coefficient, and *r* will be used interchangeably in this chapter.

Basic Formula for *r*

We are now ready to state the definition of the Pearson correlation coefficient. The value of this coefficient (*r*) is equal to the mean of the *z*-score products for the X and Y pairs. This definition is stated algebraically below:

$$r = \frac{\Sigma z_X z_Y}{N}$$

$$\text{where } z_X = \frac{X - M_X}{\sigma_X} = \frac{X \text{ score} - M \text{ of } X}{SD \text{ of } X}$$

$$z_Y = \frac{Y - M_Y}{\sigma_Y} = \frac{Y \text{ score} - M \text{ of } Y}{SD \text{ of } Y}$$

$$N = \text{the number of pairs}$$

According to this formula, we find *r* by first calculating each person's *z*-score on X and his *z*-score on Y. (Notice that *z* means exactly the same thing here as in previous chapters.) Next we would multiply each person's z_X score by his z_Y score, giving us a ($z_X z_Y$) product for every individual. Then we would add up all these products (i.e., find $\Sigma z_X z_Y$) and divide by N to find the M of the *z*-score products. Since this value is what we have defined as *r,* our computation of *r* would then be complete.

Now that we have a definition of *r,* it is appropriate to ask if the *r* values we obtain with this definition will have the same size and direction which our early statements about correlation suggest. We have said, for example, that a positive correlation will occur if relatively high X's and Y's tend to be paired and if relatively low X's and Y's tend to be paired. Can we say that r will be positive when these conditions are met? To answer this question, we will study how the value of r changes for different arrangements of z-scores.

If X is larger than M_X, z_X will be positive because the formula $z_X = \dfrac{X - M_X}{\sigma_X}$ leads to positive z_X's in this case. Similarly, if X is smaller than M_X, z_X will be negative. Corresponding statements will be true for Y. Thus if X is larger than M_X and Y is larger than M_Y, $(z_X z_Y)$ will be the product of two positive numbers and will be positive. If X is less than M_X and Y is less than M_Y, $(z_X z_Y)$ will still be positive because it will be the product of two negative numbers. Consequently r, the M of the $(z_X z_Y)$'s will be positive when large X's and large Y's are paired and small X's and small Y's are paired. Since this situation is what we have called positive correlation previously, a positive r does correspond to our definition of positive correlation. Analogous reasoning could be used to show that a negative r value corresponds to the general case of negative correlation and a zero r to the case of zero correlation. Furthermore, r gives a numerical description of the degree of relationship between two variables, which is consistent with our previous definition of high and low correlation.

Having seen the connection between r and our original concept of correlation, we are ready to consider some additional characteristics which will affect our use of it. One important fact about this correlation coefficient is that *no* r *ever is less than −1 nor more than +1*, regardless of the size of the X and Y units or the number of pairs being correlated. When a perfect negative correlation exists (i.e., when all points on the scatter plot lie on a straight line with high X's paired to low Y's and low X's paired to high Y's), r is −1. When a perfect positive correlation exists (i.e., when all points on the scatter plot lie on a straight line with high X's paired to high Y's and low X's paired to low Y's), r is +1. At all other times r is somewhere between −1 and +1. This restriction of the range of possible correlation coefficient values is extremely fortunate because *it permits a direct comparison of*

r's *obtained from widely different sets of data without a correction for the size of the original X and Y values*. In this respect r is similar to z.

Two examples of the computation of r with the basic formula are presented in Table 10.1. In Case 1 most of the pairs of z's for X and Y are either both positive or both negative, producing positive values of $(z_X z_Y)$ and a positive $(z_X z_Y)$ which in turn

TABLE 10.1

An Example of the Way r Depends upon the Pairing of z-Scores

CASE 1			CASE 2		
Most $(z_X z_Y)$ products positive			Most $(z_X z_Y)$ products negative		
z_X	z_Y	$(z_X z_Y)$	z_X	z_Y	$(z_X z_Y)$
1.4	1.3	1.82	−1.4	1.3	−1.82
1.9	1.3	2.47	−1.9	1.3	−2.47
1.0	1.1	1.10	−1.0	1.1	−1.10
0.0	0.5	0.00	0.0	0.5	0.00
−0.7	0.4	−0.28	0.7	0.4	0.28
−0.8	−0.4	0.32	0.8	−0.4	−0.32
−0.2	−0.5	0.10	0.2	−0.5	−0.10
−0.9	−1.1	0.99	0.9	−1.1	−0.99
−0.8	−1.3	1.04	0.8	−1.3	−1.04
−0.9	−1.3	1.17	0.9	−1.3	−1.17

$$\Sigma (z_X z_Y) + \text{'s} = +9.01 \qquad \Sigma (z_X z_Y) + \text{'s} = +0.28$$
$$\Sigma (z_X z_Y) - \text{'s} = -0.28 \qquad \Sigma (z_X z_Y) - \text{'s} = -9.01$$
$$\Sigma (z_X z_Y) \quad = \quad 8.73 \qquad \Sigma (z_X z_Y) \quad = -8.73$$

$$r = \frac{\Sigma z_X z_Y}{N} \qquad\qquad r = \frac{\Sigma z_X z_Y}{N}$$

$$r = \frac{8.73}{10} \qquad\qquad r = \frac{-8.73}{10}$$

$$r = .873 \qquad\qquad r = -.873$$

produces a positive r of .873.[4] In Case 2 the z_X values are the same as those of Case 1, except that the z_X's which were positive have been changed to negative and those which were negative have been changed to positive. In other words, persons whose X scores were above M_X in Case 1 are now below M_X in Case 2, and

[4] In this book no sign is attached to an r value unless it is negative. Consequently, an r value of .873 is positive and an r value of $-.873$ is negative.

persons whose X scores were below M_X in Case 1 are now above M_X in Case 2. Consequently most of the $z_X z_Y$ products in Case 2 are negative, producing a negative r value of $-.873$. The size of r is the same as before, but its direction has been changed from positive to negative. This illustrates the fact that the direction of correlation depends upon whether positive z_X's are paired with positive z_Y's and negative z_X's are paired with negative z_Y's or the reverse.

The Computational Formula for r

Despite the ease with which our basic formula for r can be remembered, a different equation is more useful for computing r. From the definitions of z_X and z_Y a computational formula has been developed:

$$r = \frac{\dfrac{\Sigma XY}{N} - M_X M_Y}{\sigma_X \sigma_Y}$$

This equation gives exactly the same results as the previous one and has the great advantage that it permits use of raw scores (X and Y) in place of z-scores. Therefore, we need not perform the tedious process of converting each raw score into a z-score before computing the correlation coefficient. The use of this computational formula for r is quite easy because there is only one new expression in the formula. That expression is ΣXY, the sum of the products of each X and its corresponding Y value. This value is found by multiplying each X by the Y value paired with it and adding these products. Then $\Sigma XY/N$ may be found by dividing ΣXY by N, the number of pairs, of course.

You should beware of one error which you may make as you learn to calculate r. "Perhaps," you might say, "I could find ΣXY by multiplying ΣX times ΣY instead of multiplying each X by the corresponding Y before summing." *Do not do this*. Your idea is like a famous round battleship in Russian history: it sounds fine, but it really won't work. Unfortunately ΣXY must be found by the way described in the previous paragraph; it is not equal to $(\Sigma X)(\Sigma Y)$.

The way to use the computational formula to find r is shown in Table 10.2, which shows the steps necessary to find the r

TABLE 10.2

Demonstration of the Use of the Computational Formula for r

X (Pre-shock)	X^2	Y (Post-shock)	Y^2	XY
5.0	25.00	7.0	49.00	35.00
6.0	36.00	5.8	33.64	34.80
6.5	42.25	7.8	60.84	50.70
4.7	22.09	5.9	34.81	27.73
5.8	33.64	6.8	46.24	39.44
7.4	54.76	8.0	64.00	59.20
5.0	25.00	4.0	16.00	20.00
5.2	27.04	6.4	40.96	33.28
4.5	20.25	5.1	26.01	22.95
5.8	33.64	7.7	59.29	44.66
5.6	31.36	5.8	33.64	32.48
8.0	64.00	8.5	72.25	68.00
6.3	39.69	9.0	81.00	56.70
5.5	30.25	7.6	57.76	41.80
6.9	47.61	8.4	70.56	57.96
5.2	27.04	6.6	43.56	34.32
3.3	10.89	3.6	12.96	11.88
5.5	30.25	7.3	53.29	40.15
5.8	33.64	7.0	49.00	40.60
7.4	54.76	9.5	90.25	70.30
$\Sigma X = \overline{115.4}$	$\Sigma X^2 = \overline{689.16}$	$\Sigma Y = \overline{137.8}$	$\Sigma Y^2 = \overline{995.06}$	$\Sigma XY = \overline{821.95}$

$$M_X = \frac{\Sigma X}{N} = \frac{115.4}{20} = 5.77 \qquad M^2{}_X = 33.2929$$

$$\sigma_X = \sqrt{\frac{\Sigma X^2}{N} - M^2{}_X} = \sqrt{\frac{689.16}{20} - 33.2929} = 1.08$$

$$M_Y = \frac{\Sigma Y}{N} = \frac{137.8}{20} = 6.89 \qquad M^2{}_Y = 47.4721$$

$$\sigma_Y = \sqrt{\frac{\Sigma Y^2}{N} - M^2{}_Y} = \sqrt{\frac{995.06}{20} - 47.4721} = 1.51$$

$$r = \frac{\dfrac{\Sigma XY}{N} - M_X M_Y}{\sigma_X \sigma_Y} = \frac{\dfrac{821.95}{20} - (5.77)(6.89)}{(1.08)(1.51)} = \frac{41.0975 - 39.7553}{1.6308}$$

$$r = \frac{1.3422}{1.6308} = .823$$

between two sets of data obtained in an experiment on the effects of electric shock upon drinking rate.[5] The amount of water that each of 20 animals drank in a test period before shock (pre-shock) is called X, and the corresponding amount drunk in a test period after shock (post-shock) is called Y. For example, the first row in the table indicates that one animal had a pre-shock score (X) of 5.0 and a post-shock score (Y) of 7.0. Because the M's and SD's for X and Y are part of the formula for r, their calculation is included in Table 10.2 with the other steps involved in computing r.

As Table 10.2 shows, the r for these two distributions is .823. We may draw the conclusion that there was a strong tendency in this experiment for rats that drink a good deal before shock to drink a good deal after shock and for those that drank little before shock to drink little afterward. A more complete interpretation of this r of .823 will be made as soon as we have discussed a few other properties of r.

WHAT r MEANS

The Pearson or product-moment correlation coefficient for a particular set of data measures a specific type of relationship: the *linear correlation* between two variables. By this, we mean that r measures the *degree* to which a straight line relating X and Y can summarize the trend in a scatter plot. Figure 10.2 presents two such scatter plots, Figure 10.2 A exhibiting a linear correlation and Figure 10.2 B exhibiting a non-linear (or curvilinear) relationship between X and Y.

Although the data of Figure 10.2 B are best described by the dotted curved line of that figure, the straight line drawn through the same figure does come close to many of the data points. Thus a straight line has some usefulness for summarizing the relationship between X and Y in this case.

What would happen if we computed r, a measure of linear correlation, for data which have a curvilinear relation? The answer

[5] Amsel, A., and Maltzman, I. The effect upon generalized drive strength of emotionality as inferred from the level of consummatory responses. *J. exp. Psychol.*, 1950, 40, 563-569.

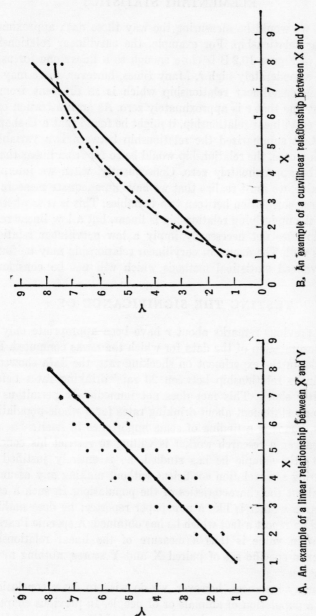

A. An example of a linear relationship between X and Y

B. An example of a curvilinear relationship between X and Y

FIG. 10.2. Scatter plots of two hypothetical sets of data showing different kinds of relationships between X and Y

is that we would be measuring the way those data approximate a linear relationship. For example, the curvilinear relationship shown in Figure 10.2 B is close enough to a linear one for us to expect a moderately high r. Many times, however, there may be a strong curvilinear relationship which is so different from a straight line that r is approximately zero. As an illustration of a highly curvilinear relationship, it might be found that a U-shaped curve best summarized the relationship between two variables. In such a case, the relationship would be so far from linear that r might be approximately zero. Consequently, when we interpret an r value, we must realize that we have an adequate measure of the *linear* correlation between two variables. This is true whether or not the underlying relationship is linear, but a low linear relationship does not necessarily imply a low curvilinear relationship as well. The degree of curvilinear relationship may be found by advanced statistical methods which will not be considered here.

TESTING THE SIGNIFICANCE OF r

Our previous remarks about r have been appropriate only to the interpretation of the data for which the r was computed. For example, in the experiment on shocking rats, the data showed a high linear relationship between 20 rats' drinking rates before and after shock. This fact does not immediately permit us to make any statement about drinking rates for a whole population of rats, but it is a finding of some importance in itself.

Whenever a research worker is willing to restrict his conclusions to the sample he has studied, he is entirely justified in computing a correlation coefficient without making any assumptions about the characteristics of the population. In such a case a research worker is like a newspaper reporter: he does nothing more than report a fact which he has obtained. A specific Pearson correlation value is thus a measure of the linear relationship between a specific set of paired X and Y scores, nothing more, nothing less.

In many instances, however, we do wish to draw conclusions about a population of animals or of people. In previous chapters we wanted to know whether two sample M's were drawn from populations with the same M's. At the present time we wish to make inferences about the population r from the r of a sample. In particular, we wish to know whether a sample r of a given value would have been likely to occur if the population r were zero. This amounts to a test of a new null hypothesis which asserts that the value of the population r is zero.

Testing the significance of r is quite easy to do because no formulas are needed. Table D in the back of this book lists the significant values of r for the 5% and 1% levels of confidence. Whenever r is equal to or greater in absolute size than the appropriate significant value, regardless of whether r is positive or negative, we can conclude that it is significant at the level of confidence we are using. You will notice that the significant values of r depend upon the number of degrees of freedom (df) just as the significant values of t do. This is true because the probability of obtaining any specific r value varies with the size of the sample. Notice that the df is N-2 for this test, one less than you might have expected. As we have said, N is the number of *pairs* of scores.

The procedure for testing the significance of r can now be illustrated by testing the significance of the .823 value of r obtained from the rat experiment previously mentioned. Since this r was based on 20 pairs of measurements, there are 20 — 2 or 18 df. Table D shows that for 18 df the smallest significant r at the 1% level is .561. Therefore, the obtained r of .823 is clearly significant at that level. Consequently, we reject the hypothesis at the 1% level that r is zero in the population from which the 20 rats were drawn. We do this because the logic of our statistical test implies that there would be less than 1 chance in 100 of obtaining a sample r of .823 if the population r were zero. Thus, unless we have failed to meet the statistical assumptions for this test, we can conclude that there is some linear correlation between drinking rates before and after shock in the population from which the experimental subjects were drawn.

The Assumptions Involved in Testing r for Significance

Assumptions are merely conditions that must be met for a statistical test if the test is to be appropriate. For example, the *t*-test depends upon the assumption or requirement that the experimental data are random samples from the populations being studied. Assumptions like this are important because they are used in developing the statistical tests. Unless the assumptions of a test are met, then, the results of a test may be false and misleading.

Only two assumptions are required for testing the significance of *r*. First, the sample used must have been obtained by random sampling from the population concerned. Second, the population of X and Y scores must have a distribution which we will characterize by saying that X and Y must each be normally distributed, and that the relationship between X and Y must be linear. This is by no means a complete statement of the second assumption, but it suggests what to consider before testing *r* for significance. If the sample is randomly drawn, if X and Y are each normally distributed, and if the correlation between X and Y is linear, one may reasonably decide to perform this significance test.

Another Illustration of the Use of Table D

Another example of a test for the significance of *r* can be taken from a study [6] of the selection of police officers. The research workers in this study were attempting to discover whether tests of various abilities would be useful in predicting which policemen would be the most competent in their jobs. They found that marksmanship and scores on a mechanical comprehension test exhibited a Pearson correlation value of .27 when 129 St. Louis patrolmen were tested. For 125 degrees of freedom, which is the tabled value just lower than the 127 which we would use if the table were more complete, the 1% level *r* is .228. Therefore the .27 *r* which these investigators obtained is significant at better than the 1% level. We conclude that there is some positive correlation between marksmanship and the mechanical comprehension scores in the population being sampled, an indication that a mechanical comprehension test might be useful in selecting the persons to be hired as patrolmen. Of course, the finding of sig-

---

[6] DuBois, P. H., and Watson, R. I. The selection of patrolmen. *J. appl. Psychol.*, 1950, 34, 90-95.

nificant correlations like this one is only the first step in the selection of patrolmen. A more complete discussion of the use of tests for selection purposes may be found in most texts on industrial psychology or test construction.

THE USE OF r IN PREDICTING Y FROM X

Once a relationship between two variables has been found, it is often desirable to predict the value of one variable to be expected when a particular value of the other is obtained. For example, a university registrar might wish to predict college grades (Y) from performance on an aptitude test (X). If a method for such prediction were available, he could tell from the aptitude test scores which applicants for admission would be most likely to succeed in college and which would be most likely to fail. Then he would be able to admit only those students with reasonable chances of success. This is exactly what is done in many colleges. Another situation in which this type of prediction would be important is the case where some performance measure increases in a linear fashion with amount of practice. Through a study on the effects of practice in reading, it would be quite useful, if this were possible, to predict reading speed (Y) after different amounts of practice (X). This could serve two purposes: to indicate how much a specific person could improve his reading speed and to formulate a scientific law about the relationship between practice and reading speed.

To predict scores on one variable (Y) from scores on another (X), we first obtain pairs of data in which one X and one Y appear in each pair. Then we determine what would be the best Y value to predict for each X value if the actual Y value were not known to us. The predicted Y's can be compared with the obtained Y values to indicate the success of the predictions. The ultimate usefulness of this technique will be in predicting Y values when only X values are known.

Now that we know our goals in the prediction of one variable from another, we can turn our attention to the method of making such predictions. First, we recall that Figure 10.1 A was said to represent a high correlation because the straight line drawn through that graph came close to most of the plotted points. This line is a prediction line or, as it is often called, a *regression line*.

Another example of a regression line is given for the scatter plot presented in Figure 10.3, which shows the relationship between body weight (X) and ability to maintain bodily equilib-

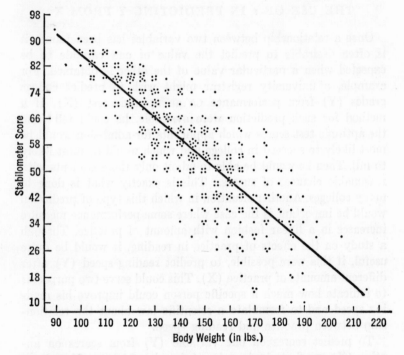

FIG. 10.3. A scatter plot and regression line relating stabilometer scores to body weight

rium (Y) observed with an instrument called a stabilometer.[7] This figure shows that subjects whose body weight is great have less ability to maintain equilibrium than those whose body weight is small. Thus there is a negative correlation between body weight and ability to balance oneself, and the regression line goes from the top left of the graph to the bottom right.

[7] Travis, R. C. An experimental analysis of dynamic and static equilibrium. *J. exp. Psychol.*, 1945, 35, 216-234.

Notice that the regression line comes close to many data points, showing that good predictions can be made on the basis of negative correlations as well as positive ones.

Although the regression line shown in Figure 10.3 seems to conform to the relationship between the X and Y scores in that figure, other straight lines could be drawn which would seem just as satisfactory for predicting Y from X. In fact, if 20 people each drew a straight line through this figure to indicate where the regression line should be, 20 different regression lines might result. Therefore, we cannot trust ourselves to decide where a regression line should lie by simply looking at a graph. To make certain that everyone will make the same predictions of Y from X for any set of data we must have a procedure for finding the "best" regression line.

The Equation of a Regression Line

If there is a best regression line, there is also an equation for that line. The rules for finding this equation, called the *regression equation*, are simple but very important. The regression equation for finding the predicted Y (Y_{pred}) from X is given below:

$$Y_{pred} = \left(\frac{r\,\sigma_Y}{\sigma_X}\right) X - \left(\frac{r\,\sigma_Y}{\sigma_X}\right) M_X + M_Y$$

With this equation we can determine what value of Y to predict from any X value, provided that we know the values of r, σ_Y, σ_X, M_Y, and M_X.

The use of this equation may be illustrated by reference to the experiment we previously mentioned on the effect of shock upon drinking rate. Table 10.2, which presented the data from that experiment, contains the information we need in order to develop a regression equation for predicting post-shock drinking rate (Y) from the pre-shock rate (X). With the aid of that table we substitute the values $r = .823$, $\sigma_Y = 1.51$, $\sigma_X = 1.08$, $M_Y = 6.89$, and $M_X = 5.77$ into the regression equation just presented and find:

$$Y_{pred} = \frac{(.823)\,(1.51)}{(1.08)} X - \frac{(.823)\,(1.51)}{(1.08)} (5.77) + 6.89$$

After the appropriate multiplications and divisions have been performed this equation reads:

$$Y_{pred} = 1.15X - 6.64 + 6.89$$

Finally, the subtraction of 6.64 from 6.89 leads us to the final form for this regression equation:

$$Y_{pred} = 1.15X + .25$$

We can now predict Y for each X in Table 10.2. Table 10.3 shows how each prediction is made. It also presents the actual Y values in order to permit a comparison of Y_{pred} values with the actual

TABLE 10.3

An Application of the Regression Equation in Predicting Post-shock Drinking (Y) from Pre-shock Drinking (X)

X	1.15X	Y_{pred} (1.15X + .25)	Y (Actual)
5.0	5.75	6.00	7.00
6.0	6.90	7.15	5.80
6.5	7.48	7.73	7.80
4.7	5.40	5.65	5.90
5.8	6.67	6.92	6.80
7.4	8.51	8.76	8.00
5.0	5.75	6.00	4.00
5.2	5.98	6.23	6.40
4.5	5.18	5.43	5.10
5.8	6.67	6.92	7.70
5.6	6.44	6.69	5.80
8.0	9.20	9.45	8.50
6.3	7.24	7.49	9.00
5.5	6.32	6.57	7.60
6.9	7.94	8.19	8.40
5.2	5.98	6.23	6.60
3.3	3.80	4.05	3.60
5.5	6.32	6.57	7.30
5.8	6.67	6.92	7.00
7.4	8.51	8.76	9.50

Y's. This comparison indicates that the regression equation for these data leads to rather successful predictions. For example, when X = 3.3, $Y_{pred} = 4.05$ and Y = 3.60. When X = 8.0, then $Y_{pred} = 9.45$ and Y = 8.50.

No experimenter expects predictions based upon a regression equation to be perfect. In fact, several Y_{pred} values in Table 10.3 are badly in error. However, if r is not zero, the use of a regression equation is a better method of prediction than any alternative such as using M_Y as the value of Y_{pred}, regardless of the X value. Furthermore, a very large r, near either -1 or $+1$, leads to predictions which are nearly perfect. In general, as the size of r becomes greater, the predictions become more accurate.

THE RANK ORDER CORRELATION
COEFFICIENT (ρ)

Occasionally sets of data either are reported by their rank orders only, or it seems desirable to assign ranks to them and work with the ranks rather than the raw scores. Thus a collection of rocks might be ranked in order from hardest to softest even though no other measurement of hardness had been made first; or the performance of baseball teams, first reported as percentages of games won, might be converted to ranks by giving the team with the highest percentage rank number 1, the next team rank number 2, and so on. In these situations the r between the ranks themselves could be determined by means of our computational formula. However, a new formula will give exactly the same results with even less computational work. This formula, which is called the formula for the rank order correlation coefficient, ρ (the Greek letter *rho*), follows:

$$\rho = 1 - \frac{6\Sigma d^2}{N(N^2 - 1)}$$

where N is the number of pairs of ranks and d is the difference between a pair of ranks (never the difference between a pair of scores). You should notice that the 1 and the 6 in the formula are always used when ρ is to be found. They are constant regardless of the values of N or of d.

The application of this formula for the rank-order correlation coefficient may be illustrated by showing the computations required to find the correlation between the final standings of the American League baseball clubs for 1951 and 1952. Table 10.4

presents these computations. The ranks or final standings for the 1951 season are listed as X, and the standings for the 1952 season are listed as Y. The difference, d, for each team is equal to $X - Y$. The value of ρ proves to be .667. This indicates a sizeable relationship between the final standings for the two years.

TABLE 10.4

Computation of ρ for the Final Standings of the American League Baseball Clubs in 1951 and 1952

TEAM	(RANKS FOR 1951) X	(RANKS FOR 1952) Y	$d = X - Y$	d^2
New York	1	1	0	0
Cleveland	2	2	0	0
Boston	3	6	−3	9
Chicago	4	3	1	1
Detroit	5	8	−3	9
Philadelphia	6	4	2	4
Washington	7	5	2	4
St. Louis	8	7	1	1
				$\Sigma d^2 = 28$

$$\rho = 1 - \frac{6\Sigma d^2}{N(N^2 - 1)}$$

$$\rho = 1 - \frac{6(28)}{8(63)} = 1 - \frac{168}{504} = .667$$

The Case of Tied Ranks

The rules for calculation of ρ must include what to do if there are ties for some ranks. If, for example, Cleveland and Boston had tied for second place in 1951, one would need to know how to treat their ranks before finding the correlation. A simple method is to assign each of the two tied teams the rank of 2.5, the average of the second and third ranks, since Cleveland and Boston together must account for the ranks 2 and 3, i.e., the ranks *between* 1 and 4. Then ρ is computed as before.

We illustrate the assignment of values for the case of tied ranks by the following example listing the intelligence quotients (IQ's) and ranks of ten persons whom we designate by the letters A through J:

Persons	A	B	C	D	E	F	G	H	I	J
IQ	130	128	128	122	115	110	100	100	100	95
Rank	1	2.5	2.5	4	5	6	8	8	8	10

First of all we notice that B and C tied for the second place in their IQ's. Since B and C together account for the second and third persons in order of rank, 2 and 3 were averaged, giving 2.5 for B and 2.5 for C. Then D was assigned the fourth rank since three persons were superior to him. Finally, G, H, and I were all assigned rank 8 because they were all tied and together represent the three ranks of 7, 8, and 9, which have an average of 8; and J, the last person, received a rank of 10 because nine persons were superior to him.

Interpreting the Rank-order Correlation Coefficient

When ρ is found for data originally measured in ranks, ρ has the same value that r would have (except in the case where ties have occurred) and may, therefore, be interpreted as a measure of the amount of linear correlation between ranks. If the data were originally expressed in other units than ranks (e.g., in intelligence scores), ρ (which is, of course, the correlation between *ranks*) is not equal to the r between the original scores. However, since ρ and r will have similar values, we are permitted to infer the approximate size of the r between the original variables from the size of ρ.

Despite the similarity between ρ and r, we cannot test the significance of ρ by means of Table D, the table of significant r's. Table D is inappropriate because the assumptions underlying r are not met with ρ. However, the significance of ρ may be tested by another method. If we assume that there is no relationship between the ranks obtained on X and those obtained on Y, then there is a specific probability value that a ρ as large in absolute value as the one obtained in a particular study could arise. If this probability is less than 5%, we reject the hypothesis of no relationship at the 5% level. If this probability is greater than 5%, we accept the hypothesis.

Table E in the back of the book presents the values of ρ required for significance at the 5% level and at the 1% level. As in the case of r, the required values for significance depend upon the number of pairs, N. In Table E, N is used directly without the necessity of finding a df value first. We will now use this table to determine whether the ρ for the final standings of American League teams in 1951 and 1952 is significant. As we have said, ρ is .667 and is based upon an N of 8. When we refer to Table E, we see that a ρ of .738 is required for significance at the 5% level. Since our obtained ρ is below this, we would accept the hypothesis of no relationship between 1951 and 1952 standings at the 5% level. Notice that this is a case in which a ρ which seems quite large (.667) is not significant at the 5% level because it is based upon a relatively small N.

We may summarize the facts about ρ by saying that it is a measure of the correlation between ranks and has the same value as would the r between ranks, assuming there are no ties in rank. Although ρ does not have the same value as the r between the scores on which the ranks were based, one would expect ρ and this r to have similar values. A significance test for ρ may be made with Table E which is used in the same way that Table D was used for r.

11

Statistics and the Design of Experiments

EXPERIMENTATION AND THE *t*-TEST

In Chapter 9 we learned how to determine, by means of the *t*-test, whether the difference between two random sample M's is significant. To repeat briefly what was said at that time, we measure two random samples on a certain trait or characteristic and find that their M's differ. We assume the null hypothesis, the hypothesis that our two samples were randomly drawn from populations that have the same M on the trait we are measuring. From the results of the *t*-test we state whether we will or will not reject the null hypothesis at a certain level of probability. If we reject the null hypothesis, we are saying that our sample M's come from populations whose M's *do* differ with respect to this characteristic.

The *t*-test is one of the most useful statistical methods available to the research worker. This is because much research takes the form of experiments in which the performance of at least two groups or samples of subjects is measured under *different conditions*, to determine whether or not the conditions produce different performance. Thus many investigations yield at least two mean scores, one from a group tested under one condition, the other from a group tested under another condition. If the *t*-test indicates a significant difference between M's, the experimenter concludes that the two conditions *do* produce differences in performance. Now note what this conclusion means: the investigator is assuming that the two groups would *not* have differed, except by sampling error, had they been measured under the *same* conditions. In other words, the experimenter assumes that if he had measured a large number of similar sets of two groups under the same conditions, he would have found no consistent difference between groups. If the assumption is true that the two groups of subjects would not have differed except for sampling error when measured under the same conditions, we call them *comparable groups*. Such groups may be used in research where their performance is measured under *different* conditions to find out whether the *conditions* produce significantly different performance.

It follows from what we have just said that a fundamental problem in research is the original selection of groups of subjects, selection so the groups are comparable at the beginning of the experiment. If groups are not comparable originally, conclusions drawn about the conditions studied may be in error no matter whether the conditions did or did not have different effects. It is the purpose of this chapter to describe the methods used to obtain comparable groups for research, and to present the appropriate statistics for each case.

Illustration of an Experiment

Before we take up the first method (random samples), we shall present an illustrative experiment. By doing this first, we can be a little more concrete about some of the aspects of an experiment mentioned earlier, and we shall have an illustration to which we can refer in order to clarify points to be taken up later.

Let us say an investigator wants to study the effect of distraction on learning. In the terminology used earlier, he is going to compare performance, as measured by speed of learning, under the conditions of distraction, with performance under the condition of no distraction. Each of his two groups of subjects consists of 20 undergraduates. The group that serves under the distraction condition is obtained in part from the 16 students in a senior psychology course taught by the experimenter, who requires them to serve. The experimenter then gets 24 volunteers from an introductory history course. After assigning four of these to the distraction group and the remaining 20 to the no-distraction group, he has his two samples.

The task used is the learning of a list of facts. Both groups learn the capital cities of 30 foreign nations. While learning the list, each member of the distraction group is subjected to the song *Johnson Rag* played on a tape recorder and heard by him through earphones. The no-distraction group learns the list without being subjected to sound.

At the conclusion of the study the investigator has, as a score for each subject, the number of trials (number of times through the list) required to learn. He computes M for each group and finds a greater mean number of trials to learn for the distraction group. The difference between the M's is tested by the *t*-test and found to be significant at better than the 5% level of confidence. The experimenter concludes that the sound was an effective distraction, producing slower learning in the distraction group.

We now ask: Shall we accept the investigator's conclusion? We should *not* accept his conclusion, because it is entirely possible, even probable, that the groups were not comparable originally. A senior psychology class and an introductory history class are very probably different in many respects. For one thing, the group containing more history students may have known more foreign capitals to begin with. As we said earlier, *the groups in an experiment must be chosen so they would not differ except for sampling error if they were tested under the same conditions.* In this study this basic requirement probably was not met. The groups differed in too many ways for the research worker merely to assume, as he did, that they were alike at the outset on characteristics that could bias the results. There are other biasing characteristics (in addition to original knowledge of foreign capitals) on which the groups may well have differed originally. One such factor is ability to learn lists of specific facts; one group may have consisted, on the average, of faster learners. Another bias is that one group consisted of volunteers, while most of the other group were required to serve.

Prepared by this example of a poorly designed experiment, which no resort to a *t*-test could save, let us take up an acceptable way of choosing groups for research, namely, random sampling.

RANDOM SAMPLES

Earlier, we referred to the groups in an experiment as samples. We shall now take up the case where the groups are *random samples*. As we already know, a random sample is one drawn such that every member of the population from which the sample is taken has an equal chance of being chosen. In an experiment we need two groups, both of which are to be random samples. We can achieve this if each subject is drawn randomly from the population, and if the assigning of each subject to a group is also random.

How would random sampling work in the case of our illustrative experiment on distraction during learning? First, the experimenter would have to define the population. Let us say he defines the population as all undergraduates in the college where he is working. Then the actual mechanics of drawing the two random samples could be carried out in a number of ways, e.g., by putting each student's name on a slip of paper and drawing slips from a hat in which the slips have been thoroughly mixed. Strictly speaking, to maintain the requirement of random sampling that each individual has an equal chance of being chosen, each member drawn must be returned to the population before the next is drawn. For practical reasons, we usually cannot meet this requirement. This, however, is not serious when the sample N is very much smaller than the population N, which is usually true.

Why Random Samples?

We ask you to recall once again the problem on which we are working: we want to obtain comparable groups of subjects for an experiment. How is this requirement met by random sampling? First, we remember that comparable groups were defined as those that do not differ *except for sampling errors*. Now if we draw a *single* random sample from a population, the difference between the sample M and the population M is sampling error. A large number of sampling errors is likely to be distributed normally. This means that positive and negative sampling errors would, in the long run, tend to cancel each other out; the M of a normal distribution of random sampling errors approaches zero. It also means that any one sampling error is likely to be small, since in a normal distribution values close to M occur more frequently.

If, now, we draw *two* random samples from the same population, differences *between the sample M's* are also sampling errors. Again, these sampling errors, which now are differences between M's of random samples, also tend to be distributed normally with M approaching zero. Therefore, the probability is greater of drawing two random samples that differ by a small rather than a large sampling error. It follows that a research worker can use random samples from the same population for testing under the different conditions of his investigation, with confidence that any original difference between the samples is sampling error and is probably small.

There is another reason for basing research on random samples from the same population: the probability values given in Tables B and C, which are used to evaluate *t*-ratios, are appropriate for random sampling. Recall that whenever we report that a difference between M's is significant at, say, the 1% level, we mean that the probability is no more than 1 in 100 that such a large difference would occur if the difference between population M's were zero. Such statements are appropriate if random sampling, and other assumptions of the *t*-test, are met.

The *t*-test with Random Samples

After an investigator measures the performance of his random samples under different conditions, he computes the two M's and finds they differ numerically. It is now meaningful to test whether the M's differ significantly. We have already learned in Chapter 9 the necessary computations for the *t*-test in this case. We wish here only to draw your attention again to the standard error of the difference (σ_{diff}), the denominator of the *t*-ratio. When the samples are chosen randomly, the σ_{diff} is given by,

$$\sigma_{\text{diff}} = \sqrt{\sigma_{M_1}{}^2 + \sigma_{M_2}{}^2}$$

This is the formula that was given in Chapter 9. We merely add here that it is the formula for σ_{diff} to be used for random samples, and that when we take up the case of matched samples we shall find that another term must be added to the formula.

MATCHED SAMPLES

So far in our discussion of the problem of obtaining comparable groups for research we have considered only the case where each subject needed is randomly and independently drawn from the population. There exist, however, some populations where the members occur in *pairs*. By this we mean that for each member of the population there is another member who is similar or in some way related. For example, in a population made up of a large number of sets of identical twins, each individual is quite similar, on many characteristics, to the other member of the population who is his twin. Even a population of boys and their sisters can be considered a population of pairs, since on some characteristics a boy will be more similar to his sister than he would be to a girl chosen at random.

Whenever we sample from a population of pairs of individuals to obtain comparable groups for research, we usually do *not* draw each sample randomly. Instead, we first draw a random sample of the *pairs;* that is, the two persons forming a pair are drawn simultaneously but randomly with respect to any other pair. We then form groups of subjects by picking randomly one member of each pair to be assigned to one group. The other member of each pair goes into the other group. Thus, if our population is composed of brothers and sisters, we would first select a random sample of pairs, each pair consisting of a boy and his sister. Then one member of each pair is picked *randomly* and assigned to one group; the other group is made up of the remaining member of each pair. The result will be that *each* group contains *both* boys and girls. Then, as usual, one group is tested under one condition, the other group under the other condition; we compare conditions or groups, not boys and girls.

Such samples are called *matched* or *correlated* samples and it will be worth while to examine how they differ from random samples. Let us first assume the drawing of a large number of sets of *random* samples (two samples in each set) from some defined population. If the samples are random, there will *not* be a tendency for the M's of the two samples in a set to be similar. If M of one sample of a set is a relatively high value, M of the other sample is just as likely to be relatively low as high. We are saying that *random samples are not correlated*. Furthermore, if we plot a distribution of the *differences* between M's of sets of random samples, we find that the *variability* of the distribution is relatively large because in some sets the M's are quite far apart. In other words, the σ_{diff}, the measure of variability of differences, is relatively large for M's of random samples.

Suppose, on the other hand, we have a population from which we can draw sets of *matched* samples (two samples per set), and again assume we draw a large number of sets of such samples. In this case we will find that the M's of the two samples of a set *do* show a tendency to be related in some way. If the pairs of scores are *positively correlated*, then when M of one sample of a set is a high value, M of the other sample also tends to be high. Similarly, low values tend to go together. For example, the IQ's of brothers and sisters are positively correlated. Suppose we draw sets of samples such that in each set one sample consists of boys and the other sample their sisters; that is, we draw matched samples. In a set where the boys have a high mean IQ, the mean IQ of their sisters will tend to be relatively high, and when the boys' M is low, the girls' M tends to be low. The result is that differences between M's of sets of positively correlated samples tend to be smaller than differences between M's of sets of random samples. *This means that the variability of a distribution of such differences, i.e., the σ_{diff}, will be less for positively correlated samples than for random samples.* Because of this, when we wish to test for the significance of a difference between M's of matched samples, we must use a different formula for the σ_{diff} than we use for random samples. Let us see what this formula is.

The *t*-test with Matched Samples

When an investigator has used matched samples in his research, the samples having been measured under different conditions, he will, as usual, have two distributions of scores at the conclusion of his research. As always, the distributions represent performance under the different experimental conditions, and the difference between the M's is to be evaluated by the t-test. For matched samples, the formula for σ_{diff} (again, the denominator of the t-ratio) is:

$$\sigma_{\text{diff}} = \sqrt{\sigma_{M_1}{}^2 + \sigma_{M_2}{}^2 - 2r_{12}\sigma_{M_1}\sigma_{M_2}}$$

where: σ_{M_1} = standard error of the mean of one group
σ_{M_2} = standard error of the mean of the other group
r_{12}(read: r sub one two) = the Pearson product-moment correlation coefficient between the two groups, i.e., between the two distributions being tested for significance of difference.

Note that this formula is the same as the σ_{diff} formula for random samples except for the term, $2r_{12}\sigma_{M_1}\sigma_{M_2}$, after the minus sign. Let us consider the correlation coefficient, symbolized by r_{12}. *It is the correlation between the two distributions, the M's of which are to be tested for significance.* Recall that to compute a Pearson r between two distributions we must be able to pair a score from one distribution with a score from the other. In any experiment using matched groups each pair of scores comes from the already-paired subjects. Thus, *all* the terms under the radical sign in the σ_{diff} formula, the standard errors and the correlation, are obtained from the two distributions of scores resulting from the experiment. Either of these distributions may be identified by the subscript 1 and the other by the subscript 2.

What happens to the σ_{diff} for matched groups as r_{12} takes various values? When r_{12} is zero, the last term under the radical (everything after the minus sign) becomes zero, and we have the σ_{diff} formula for random groups. If there is no correlation between the groups they are, in that respect, the same as random groups. If r_{12} is some positive value, the σ_{diff} will be *smaller* than when r_{12} is zero, and the higher the r_{12} the greater the reduction in the σ_{diff}. Thus we can see that if the difference between two M's (the numerator of the t-ratio) is the same whether the difference is between two random groups or two matched groups, the difference is more likely to result in a significant t, when divided by the appropriate σ_{diff}, in the matched groups. We can also see why there would be little point in using matched samples in an experiment unless the members of a pair are originally fairly similar. Unless the r_{12} is at least some medium to high value, there will be little reduction in the σ_{diff}.

Same Subjects in Both Groups

There is another case in which the σ_{diff} formula for matched groups is used. This is the case in which a *single* random sample of subjects serves in *both* conditions of the experiment.

Recall that our major concern, as we have harped so incessantly, is to obtain comparable groups for research. The two ways to obtain comparable groups that we have discussed, namely, random samples and matched samples, both involve different individuals in the two groups. Most research requires that the groups contain different individuals, and this is the root of our problem; we must get different groups that can be considered comparable for the purposes of some experiment. This is not always easy to do because people vary widely on almost every measurable characteristic. Therefore, it is especially pleasing to the research worker that in some studies he can use the same group of people in both conditions of the study. Whether or not he can use only one group depends upon the conditions being studied and the performance to be measured, but if he can, the group's performance is measured once under one condition and again under the other condition. Thus, two scores are obtained for each subject, each score obtained under a different condition.

Whenever possible, it is advantageous to use the same subjects in both conditions. In the first place, the actual mechanics of getting the subjects and running them in the experiment are usually simpler because only a single random sample is used. More importantly, there is no problem of obtaining comparable groups. The subjects serving in the different conditions are ideally matched; they are highly correlated because they are the same people. An individual is likely to be a better match for himself than is any other individual.

The Direct-Difference Method

We have discussed two cases, matched samples, and same subjects in both groups, where we must take account of the correlation between groups when we compute the σ_{diff} for a t-test. Let us consider an example, an experiment where such a correlation existed.

The example we have chosen here is a case where the same subjects were used in both conditions of the study. The investigators [1] measured the number of times it was necessary to expose a word before the word could be correctly recognized, when the time of exposure was only a fraction of a second. They wished to compare the speed with which taboo words, such as those with a sexual meaning, are recognized, with the speed of recognition of neutral words. So they measured the number of brief exposures necessary to recognize each taboo word, as one condition, and each neutral word, as the other condition. The same group of 20 subjects served in both conditions. The raw data are presented in Table 11.1. The table shows the total number of exposures before recognition of all taboo words and of all neutral words for each subject.

We want to determine whether the difference between the M's of the two raw score distributions in Table 11.1 is significant. For the t-test we need the difference between M's and the σ_{diff}. The formula for the σ_{diff} for matched groups requires that we compute the σ_M of each distribution, and the correlation (r_{12}) between the distributions. This is a lot of computation, so it is pleasant to be able to state that there is a much shorter method of doing the computations for the t-test for matched groups. We shall call it the *direct-difference method*. It can be used either with matched samples of different subjects or with same subjects in both groups.

To do the t-test for matched groups by the direct-difference method the *first* step is to obtain for each subject the *difference* between his two raw scores. This has been done in Table 11.1 in the column labeled "Difference." In subtracting one raw score from the other to get the difference score for a subject, it does not matter which is subtracted from which as long as it is done in the same way for every subject. In Table 11.1 the neutral-word score is subtracted from the taboo-word score; thus the

[1] McGinnies, E. and Sherman, H. Generalization of perceptual defense. *J. abnorm. soc. Psychol.*, 1952, 47, 81-85.

TABLE 11.1

Total Number of Exposures Required to See Taboo Words and
Neutral Words

SUBJECT	TABOO WORDS	NEUTRAL WORDS	DIFFERENCE	(DIFFERENCE)^2
1	10	12	−2	4
2	49	28	21	441
3	9	9	0	0
4	10	7	3	9
5	21	9	12	144
6	8	8	0	0
7	25	12	13	169
8	56	18	38	1444
9	6	9	−3	9
10	5	5	0	0
11	8	13	−5	25
12	8	7	1	1
13	14	6	8	64
14	21	13	8	64
15	31	32	−1	1
16	17	13	4	16
17	14	12	2	4
18	75	65	10	100
19	46	6	40	1600
20	68	20	48	2304

$$N = 20 \quad M_1 = 25.05 \quad M_2 = 15.20 \quad \Sigma D(+) = +208 \quad \Sigma D^2 = 6399$$
$$\Sigma D(-) = -11$$
$$\Sigma D = 197 \quad M_D = \frac{197}{20} = 9.85$$

$$\sigma_D = \sqrt{\frac{\Sigma D^2}{N} - (M_D)^2} \qquad \sigma_{MD} = \frac{\sigma_D}{\sqrt{N-1}}$$

$$\sigma_D = \sqrt{\frac{6399}{20} - (9.85)^2} \qquad \sigma_{MD} = \frac{14.93}{\sqrt{19}}$$

$$\sigma_D = 14.93 \qquad \sigma_{MD} = 3.43$$

$$t = \frac{9.85}{3.43} = 2.87$$

difference score is negative whenever the neutral-word score is larger. The difference scores, for which we shall use the symbol D, can be considered and treated in the same way as a distribution of raw scores.

Once the distribution of direct differences, each difference having its correct algebraic sign, has been obtained, *all* further computations are based on it. First, we compute the algebraic M of the differences. This is done by summing all the positive values, summing all the negative values, subtracting the sum of the negative from the sum of the positive to get ΣD, and then dividing by N to get M. In any matched groups experiment N is always the number of *pairs* of raw scores, or the number of direct differences; thus, in this experiment N is 20.

The algebraic M of the differences (M_D) is *always* the same as the difference between the M's of the two raw score distributions. Accordingly, in Table 11.1 M_D is 9.85, identical with the difference between the two raw score M's (25.05 and 15.20). The M_D is therefore the *numerator* in the *t*-ratio; it is not necessary to compute the M's of the raw score distributions, except as a check on accuracy of computation.

The σ_{diff} needed is obtained by computing the standard error of the mean difference (σ_{MD}). The σ_{MD} is obtained in the usual way: first compute SD of the distribution of differences (σ_D). Again letting D stand for difference, we can write the SD formula as:

$$\sigma_D = \sqrt{\frac{\Sigma D^2}{N} - (M_D)^2}$$

Then compute σ_{MD} by:

$$\sigma_{MD} = \frac{\sigma_D}{\sqrt{N-1}}$$

The standard error of the mean difference (σ_{MD}) is identical with the standard error of the difference that would be obtained by use of the long formula involving the correlation. We can express the long method of doing a *t*-test for matched groups, the direct-difference method, and the fact that the two methods give the same results by the following:

$$t = \frac{M_1 - M_2}{\sqrt{\sigma_{M_1}{}^2 + \sigma_{M_2}{}^2 - 2r_{12}\sigma_{M_1}\sigma_{M_2}}} = \frac{M_D}{\sigma_{MD}}$$

For the data in Table 11.1, $\sigma_{MD} = 3.43$. Our *t*-ratio is therefore 9.85/3.43, giving $t = 2.87$. In any experiment using matched groups the number of degrees of freedom for evaluating the t is $N - 1$, where again N is the number of *pairs* of subjects. With 19 df, this t is significant at the 1% level; we conclude that the taboo words were not recognized as rapidly as the neutral words.

The direct-difference method automatically takes into account the correlation that exists between the raw score distributions (r_{12}), regardless of the size or algebraic sign of the correlation. Therefore, as we have said, the t-value obtained by this method will be identical with the t-value obtained by use of the long formula for the σ_{diff}. We rarely use the long formula. It would probably save time only if we wanted to know the value of the correlation and already had r_{12} computed.

The r_{12} affects the *variability* of the distribution of direct differences. With a positive r_{12}, the SD of these differences is reduced (as compared to the σ_D if r_{12} is zero), and the higher the r_{12} the smaller the σ_D. And, of course, the smaller the σ_D the smaller the σ_{MD}.

Before leaving our example we may note that if we had incorrectly used the random groups formula for the σ_{diff}, we would have obtained a σ_{diff} value so large that the t would not have been significant. This would have led to the incorrect conclusion of no difference in speed of recognition of taboo words and neutral words. In this experiment the correlation (r_{12}) between the two raw score distributions is .717. This is the value that would be used in the long formula for matched groups; the result would be a σ_{diff} value of 3.43, the same as was obtained by the direct-difference method. However, using the random groups formula, ignoring the correlation, gives 5.76 as the σ_{diff} value. Then t would be 9.85/5.76, or 1.71, a value which is not significant at the 5% level. Thus the correct use of a method which takes the correlation into account reduced the σ_{diff} from 5.76 to 3.43, resulting in a significant t.

NONRANDOM SAMPLES

All of the methods of obtaining comparable groups for research that we have discussed so far require random sampling from a defined population. Unfortunately, these requirements are ideals that seldom can be met in practice. Actually, it is not an exaggeration to say that much, perhaps most, research in the biological and social sciences is based on groups that were not randomly drawn from a defined population. In order to get any research done at all, the investigator may have to use whatever subjects are available to him. There are certain disadvantages to this procedure that do not occur when random samples are used. We shall take up those matters later, but first let us describe some of the situations where random sampling is not feasible.

Groups Formed by the Investigator

A case that arises frequently is the one in which there are a certain number of subjects available, and where the investigator has control over what subjects are assigned to what groups. Thus, the investigator might have a group of volunteers from his classes, or, if he is using animals, a group bought from a biological supply house. Such groups cannot be considered random samples from a defined population. Usually, however, the subjects *can* be assigned at random to the different conditions of the experiment. This is advisable, since it would result only in chance differences between the groups. If the subjects cannot be assigned strictly at random to the groups, the groups must be tested for comparability. The method for doing this is described in the next section.

Intact Groups

Sometimes an investigator has to use, as his groups of subjects, individuals already organized into groups. Suppose, for example, he wants to compare two different methods of teaching introductory psychology. The only available subjects are the students taking the course. Suppose further that these students are divided into two sections meeting at different times. Very probably, the experimenter will have to use the sections as they exist, applying one method to one section, the other method to the other section.

In a case such as this the investigator must demonstrate that the groups are comparable for the purposes of the study. The problem of comparability is usually handled by comparing the groups' performance *before* introducing the different conditions. A pre-test is given that measures the same kind of performance as the post-test (the measure that will be used to compare the different conditions). Thus, in our example of different methods of teaching psychology, the students could first be given an examination on the same kind of material that will be used at the end of the course to measure the effects of the different methods. The experimenter compares the mean scores of the two groups on this pre-test, using the random groups t-test, and if the t-value is not significant, he considers the groups sufficiently comparable for the purposes of the study.

What happens if, upon pre-testing, the investigator finds a significant difference between groups? The common procedures are either to throw out some subjects, or to add further subjects, in order to make the groups comparable. If more subjects are available than are needed, as may be the case when the groups are formed by the experimenter, usually more subjects are added until comparable groups are achieved. With intact groups there may not be an extra supply of subjects. Comparable groups may be obtained in this case if enough of those subjects who got extremely high or low scores on the pre-test are, in effect, eliminated by omitting their scores. Subjects can also be added to intact groups by using other sets of such groups when they become available.

Advantages of Random Sampling

One of the advantages of random sampling from a specified population is, as we have said, the assurance that differences between samples are not systematic or consistent differences. There is another important advantage. Since the basic requirement of random sampling, (that every member of the population have an equal chance of being drawn), cannot be met without specifying the population, the limits within which an investigator can generalize his results are known. He can generalize to the population, and the sampling error formulas enable him to state the confidence intervals for the population values.

In contrast, when an experimenter uses groups that are not

random samples, he usually cannot specify the population. He is therefore in doubt about the generalizability of his results. Because of this, the research worker is very cautious in his generalizations. He makes no pretense that his results apply to any additional groups except perhaps those very similar to the ones he used. Although he may wish he could make predictions for larger groups, he will nevertheless have made a contribution if he shows whether or not the conditions he compared produced any difference in behavior, even if only in the groups he used. In short, much research still is needed to determine whether or not certain conditions have *any* effect on performance; such research may profitably proceed without precise specification of the population from which the samples were drawn.

12

Simple Analysis of Variance

<hr>

THE PURPOSE OF ANALYSIS OF VARIANCE

In previous chapters of this book we have explained techniques for analyzing data from two different experimental conditions in order to test hypotheses about the effects of those conditions. We saw how to test the significance of differences between M's for two separate groups treated differently and also how to test the significance of differences between M's for the same group of subjects tested under two different conditions. Yet we have paid little or no attention to the statistical analysis of findings based upon three or more conditions. The purpose of this chapter is to describe one of the most widely used methods for making such analyses.

First of all, we ask why an experiment should ever include more than two conditions. Two answers may be given to this question: (*a*) we may be interested in studying more than two conditions at a time, and (*b*) the data obtained with two conditions may give quite a different answer to our experimental problem than would comparable data from three or more conditions. Referring to our first point, we can see that an investigator might have three, four, or even more methods of teaching French which he would like to compare rather than only two methods. However, (and this is our second point) if the experimenter studied only two teaching methods and found no differences in the results, he might conclude that teaching methods never affect learning when, in fact, some other method which could have been included in an experiment with more than two conditions would have affected learning appreciably.

Let us consider another experiment in which more than two conditions would be desirable. If we wished to determine the course of forgetting with the passage of time, we could train each of two groups of people to recite a list of 12 nonsense syllables and test one group for retention one hour after training and another group 24 hours after training. This would give us two points on the forgetting curve, i.e., the curve showing how much is remembered at various lengths of time after training, but it certainly would not give us enough information to permit us to plot the intermediate points on the curve or even to estimate the amount of forgetting after, say, six hours. Here too, we need more than two experimental conditions in order to obtain an adequate picture of the relationship between experimental conditions and the behavior being observed.

Once it is agreed that experiments involving more than two groups or conditions are sometimes desirable, we are faced with the necessity of testing the significance of the differences among the M's obtained with the several conditions. Our first thought would surely be to compute t-ratios and test the significance of the differences between M's for all possible pairs of conditions. But this has certain disadvantages. For one thing, there may be a great number of pairs of conditions to be studied. If four methods of teaching French were to be compared, there would be six different t-ratios to be found. This fact is shown in the following list of pairs of methods whose data would form the basis for individual t-tests.

Pair 1 : Method A and Method B
Pair 2 : Method A and Method C
Pair 3 : Method A and Method D
Pair 4 : Method B and Method C
Pair 5 : Method B and Method D
Pair 6 : Method C and Method D

Not only would a great deal of numerical work be required, but the use of separate t-tests for analyzing the results of an experiment based upon more than three groups would lead to results which could not easily be interpreted. If we obtain one significant t-value out of six, what does this mean? Had we performed a single t-test, we would have had 5% probability of obtaining a t significant at the 5% level by random sampling alone, but with six t-tests our chances of having at least one of them significant because of random sampling is much larger. To carry this argument to its extreme, if a million t-tests were involved in an experiment, a single significant t-value would certainly be no indication that the conditions being varied had an effect.

We would not be handicapped by the fact that increasing the number of t-ratios to be computed for an experiment increases the probability that a significant t will be found if we could state how this probability changes with the number of t-values which are to be computed. Unfortunately this cannot be done, and so our use of t leads us to results which we cannot evaluate easily.[1] Consequently, a single test for the significance of the differences among all the M's of the experiment seems necessary as a means of reducing computational effort and permitting a more correct determination of the significance of differences obtained in the experiment. This chapter will introduce you to one such test, the *analysis of variance* technique. This technique is appropriate for use with two or more groups. However, it is most frequently employed with three or more groups, since the t-test is available for experiments involving two groups. First we will describe the principles of analysis of variance, and then we will show how to apply that method to scientific data.

THE ABC's OF ANALYSIS OF VARIANCE

Our purpose in this section is to describe the analysis of variance technique in very general terms. The basic fact which underlies the technique known as analysis of variance is that the

[1] If each of the t-ratios had been computed from a completely different set of data, we could employ the tables presented in the article: Wilkinson, B. A statistical consideration in psychological research. *Psychol. Bull.*, 1951, 48, 156-158.

However, when all possible pairs of conditions in a single experiment are compared, the same M and SD values are used several times, and the t-ratios are not independent of each other.

total variability of a set of scores from several groups may be divided into two or more categories. In the type of experimental design we are considering, there are two categories of variability: the variability of subjects within each group and the variability between the different groups. To visualize these two kinds of variability, imagine that we have four experimental conditions, each of which is applied to a different group. Suppose each condition yields widely different scores, so that members of Group 1 all have smaller scores than members of Group 2, who in turn have smaller scores than members of Group 3, and so on. This gives us the situation graphed in Figure 12.1. Notice that M values are given for each group separately and also for the set of four groups combined, in the latter case M being called M_{tot} (M of total). Now we can identify the variability observed in the experiment: the variability of the scores from M_{tot} is called the *total variability*, the variability of the scores from their group M's is called the *variability within groups*, and the variability of the group M's from M_{tot} is called the *variability between groups*. Consider, for example, the people who have the score marked X_2. The deviation $(X_2 - M_{tot})$ contributes to the total variability, but that deviation is composed of the two quantities $(X_2 - M_2)$ and $(M_2 - M_{tot})$ as Figure 12.1 makes clear. Since $(X_2 - M_2)$ is the difference between a score and its group M, and $(M_2 - M_{tot})$ is the difference between group M and M_{tot}, the contribution of X_2 to the total variability is made up of one part which is variability within a group, and another which is variability between groups. Since any score's deviation from M_{tot} may be divided algebraically into these two parts, it is possible to express the over-all variability observed in an experiment as the sum of these two types of variability, i.e., the sum of the variability between groups and the variability within groups.

Once we have assimilated the idea that one kind of variability in an experiment is variability between groups and another kind is variability within groups, we can let our previous experience with statistical tests suggest how this idea can be employed in analyzing differences in M values obtained from several groups. Thinking back to our study of t, we remember that the numerator of the t-ratio is equal to $M_1 - M_2$ and that the denominator is σ_{diff}. Since $M_1 - M_2$ is a measurement of the difference between groups, it could be called an expression of the variability between groups. Similarly, σ_{diff} could be considered a measurement of the

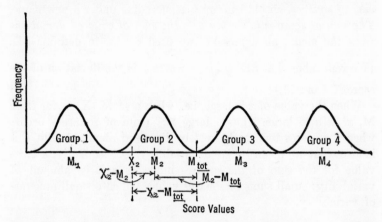

FIG. 12.1. An example of four groups of scores illustrating variability within groups and variability between groups

variability within groups, making t the ratio of variability between groups to variability within groups. In that case we could say that a significant t occurs only when the ratio of between groups variability to within groups variability is as large as the significant t's presented in Table C. Applying the same reasoning to experiments involving more than two groups, we decide that we again want to obtain a ratio of these two types of variability and, provided this ratio is sufficiently large, we call the differences among M's significant. The analysis of variance technique is simply a method which provides an objective criterion for deciding whether the variability between groups is large enough in comparison with the variability within groups to justify the inference that the M's of the populations from which the different groups were drawn are not all the same.

THE CONCEPT OF SUMS OF SQUARES

Basic Ideas

The cornerstone in the analysis of variance technique is the *sum of squares,* an old concept masquerading under a new name. *The sum of squares is simply* Σx^2, *the sum of squared deviations from the mean,* an expression we used earlier in defining SD. (We remember that $SD = \sqrt{\dfrac{\Sigma x^2}{N}}$ where x is the deviation of the score X from M.)

When the value of x is large, i.e., when a score (X) is far from M, x^2 is also large. Thus a large Σx^2 (sum of squares) occurs when the scores tend to be widely dispersed about M. But this is also what we mean by great variability. Consequently, a large value for the sum of the squares indicates a large amount of variability; small sums of squares values indicate small amounts of variability.

Types of Sums of Squares Values

We have already stated that the total variability in an experiment may be divided into two parts: the variability of subjects within groups, and the variability between different groups. Now we wish to find ways of computing sums of squares which will correspond to the total variability and to its two parts. These three sums of squares, which we shall call, respectively, total sum of squares (SS_{tot}), within-groups sum of squares (SS_{wg}), and between-groups sum of squares (SS_{bg}), will be discussed presently. First, however, we must list some new symbols which will be used in the remainder of this chapter:

M_{tot} = the mean of all the scores in the experiment. (Also called the grand mean or the over-all mean.)

M_g = a general expression for the mean of the scores in any group.

M_1 = the mean of the scores in Group 1.

M_2 = the mean of the scores in Group 2.

M_3 = the mean of the scores in Group 3.

N_{tot} = the number of scores in the experiment.

N_g = a general expression for the number of scores in any group.

N_1 = the number of scores in Group 1.

N_2 = the number of scores in Group 2.

N_3 = the number of scores in Group 3.

k = the number of groups.

X_1 = a score from Group 1.

X_2 = a score from Group 2.

X_3 = a score from Group 3.

The definition of SS_{tot}. The total sum of squares (SS_{tot}) is just what our previous statement would suggest: *the sum of squared deviations of every score from the mean* (M_{tot}) *of all the scores in the experiment.* This definition may also be expressed in an equation:

$$SS_{tot} = \Sigma(X - M_{tot})^2$$

Because SS_{tot} is to represent all the variability recorded in an experiment, we must find $(X - M_{tot})^2$ for each X in the entire experiment and then sum all of these $(X - M_{tot})^2$ quantities. Accordingly, the number of squared deviations to be added will be equal to the total number of subjects in the experiment (N_{tot}). We subtract M_{tot} from each person's score (X), square this deviation $(X - M_{tot})$, and then sum these squared deviations.

The definition of SS_{wg}. The sum of squares within groups is most easily understood as a combination of sums of squares within separate groups. For example, we define the sum of squares within Group 1 (SS_{wg1}) by the following equation:

$$SS_{wg1} = \Sigma(X_1 - M_1)^2$$

(Note that X_1 is a score in Group 1 and that we must find $(X_1 - M_1)^2$ for every X_1 in Group 1.) This is an expression of the variability within Group 1. Notice that it serves the same purpose for Group 1 that SS_{tot} does for the entire experiment.

The sum of squares within Group 2 (SS_{wg2}) is defined by writing the preceding equation in terms of X_2 and M_2 rather than X_1 and M_1. A similar change is made for Group 3, and for any other group in the experiment. Once the sum of squares within each of the groups is known, we add them because we want only one SS_{wg} expression. Accordingly, we define SS_{wg} for the entire experiment as the sum of the SS_{wg}'s for the separate groups. Writing this definition in terms of the quantities which make up the individual SS_{wg}'s, we have:

$$SS_{wg} = SS_{wg1} + SS_{wg2} + SS_{wg3}$$

or

$$SS_{wg} = \Sigma(X_1 - M_1)^2 + \Sigma(X_2 - M_2)^2 + \Sigma(X_3 - M_3)^2$$

for the case of 3 groups. With a different number of groups (k) the number of terms on the right hand side of the above equation would equal the new value of k. For example, with five groups (when $k = 5$) SS_{wg} would be defined as $SS_{wg} = SS_{wg1} + SS_{wg2} + SS_{wg3} + SS_{wg4} + SS_{wg5}$.

The definition of SS_{bg}. From the above we would expect that SS_{bg} would be based upon the squared deviation of each M_g from M_{tot}, just as other SS's are based upon deviations of scores from M's. This is exactly what is done. First we find $(M_g - M_{tot})^2$ for each M_g. Then we weight each $(M_g - M_{tot})^2$ quantity with the number of cases in its group (N_g) and add the weighted quantities $N_g(M_g - M_{tot})^2$ to find SS_{bg}. In general, then, we can say the following:

$$SS_{bg} = \Sigma N_g(M_g - M_{tot})^2$$

Taking a specific number of groups $(k = 3)$, we can write the above equation in a new form:

$$SS_{bg} = N_1(M_1 - M_{tot})^2 + N_2(M_2 - M_{tot})^2 + N_3(M_3 - M_{tot})^2$$

since N_g is N_1 for the first group, N_2 for the second group, and N_3 for the third group and M_g has comparable values.

Relationship Between SS_{tot} and SS_{wg}

We have been told that SS_{wg} accounts for part, but not all, of SS_{tot}. For instance, if we compared the mechanical aptitude scores of men and women, the variability of scores within the two groups would account for part of the total variability (SS_{tot}). This is not the sole source of variability, however; we would expect the men to exhibit greater mechanical aptitude than the women, and this difference between groups would be reflected in an SS_{bg} value, which would also be part of SS_{tot}.

In some other experiments there might be no difference, or almost no difference, between the groups. For example, three teaching methods—a lecture method, a discussion method, and a project method—used with three different groups of students of freshman history might result in identical M's on their exams. Then each M_g would equal M_{tot}, and there would be no SS_{bg}. In such a case all of SS_{tot} would be accounted for by SS_{wg}. In the next three paragraphs this fact, that SS_{wg} is *part* of SS_{tot} when there are differences between groups, and that SS_{wg} is *all* of SS_{tot} when there are no differences between groups, is elaborated for the case of three groups.

If all groups have the same M, then $M_1 = M_2 = M_3$. Furthermore, each M_g (group M) is equal to M_{tot}. Consequently, we may substitute $(X - M_{tot})$ for each $(X - M_g)$ value in our definition of SS_{wg}. But $(X - M_{tot})$ is the basic component in the computation of SS_{tot}. Therefore, SS_{tot} will now equal SS_{wg}, as the set of balances below shows.

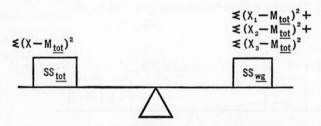

The reason that SS_{wg} balances SS_{tot} is suggested by the objects in the scale above. Because every X must come from some group, it is either an X_1, and X_2, or an X_3 in this situation. Therefore, the quantity on the right of the balance is exactly the same as that on the left; on each side of the balance, we are subtracting M_{tot} from each score separately, squaring the differences and summing them. Accordingly $SS_{tot} = SS_{wg}$ when all M_g's are equal, as in the case of the three teaching methods which proved equally effective.

Of course the situation above is an exceptionally rare one.

Even when three experimental conditions are nearly identical, the M_g's usually differ slightly from one another. In this case the M_g's are not equal to M_{tot}. SS_{tot} is greater than SS_{wg}, and the scale no longer balances.

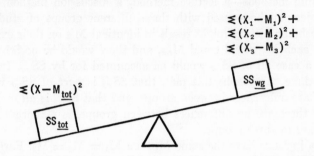

We can put the scale in balance again if we add an appropriate amount to the right hand side. This amount will always be the value of SS_{bg}. However, SS_{bg} is not simply a convenient quantity dreamed up to account for the difference between SS_{tot} and SS_{wg}. It is a meaningful measurement of the difference between group M's and will prove extremely useful to us.

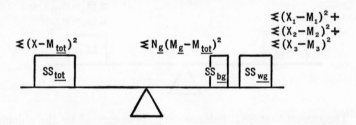

We now know the definitions of SS_{tot} and its two components, SS_{bg} and SS_{wg}. We also understand how the differences among M_g's affect these SS values. Before we can apply our knowledge in a practical way, however, we must know how to compute the values of SS_{tot}, SS_{bg}, and SS_{wg}. Directions for performing these computations are presented in the next section of this chapter.

Computational Steps in Finding Sums of Squares

Use of the basic formulas. Now that we have equations for SS_{tot}, SS_{wg}, and SS_{bg}, we can illustrate their use with a specific set of scores. Table 12.1 presents the results of a hypothetical experiment on the effects of courses in music appreciation upon attitudes toward classical music. Group 1 members took no courses in music appreciation, Group 2 members took one course, and Group 3 members took two courses in this field, before having their attitudes measured. Table 12.1 also shows the computational steps required in finding SS_{tot}, SS_{bg}, and SS_{wg}. In the left hand side of the table the deviation of each of the 30 scores from M_{tot} is determined and then squared. The sum of these squared deviations, 9680, is SS_{tot}. On the right hand side of the table the X values for the three groups are arranged separately and M's are computed for each group in order to permit computation of SS_{bg} and SS_{wg}. Also, on the right of the table, the deviation of each score from its M_g is determined and squared. According to our definitions, the sum of these squared deviations for Group 1 is SS_{wg1}, that for Group 2 is SS_{wg2}, and so on. Since there are three groups in this experiment, SS_{wg} is equal to $SS_{wg1} + SS_{wg2} + SS_{wg3}$ or 7260. The determination of SS_{bg} shown near the bottom of Table 12.1 begins with the calculation of each $(M_g - M_{tot})$ quantity. Then the $(M_g - M_{tot})^2$ values are determined and each multiplied by N_g, which is 10 for every group in this experiment. The sum of these $N_g(M_g - M_{tot})^2$ quantities proves to be 2420. We note that the sum of SS_{bg} and SS_{wg} is 9680, supporting our previous statement that SS_{bg} plus SS_{wg} is always equal to SS_{tot}.

Computational formulas. Just as was the case with SD and r, we can simplify our work with SS values by using special computational formulas in place of the basic formulas given above. The computational formulas lead to precisely the same answers as do the basic formulas but usually require less time for their use. Although these new equations can be derived algebraically from the basic definitions, we present them without any proof. First of all, SS_{tot} is found with the computational formula:

$$SS_{tot} = (\Sigma X^2) - (N_{tot}M^2_{tot})$$

TABLE 12.1

Application of the Basic Formulas for SS_{tot}, SS_{bg}, and SS_{wg}, to the Data from the Hypothetical Attitude Experiment

X	$(X - M_{tot})$	$(X - M_{tot})^2$	X_1	$(X_1 - M_1)$	$(X_1 - M_1)^2$	X_2	$(X_2 - M_2)$	$(X_2 - M_2)^2$
68	15	225	68	26	676			
63	10	100	63	21	441			
58	5	25	58	16	256			
51	-2	4	51	9	81			
41	-12	144	41	-1	1			
40	-13	169	40	-2	4			
34	-19	361	34	-8	64			
27	-26	676	27	-15	225			
20	-33	1089	20	-22	484			
18	-35	1225	18	-24	576			
78	25	625	$\Sigma X_1 = 420$	$\Sigma x_1 = 0$	$\Sigma x_1^2 = 2808$	78	25	625
69	16	256				69	16	256
58	5	25				58	5	25
57	4	16				57	4	16
53	0	0				53	0	0
52	-1	1				52	-1	1
48	-5	25				48	-5	25
46	-7	49				46	-7	49
42	-11	121				42	-11	121
27	-26	676				27	-26	676
94	41	1681				$\Sigma X_2 = 530$	$\Sigma x_2 = 0$	$\Sigma x_2^2 = 1794$
82	29	841						
73	20	400						
67	14	196						
66	13	169						

$$M_1 = \frac{\Sigma X_1}{N_1} = \frac{420}{10} = 42$$

$$SS_{wg1} = \Sigma (X_1 - M_1)^2 = 2808$$

$$M_2 = \frac{\Sigma X_2}{N_2} = \frac{530}{10} = 53$$

$$SS_{wg2} = \Sigma (X_2 - M_2)^2 = 1794$$

$$M_3 = \frac{\Sigma X_3}{N_3} = \frac{640}{10} = 64$$

$$SS_{wg3} = \Sigma(X_3 - M_3)^2$$
$$= 2658$$

X_3	$(X_3 - M_3)$	$(X_3 - M_3)^2$
94	30	900
82	18	324
73	9	81
67	3	9
66	2	4
62	−2	4
60	−4	16
54	−10	100
50	−14	196
32	−32	1024
$\Sigma X_3 = 640$	$\Sigma x_3 = 0$	$\Sigma x_3^2 = 2658$

62	9	81
60	7	49
54	1	1
50	−3	9
32	−21	441
$\Sigma X = 1590$	$\Sigma x = 0$	$\Sigma x^2 = 9680$

$$M_{tot} = \frac{\Sigma X}{N} = \frac{1590}{30} = 53$$

$$SS_{tot} = \Sigma(X - M_{tot})^2$$
$$= 9680$$

$$SS_{bg} = \Sigma N_g(M_g - M_{tot})^2$$
$$= N_1(M_1 - M_{tot})^2 + N_2(M_2 - M_{tot})^2 + N_3(M_3 + M_{tot})^2$$
$$= 10(42 - 53)^2 + 10(53 - 53)^2 + 10(64 - 53)^2$$
$$= 10[(42 - 53)^2 + (53 - 53)^2 + (64 - 53)^2]$$
$$= 10[121 + 121]$$
$$= 2420$$

$$SS_{wg} = SS_{wg1} + SS_{wg2} + SS_{wg3}$$
$$= 2808 + 1794 + 2658$$
$$= 7260$$

This formula states that SS_{tot} is computed by squaring every X, adding all the X^2 values together, and subtracting the product of N_{tot} and M^2_{tot}. Then SS_{bg} is found with the formula:

$$SS_{bg} = (\Sigma[N_g M_g^2]) - (N_{tot}M^2_{tot})$$

Thus SS_{bg} is determined by finding each M_g, squaring it, multiplying M_g^2 by the corresponding N_g, adding these $N_g M_g^2$ quantities together, and subtracting $N_{tot}M^2_{tot}$ from that sum. This computational formula for SS_{bg} could be rewritten as follows for the case where $k = 3$:

$$SS_{bg} = N_1 M_1{}^2 + N_2 M_2{}^2 + N_3 M_3{}^2 - N_{tot}M^2_{tot}$$

If k had some other value there would still be $k(N_g M_g^2)$ quantities to be added before subtraction of $N_{tot}M^2_{tot}$.

Finally, since we know that SS_{tot} is composed of SS_{bg} and SS_{wg}, we can find SS_{wg} by subtraction:

$$SS_{wg} = SS_{tot} - SS_{bg}$$

With the computational formulas for SS_{tot}, SS_{bg}, and SS_{wg} before us, we can recalculate the SS value for the data from our hypothetical experiment on attitudes toward classical music. Table 12.2 shows the steps involved in this recomputation.

As we expected, the SS values obtained in Table 12.2 are exactly the same as those arrived at in Table 12.1. This gives us a practical (and perhaps desperately needed) bit of assurance that the computational formulas are appropriate for finding SS values.

One more fact about the computation of SS values is important to us. If we look carefully at the basic formulas for SS values, we see that no SS can ever have a negative value. This is not obvious from the computational formulas, but must also be true for them. Consequently, a negative SS value is always a sign that a mistake in arithmetic has been made and that recalculations are necessary.

TABLE 12.2

Application of the Computational Formulas for SS_{tot}, SS_{bg}, and SS_{wg} to the Data of Table 12.1

X	X²	X₁	X₂	X₃
68	4624	68	78	94
63	3969	63	69	82
58	3364	58	58	73
51	2601	51	57	67
41	1681	41	53	66
40	1600	40	52	62
34	1156	34	48	60
27	729	27	46	54
20	400	20	42	50
18	324	18	27	32
78	6084	420	530	640
69	4761			
58	3364			
57	3249			
53	2809			
52	2704			
48	2304			
46	2116			
42	1764			
27	729			
94	8836			
82	6724			
73	5329			
67	4489			
66	4356			
62	3844			
60	3600			
54	2916			
50	2500			
32	1024			
1590	93950			

$$M_1 = 42 \qquad M_2 = 53 \qquad M_3 = 64$$

$$SS_{tot} = \Sigma X^2 - N_{tot}M^2{}_{tot}$$

$$= 93,950 - 30(53)^2$$

$$= 93,950 - 30(2809)$$

$$= 93,950 - 84,270$$

$$= 9,680$$

$$SS_{bg} = \Sigma N_g M_g{}^2 - N_{tot}M^2{}_{tot}$$
$$= 10(42^2) + 10(53^2) + 10(64^2) - 84,270$$
$$= 10(1764 + 2809 + 4096) - 84,270$$
$$= 10(8669) - 84,270$$
$$= 86,690 - 84,270 = 2420$$

$$SS_{wg} = SS_{tot} - SS_{bg}$$
$$= 9680 - 2420$$
$$= 7260$$

THE CONCEPT OF VARIANCE OR MEAN SQUARE

The use of sums of squares as measurements of variability has only one disadvantage: the size of SS depends very much upon the number of measurements upon which it is based. Other things being equal, a sample of 100 measurements from a given population will yield about twice as large an SS as a sample of 50 from that population because there will be twice as many squared deviations involved in the former. For this reason, a large SS may result either from a large variability of the characteristic being measured or from having a large N in the sample. Consequently, the interpretation of an SS value is more complicated than the interpretation of SD, for example. In this respect an SS is an unsatisfactory measurement of variability, and can only be of limited usefulness unless it leads to some new statistic which does not depend so greatly upon N.

Fortunately such a statistic does exist, and we have had some previous acquaintance with it. Recall that when we first discussed SD, the *variance* was defined as equal to σ^2 or SD^2. However, in the present context we will call this quantity the *mean square* rather than the variance because *mean square* (MS) has come to be used in place of variance in discussing the analysis of variance technique. As we said when we discussed the ABC's of analysis of variance, we want to judge whether our group M's differ significantly by comparing a measure of variability between groups, which we now surmise to be a mean square between groups, with a measure of variability within groups which will be the mean square within groups. We then discover how large a value of the ratio of these two variabilities is required to indicate that the group M's differ more than would be expected if the null hypothesis were true. With this in mind, it appears that what we want now is to find one MS (mean square) value to represent variability between groups and another MS value to represent variability within groups. Once these values (MS_{bg} and MS_{wg} respectively) are known for any experiment, the size of their ratio can be used as the basis for drawing statistical conclusions about the data being analyzed.

To find an MS value, we simply divide the appropriate SS

by its df, just as we divided Σx^2 by N to find σ^2 in Chapter 6. MS_{bg} is based upon SS_{bg} and df_{bg}, the number of degrees of freedom between groups:

$$MS_{bg} = \frac{SS_{bg}}{df_{bg}}$$

where $\quad df_{bg} = k - 1$

We note that df_{bg} has a meaning similar to that of df in the t-test. However, it is based upon k, the number of groups, rather than upon the number of subjects as with the t-test.

The second MS value, MS_{wg}, is the ratio of SS_{wg} to df_{wg}:

$$MS_{wg} = \frac{SS_{wg}}{df_{wg}}$$

where $\quad df_{wg} = N_{tot} - k$

The value of df_{wg} may easily be remembered by saying that the df within a single group would be one less than the number of scores in the group (i.e., $N_g - 1$) making the df within all k groups equal to $(\Sigma N_g) - k$ or $N_{tot} - k$ since 1 df is lost in each of the k groups.

We now illustrate the determination of MS_{bg} and MS_{wg} with a computational example. By referring to either Table 12.1 or Table 12.2, we find that $SS_{bg} = 2420$ and $SS_{wg} = 7260$ in our hypothetical attitude experiment. Since $N_{tot} = 30$ and $k = 3$ for this experiment, $df_{bg} = 3 - 1 = 2$, and $df_{wg} = 30 - 3 = 27$. First we find MS_{bg}:

$$MS_{bg} = \frac{2420}{2} = 1210$$

Then we compute MS_{wg}:

$$MS_{wg} = \frac{7260}{27} = 268.9$$

As we said earlier, MS_{bg} and MS_{wg} will not be greatly different in an experiment unless the group M's differ significantly. We have just found an MS_{bg} of 1210, compared with an MS_{wg} of 268.9, which leads us to suspect that the variability between group M's is too great to be attributed to random differences between samples from populations with identical M's. In order to make a more precise comparison of these MS values, we now form what is called the F-ratio and evaluate it. The succeeding paragraphs describe this process, the final part in the analysis of variance procedure.

THE F-RATIO

The F-ratio, which is simply a numerical expression of the relative size of MS_{bg} and MS_{wg}, is defined by the equation below:

$$F = \frac{MS_{bg}}{MS_{wg}}$$

When an F-ratio has been found in an experiment, a decision regarding the significance of the differences in group M's is made by comparing that ratio with the F-values to be expected if the null hypothesis were true. The information necessary for this comparison is presented in Table F in the back of the book. (Note the happy accident that the values of F appear in Table F.) Table F shows the F-values required at the 5% and 1% levels of significance. That is, this table presents the F-values which are so large that they would be exceeded only 5% or 1% of the time by random sampling if the null hypothesis were true. If MS_{bg} is enough greater than MS_{wg}, so that the resulting F-ratio exceeds the tabled F at the 5% (or 1%) level, then we realize that it would be very unlikely that such an F would occur unless the null hypothesis were false. Therefore, we would reject the null hypothesis and say that our obtained F is significant at the 5% (or 1%) level.

One step in this procedure remains to be explored: we must know where to look in Table F for the significant values of the F-ratio with which to compare the F obtained in a particular experiment. This step is much like the procedure for finding a significant t-value in Table C. There we had to look for a t associated with a df value. Now we must find an F associated with two df values because the degree of significance of any obtained F depends upon two factors, the number of groups and the number of subjects within the groups. Accordingly we employ the values of df_{bg} and df_{wg} in using Table F.

Knowing that $df_{bg} = 2$ and $df_{wg} = 27$ in our attitude experiment, we can find a cell in Table F which is appropriate for that experiment. Since the df for the MS in the numerator of the F-ratio is df_{bg} and the df for the MS in the denominator is df_{wg}, we see from the table that we must go to the *column* labelled $df = 2$ and proceed down to the *row* labelled $df = 27$. There we find two F values, one for the 5% level of significance and the other for the 1% level of significance. The F-ratio at the 5% level of significance is 3.35 and the F-ratio at the 1% level of significance is 4.60. An F obtained in an experiment with three groups, each of 10 subjects, must be compared with these values to determine whether or not it is significant.

To illustrate the use of the F-ratio, we again employ our data from the attitude experiment. Since $MS_{bg} = 1210$ and $MS_{wg} = 268.9$, we find F with the following equation:

$$F = \frac{1210}{268.9} = 4.50$$

This F-ratio of 4.50 is significant at the 5% level because it is greater than 3.35, the F-value tabled at the 5% level for 2 and 27 df. However, it is not significant at the 1% level because it is less than 5.49, the value required for significance at the 1% level. Thus this is a situation in which we would reject the null hypothesis if we were using a 5% level of significance but would accept that hypothesis if we were using a 1% level of significance. We may notice that, if df_{wg} had been between 30 and 40 rather than at 27 as it was, Table F would not have indicated the exact F values required for significance at the 5% and 1% levels. In that case we would have used the tabled values for 2 and 30 df because they are higher than those for 2 and 40 df, thereby behaving with extra caution when we conclude that an F is significant at the 5% or 1% level.

Assumptions Underlying the Analysis of Variance

As in the case of every other statistical test we have studied, the analysis of variance involves certain assumptions which had to be made in order to derive the table of significant values for the test. Table F is known to present the F values required for significance at the 5% and 1% levels when three assumptions are satisfied: (a) Each of the k populations from which the groups in the experiment were drawn are normally distributed. (b) The σ^2 values for the k populations are equal. (c) The subjects of the experiment have been randomly and independently drawn from their respective populations.

If we know that these assumptions have been met, we can accept conclusions based upon the use of Table F at their face value. If these assumptions are not satisfied, the mathematical demonstration that the values presented in Table F are the exact values required at the 5% and 1% levels can no longer be made. However, the practical usefulness of the analysis of variance procedure may be nearly as great when one or two of these assumptions are not fulfilled as when all are satisfied. If one of these assumptions appears not to be met, the experimenter may prefer to perform the analysis of variance and interpret it conservatively (e.g., require that his F values reach the tabled values for the 1% level for significance when he would otherwise have required only a 5% level for concluding that F is significant). He prefers to do this rather than to discard his data or to seek a new statistical procedure.

To decide whether the assumptions of normality and equal σ^2's have been met is not easy. Since the groups involved in this type of experiment are small, there are seldom enough scores to indicate the shape of the distribution for each population. If the sample distribution is very far from normal, we may suspect that the distribution of the population is not normal. Similarly, very great differences among the σ^2's for the different groups suggest that the population σ^2's may be unequal. Statistical tests of normality and equality of σ^2's could be presented here but are omitted because of the space they would require and the impracticability of applying a test of normality except when N is large.

Further Examples

The case of two groups. We have a special interest in this case because of something we learned in Chapter 9. At that time we were told that the t-formula introduced in that chapter is not appropriate for small groups unless the groups are equal or very nearly equal in size. Consequently some other method of analyzing results is necessary for the case of two small groups of unequal size. Since the analysis of variance procedure is one appropriate method for use in this situation, we will now consider an example of its applicability for such a problem.

TABLE 12.3

Data from the Experiment on Perception of Barriers by the Blind; Average Distance (in ft.) of First Perception

	GROUP I Men $(N_1 = 5)$		GROUP II Women $(N_2 = 2)$	
	X_1	$X_1{}^2$	X_2	$X_2{}^2$
	9.2	84.64		
	5.9	34.81		
	5.5	30.25		
	2.5	6.25	6.1	37.21
	6.6	43.56	6.8	46.24
	$\Sigma X_1 = \overline{29.7}$	$\Sigma X_1{}^2 = \overline{199.51}$	$\Sigma X_2 = \overline{12.9}$	$\Sigma X_2{}^2 = \overline{83.45}$

$$M_1 = \frac{\Sigma X_1}{N_1} = \frac{29.7}{5} = 5.940 \qquad M_2 = \frac{\Sigma X_2}{N_2} = \frac{12.9}{2} = 6.450$$

$$\Sigma X = \Sigma X_1 + \Sigma X_2 = 29.7 + 12.9 = 42.6$$

$$M_{tot} = \frac{\Sigma X}{N_{tot}} = \frac{42.6}{7} = 6.086$$

$$\Sigma X^2 = \Sigma X_1{}^2 + \Sigma X_2{}^2 = 199.51 + 83.45 = 282.96$$

$$\begin{aligned} SS_{tot} &= \Sigma X^2 - N_{tot}M^2_{tot} \\ &= 282.96 - 7(6.086)^2 \\ &= 23.68 \end{aligned}$$

$$\begin{aligned} SS_{bg} &= \Sigma N_g M^2_g - N_{tot}M^2_{tot} \\ &= 5(5.94)^2 + 2(6.45)^2 - 7(6.086)^2 \\ &= 176.42 + 83.20 - 259.28 \\ &= .34 \end{aligned}$$

$$\begin{aligned} SS_{wg} &= SS_{tot} - SS_{bg} \\ &= 23.68 - .34 \\ &= 23.34 \end{aligned}$$

$$df_{bg} = k - 1 = 2 - 1 = 1$$
$$df_{wg} = N_{tot} - k = 7 - 2 = 5$$

Table 12.3 presents the data from one condition of an experiment in which blind persons were taught to avoid obstacles in their paths.[2] The subjects were started at some distance from a

[2] Worchel, P., and Mauney, J. The effect of practice on the perception of obstacles by the blind. *J. exp. Psychol.*, 1951, 41, 170-176.

barrier and told to walk until they were directly in front of the barrier or obstacle. Table 12.3 shows how far (in feet), on the average, each of seven blind subjects was from an obstacle at the time he first stopped walking and said it was just ahead of him. Since these data were obtained after a long training period, they show how successful the training was. A low score, of course, means that a subject estimated his position with respect to the obstacle very well. A high score means the reverse.

In Table 12.3 we have presented the data for the men and women subjects separately. Calling the men Group I and the women Group II we see from the table that $N_1 = 5$ and $N_2 = 2$. We can now compare the performance of men and women by means of the analysis of variance, treating the average performance for each person as a raw score and using the customary formulas for SS_{tot}, and SS_{bg}, and SS_{wg}. In Table 12.3 we have prepared for the application of analysis of variance to these data by including X^2 values, SS values, and df values.

TABLE 12.4

Summary of the Analysis of Variance of the Experiment on Perception of Barriers by the Blind

SOURCE OF VARIATION	SS	df	MS	F
Between groups	.34	1	.34	.07
Within groups	23.34	5	4.67	—
Total	23.68	6		

Table 12.4 summarizes the calculations of the MS and F values. This is an example of the standard method of summarizing analyses of variance. The row labelled "Between groups" shows that an MS_{bg} of .34 resulted from dividing an SS_{bg} of .34, obtained from Table 12.3 by a df_{bg} of 1 (i.e., $k - 1$). Similarly, the row labelled "Within groups" shows that an MS_{wg} of 4.67 was obtained by dividing the SS_{wg} of 23.34 by df_{wg} of 5 (i.e., $N_{tot} - k$). Finally, an F of .07 was obtained by dividing MS_{bg} (.34) by MS_{wg} (4.67). This F shows that the MS_{bg} is much less than MS_{wg}, indicating that men and women differed very little in their perception of obstacles. An F value of .07 is not signifi-

cant since it is very much less than the F of 6.61 required for significance at the 5% level with 1 and 5 df. In fact, as Table F shows, no F below 1 is significant regardless of the df values.

A step-by-step computational procedure. We conclude our discussion of the analysis of variance by first listing in sequence the steps required to perform an analysis and then illustrating each step by analyzing the results of an actual experiment.

(1) Find ΣX for every group and for the total experiment by adding all X's in the group or in the experiment.

(2) Find ΣX^2 for every group and for the total experiment by adding all X^2's in the group or experiment.

(3) Find each M_g and M_{tot} by dividing the appropriate ΣX by its N.

(4) Find SS_{tot} by the formula
$$SS_{tot} = (\Sigma X^2) - (N_{tot}M^2_{tot})$$

(5) Find SS_{bg} by the formula
$$SS_{bg} = (\Sigma [N_g M^2_g]) - (N_{tot}M^2_{tot})$$

(6) Find SS_{wg} by the formula
$$SS_{wg} = SS_{tot} - SS_{bg}$$

(7) Find df_{bg} by the formula
$$df_{bg} = k - 1$$

(8) Find df_{wg} by the formula
$$df_{wg} = N_{tot} - k$$

(9) Find MS_{bg} by the formula
$$MS_{bg} = \frac{SS_{bg}}{df_{bg}}$$

(10) Find MS_{wg} by the formula
$$MS_{wg} = \frac{SS_{wg}}{df_{wg}}$$

(11) Find F by the formula
$$F = \frac{MS_{bg}}{MS_{wg}}$$

(12) For df_{bg} and df_{wg} of the values found in steps (7) and (8), find the F's required for significance at the 5% and 1% levels from Table F.

(13) If your obtained F exceeds the required F at the 5% level (or the 1% level) reject the null hypothesis at that level, otherwise accept it.

These steps will now be illustrated by referring to the results of an experiment [3] in which four groups of rats were *trained* under different degrees of hunger and then *tested* under a single hunger condition, 1 hour of food deprivation. Group 1 was trained under 1 hour of hunger, Group 2 under 7 hours of hunger, Group 3 under 15 hours of hunger, and Group 4 under 22 hours of hunger. An analysis of variance will now be performed to find out whether the four hunger conditions during training produced significantly different numbers of correct responses during test trials. Table 12.5 presents data for these four groups together with the X^2 value for each X.

(1) Beginning with the first step, we find $\Sigma X_1 = 108$, $\Sigma X_2 = 132$, $\Sigma X_3 = 104$, and $\Sigma X_4 = 72$ by adding the numbers in the first, third, fifth, and seventh columns, respectively, of Table 12.5. Then $\Sigma X = 416$ is found by adding $\Sigma X_1 + \Sigma X_2 + \Sigma X_3 + \Sigma X_4$. These values are also presented in Table 12.5.

(2) We find $\Sigma X_1{}^2 = 2576$, $\Sigma X_2{}^2 = 4048$, $\Sigma X_3{}^2 = 2592$, and $\Sigma X_4{}^2 = 1376$ by adding the second, fourth, sixth, and eighth columns, respectively, of Table 12.5. Then $\Sigma X^2 = 10,592$ is found by adding these four sums together. These are also presented in Table 12.5.

(3) We see by counting the number of X scores in Table 12.5 that $N_1 = 5$, $N_2 = 6$, $N_3 = 5$, $N_4 = 5$, and $N_{tot} = 21$. Thus we can find M_1, M_2, M_3, M_4, and M_{tot} by dividing each ΣX by its N:

$$M_1 = \frac{\Sigma X_1}{N_1} = \frac{108}{5} = 21.6 \qquad M_3 = \frac{\Sigma X_3}{N_3} = \frac{104}{5} = 20.8$$

$$M_2 = \frac{\Sigma X_2}{N_2} = \frac{132}{6} = 22.0 \qquad M_4 = \frac{\Sigma X_4}{N_4} = \frac{72}{5} = 14.4$$

$$M_{tot} = \frac{\Sigma X}{N_{tot}} = \frac{416}{21} = 19.81$$

[3] Teel, K. S. Habit strength as a function of motivation during learning. *J. comp. physiol. Psychol.*, 1952, 45, 188-191. Raw data courtesy of the author.

We actually refer to only 4 of the 16 groups of Teel's experiment. Because the complexity of the 16 group experiment precludes its complete presentation here, we are treating the four groups under discussion as if they represented a complete experiment.

TABLE 12.5

Preliminary Steps in the Analysis of Variance of the Number of Correct Test Responses (X) by Rats Trained under Four Hunger Conditions

GROUP I 1 hr. hunger		GROUP II 7 hrs. hunger		GROUP III 15 hrs. hunger		GROUP IV 22 hrs. hunger	
X_1	X_1^2	X_2	X_2^2	X_3	X_3^2	X_4	X_4^2
24	576	16	256	8	64	28	784
24	576	8	64	36	1296	8	64
16	256	28	784	16	256	20	400
12	144	24	576	20	400	8	64
32	1024	48	2305	24	576	8	64
		8	64				
$\Sigma X_1 = 108$	$\Sigma X_1^2 = 2576$	$\Sigma X_2 = 132$	$\Sigma X_2^2 = 4048$	$\Sigma X_3 = 104$	$\Sigma X_3^2 = 2592$	$\Sigma X_4 = 72$	$\Sigma X_4^2 = 1376$

$$\Sigma X = \Sigma X_1 + \Sigma X_2 + \Sigma X_3 + \Sigma X_4 = 108 + 132 + 104 + 72 = 416$$

$$\Sigma X^2 = \Sigma X_1^2 + \Sigma X_2^2 + \Sigma X_3^2 + \Sigma X_4^2 = 2576 + 4048 + 2592 + 1376 = 10,592$$

(4) Using the formula for SS_{tot}, we find
$$SS_{tot} = (\Sigma X^2) - (N_{tot}M^2_{tot})$$
$$= 10{,}592 - (21)(19.81)^2$$
$$= 2350.84$$

(5) Using the formula for SS_{bg}, we find
$$SS_{bg} = (\Sigma[N_g M^2_g]) - (N_{tot}M^2_{tot})$$
$$= N_1M_1^2 + N_2M_2^2 + N_3M_3^2 + N_4M_4^2$$
$$\qquad - N_{tot}M^2_{tot}$$
$$= 5(21.6)^2 + 6(22.0)^2 + 5(20.8)^2 + 5(14.4)^2$$
$$\qquad - 21(19.81)^2$$
$$= 195.64$$

(6) Using the formula for SS_{wg}, we find
$$SS_{wg} = SS_{tot} - SS_{bg}$$
$$= 2350.84 - 195.64$$
$$= 2155.20$$

(7) Using the formula for df_{bg}, we find
$$df_{bg} = k - 1 = 4 - 1 = 3$$

(8) Using the formula for df_{wg}, we find
$$df_{wg} = N_{tot} - k = 21 - 4 = 17$$

(9) Using the formula for MS_{bg}, we find
$$MS_{bg} = \frac{SS_{bg}}{df_{bg}} = \frac{SS_{bg}}{k - 1} = \frac{195.64}{4 - 1}$$
$$= \frac{195.64}{3} = 65.2$$

(10) Using the formula for MS_{wg}, we find
$$MS_{wg} = \frac{SS_{wg}}{df_{wg}} = \frac{SS_{wg}}{N_{tot} - k} = \frac{2155.20}{21 - 4}$$
$$= \frac{2155.20}{17} = 126.8$$

(11) Using the formula for F, we find
$$F = \frac{MS_{bg}}{MS_{wg}} = \frac{65.2}{126.8} = .51$$

(12) Looking in Table F for the case where $df_{bg} = 3$ and $df_{wg} = 17$, we find F must be 3.20 or greater to be significant at the 5% level, and 5.19 or greater to be significant at the 1% level.

(13) Since our obtained F is smaller than 3.20, (or of course 5.19) we accept the null hypothesis that the population M's for the four training conditions are equal. This completes the analysis of variance for this experiment.

As this chapter ends, we wish to remark that the analysis of variance is one of the most versatile tools of statistics, being appropriate for testing many hypotheses about experiments of many different types. We have discussed only the simplest form of analysis of variance, the one that is used for testing a hypothesis about differences in population M's on the basis of an experiment involving several groups but only one basic variable, such as degree of hunger during training. With a few extensions of our procedure for finding SS, MS, and F values we could analyze an experiment with two variables such as one involving amount of reward as well as degree of hunger during training. Other extensions of the analysis of variance procedure are appropriate with other variations in experimental procedure. Accordingly this introduction to the analysis of variance technique becomes the first step toward the statistical analysis of many experimental problems much more complicated than those discussed in this book.

13

Chi Square

FREQUENCIES VERSUS MEASUREMENTS

We wish now to draw your attention to the fact that the data with which we have been dealing in previous chapters have almost all been what we shall call *measurements*. That is, we measure a group of subjects on some characteristic, such as height, errors in learning, digit span, and so forth, and obtain for each subject a certain value (score, measurement) of that characteristic. One of the fundamental facts we observe, and with which we have to deal, is that different people exhibit different amounts of the characteristic.

In contrast to measurement data, there are data expressed in terms of *classified frequencies*. This means that the data are recorded in terms of the *number* of subjects who fall into each of two or more categories. For example, we might ask each of 200 people chosen at random whether they believe voting should be made compulsory. We might have in this case only two categories of response, "yes" or "no," and we would record the number of people, the frequency, in each category. Let us suppose we found in this example that 116 said "yes" and 84 said "no." All of the persons included in each category have the same "score"; there is no variability in the response as classified *within* a category. Frequency data are not restricted to people; we might, for example, record the number of houses with basements and the number without in a random sample of 150 houses in a certain suburb, or we might count the number of trucks, the number of cars, and the number of motorcycles passing an intersection in a certain period of time.

Typically, the question that we want to answer when we have frequency data is *whether the frequencies observed in our sample deviate significantly from some theoretical or expected population frequencies.* We have some hypothesis about what frequencies should be expected, that is, what the population frequencies are. In some cases we may hypothesize equal frequencies in each category, so we want to determine whether the observed frequencies deviate significantly from what would be expected from a hypothesis of equal likelihood. Thus, in our voting example, with two categories, such a hypothesis would mean a 50:50 split, an equal number of people in each category. In other cases we may, on the basis of previous research or theory, adopt some other hypothesis. For example, we might hypothesize that the frequencies in the various categories should exhibit some specified ratio. Thus, suppose we knew the number of Studebakers and the number of Chryslers in a certain county in some state. These frequencies would exhibit a certain ratio, and we could use them as expected frequencies in testing whether ownership of Studebakers and Chryslers in a random sample from the whole state deviates significantly from what is true in the county.

In all these cases we have again the usual problem of determining whether the deviation of observed values (sample frequencies) from expected values (population frequencies) can be attributed to sampling errors, or whether we can conclude, at a certain level of probability, that a non-chance factor was operating. In our voting example we would not expect that if we measured another random sample of 200 people we would again get exactly 116 "yes" and 84 "no." We need, therefore, a statistical technique by which we can determine whether or not the frequencies observed in a sample depart significantly from expected frequencies. The statistic we use is called *chi square,* symbolized χ^2.

CHI SQUARE APPLIED TO ONE SAMPLE

The formula for χ^2 is:

$$\chi^2 = \sum \frac{(O - E)^2}{E}$$

where: O = observed frequency
E = the corresponding expected frequency.

According to this formula we first get the deviation of each observed frequency from its corresponding expected frequency and then square the deviations. Next, each squared deviation is divided by the appropriate expected frequency (the one used to obtain the deviation). The remaining step is to sum these quotients; the sum is the value of χ^2.

Let us see how this works with our voting example. We shall test the hypothesis that opinion neither favors nor opposes compulsory voting, that in the population from which our sample was drawn, opinion is equally divided. The expected frequency is, therefore, 100 in each category. Table 13.1, which shows the computation, indicates that for a 50:50 hypothesis with these

TABLE 13.1

A 50:50 Hypothesis Tested by χ^2

	FAVOR COMPULSORY VOTING	DO NOT FAVOR COMPULSORY VOTING	TOTAL
Observed	116	84	200
Expected	100	100	200
$O - E$	+16	−16	
$(O - E)^2$	256	256	
$\dfrac{(O - E)^2}{E}$	2.56	2.56	

$$\chi^2 = \sum \frac{(O - E)^2}{E} = 2.56 + 2.56 = 5.12$$

data, $\chi^2 = 5.12$. How is this value to be interpreted? The interpretation of a value of χ^2 is basically the same as for t. We assume a certain hypothesis; for the data in Table 13.1 this is the null hypothesis, since we have assumed that there is no difference in the population between the two categories of response. Then we ask: If the hypothesis is true, how often would values of χ^2 as large as or larger than our obtained value arise by random sampling error? If we find that values of χ^2 as large as or larger than the value obtained would occur by sampling error only 5% or 1% of the time, we reject the hypothesis at the 5% or 1% level of significance.

It appears that in order to evaluate obtained values of χ^2 we need to know the distribution of χ^2. Table G in the back of the book shows for each df value from 1 to 30 the value of χ^2 that would occur by sampling error at both the .05 and .01 levels of probability. Thus, for 1 df (first row in Table G) a value of χ^2 as large as 6.64 occurs 1% of the time by sampling error alone. Similarly, with 6 df, an obtained χ^2 would have to be at least 12.59 to be called significant at the 5% level. Note that, unlike F or t, values of χ^2 *increase* with increasing df.

Degrees of freedom. The df for a particular χ^2 does *not* depend upon the number of individuals in the sample. For χ^2, the df is determined by the number of *deviations*, between observed and expected frequencies, that are *independent*, i.e., that are free to vary. For example, what is the df for Table 13.1? First, we have to note a condition that must always be true for any χ^2: *the sum of the expected frequencies must equal the sum of the observed frequencies.* In Table 13.1 this is true; both observed and expected frequencies sum to 200. Now if, in Table 13.1, we write down 100 as the expected frequency for one category, the expected frequency for the other category (and, therefore, the deviation) is *not* free to vary; it must also be 100, in order that the expected frequencies sum to the same total as the observed frequencies. Therefore, there is 1 df for the data in Table 13.1, because only one deviation is free to vary.

We can now use Table G to evaluate the χ^2 for Table 13.1. Table G shows that for 1 df, $\chi^2 = 3.84$ at the 5% level, 6.61 at the 1% level. Our obtained value (5.12) exceeds the value at the 5% but not at the 1% level, so we may reject the null hypothesis at the 5% level of confidence. We conclude that opinion concerning compulsory voting is quite probably not evenly split in the population from which our sample was drawn.

Testing other Hypotheses

Chi square may be used to test *any a priori* or *assumed* hypothesis about the population; it is not restricted to testing the hypothesis of equally-distributed frequencies. By an a priori or assumed hypothesis we mean one which the investigator has before the research is done; the research is carried out to test the hypothesis. The hypothesis may be based on previous research or be derived from some theory. Suppose, for example, we are trying to get a congressman to introduce a bill making voting compulsory. On the basis of preliminary research or some other grounds, we claim that 75% of the voting population favor making voting compulsory. Our hypothesis is a 75:25 split. We shall not carry out the computations for this hypothesis since the method is already illustrated in Table 13.1. Our expected frequencies would show a 75:25 ratio instead of the 50:50 previously used. Whatever the N in our sample, 75% of N would be the expected frequency in the "yes" category, 25% of N the expected frequency in the "no" category.

Restrictions on the Use of χ^2

Before taking up the use of χ^2 in more complex cases, we shall note some of the conditions that must be met before data may appropriately be analyzed by χ^2. Like any statistical method, there are certain limitations on the use of χ^2; if these are kept in mind, many incorrect applications of the method will be avoided.[1]

First, χ^2 can be used only with frequency data. It is not correct, for example, to test by χ^2 the deviation between the obtained mean score on some trait for a group, and some expected or predicted mean. These are measurement data, and one of the reasons why χ^2 cannot be used with such data is that the value of χ^2 varies with the size of the unit of measurement. Thus, weight may be measured either in pounds or in kilograms. But the value of χ^2 between observed and expected weights will be different, even for the same subjects, if the score is recorded in pounds than if

[1] Lewis, D. and Burke, C. J. The use and misuse of the chi-square test. *Psychol. Bull.*, 1949, 46, 433-489.

recorded in kilograms. Who is to say which value of χ^2 is "correct"?

Second, the individual events or measures must be independent of each other. The data for the example on compulsory voting may be used as an illustration. There is no reason to think that the answer of any one of the subjects in the sample is dependent upon or correlated with the answer of any other subject; the individual responses are independent. But it would be incorrect, for example, to ask each of 50 people to make guesses as to what card will be drawn from a deck on each of five successive draws and then to claim the total frequency was 250. In such a case we would not have 250 independent responses; successive responses by the same individual are very probably related.

Third, no theoretical frequency should be smaller than 10. The distribution of χ^2, part of which is given in Table G, may take different values from those shown in the table if any expected frequency is less than 10.

Fourth, there must be some basis for the way the data are categorized. Preferably, the categories should have some logical basis, or be based on previous acceptable research, and should be set up before the data are collected. Suppose, for example, we asked a large random sample of people what magazine they would take if they could subscribe to only one. We find that, in all, 31 magazines were named, ranging from a few mentioned very frequently down to several preferred by one person each. We now categorize the data into several "types" of magazines in order to apply χ^2. Such an application would be questionable because we have not demonstrated that the types (categories) we set up are any more defensible than any others that might be used. And it would be even worse to continue reclassifying the data until we got categories that would give a significant χ^2. Our categories must be set up beforehand, and it must be demonstrated that the categories are reliable. Reliability would be demonstrated if there were a high degree of agreement among a group of qualified judges as to what magazines should be assigned to what categories.

Finally, recall that we said above that *the sum of expected and the sum of observed frequencies must be the same.* This requirement is related to another: *if we are recording whether or not an event occurs, we must include in our data, and use in computing* χ^2, *both the frequency of occurrence and the frequency of non-occurrence.* For example, suppose we roll a die 120 times and note the frequency with which a one-spot turns up. The expected frequency is 20, since a die has six sides. It would not be correct to test by χ^2 only whether the observed frequency of occurrence of the one-spot deviated significantly from the expected frequency. The χ^2 must be based *both* on the deviation of observed frequency of occurrence from expected frequency of occurrence, and the deviation of observed frequency of non-occurrence from expected frequency of non-occurrence. If we ignore the frequency of non-occurrence, the *sums* of observed and expected frequencies will not be the same, except by chance. The value of χ^2 must be based on the deviation of observed from expected frequency for both the category of occurrence and the category of non-occurrence.

TESTING SIGNIFICANCE OF DIFFERENCE BY χ^2

Chi square probably has its greatest usefulness in testing for significance of differences between groups. Although there may be any number of groups and any number of categories, apparently the situation that arises most often in research is the one in which we have two groups and two categories of response; the data are expressed in a 2×2 table. Our illustration of χ^2 as it is used to test for significance of difference will be based on a 2×2 table, although the method is the same for any number of groups and categories.

Suppose we want to determine whether there is any relation between the amount of education a person has had and his method of keeping up with the news. We ask a random sample of college graduates and a random sample of high school graduates whether they keep up with the news mostly by reading a newspaper or mostly by listening to the radio. Table 13.2 shows the data that might have been obtained, arranged in a 2×2 table.

Table 13.2 shows that 47 of the 109 college graduates in the sample said they got news mostly by listening to the radio; the other 62 relied mostly on the newspaper. Among the 97 high school graduates, 58 said the radio, 39 the newspaper. We want to know whether these frequencies indicate a significant difference between the two groups.

TABLE 13.2

Testing Significance of Difference by χ^2

	RADIO	NEWSPAPER	TOTAL
College graduates	47(55.6)	62(53.4)	109
High school graduates	58(49.4)	39(47.6)	97
Total	105	101	206

O	E	O − E	(O − E)²	$\dfrac{(O - E)^2}{E}$
47	55.6	−8.6	73.96	1.33
62	53.4	+8.6	73.96	1.39
58	49.4	+8.6	73.96	1.50
39	47.6	−8.6	73.96	1.55

$$\chi^2 = \overline{5.77}$$

When χ^2 is used to test for the significance of a difference between two or more groups it is sometimes said to be a test of *independence*. Perhaps this can best be explained by pointing out that the observed frequencies in Table 13.2 are classified two ways. One way is radio versus newspaper; the other way is by educational level. Our problem, stated above in terms of significance of difference, can therefore be restated in the form of the question: Are the two ways of classifying the observed frequencies independent of each other? If the two ways of categorizing *are* independent, then preference for radio or newspaper does *not* depend on educational level and we could combine the educational groups, categorizing merely on the basis of radio versus newspaper. This is the same as saying the groups do *not* differ significantly. On the other hand, if the classifications are *not* independent, that is, if they are correlated, then when we categorize the data one way, we must categorize the other way too. In our example this would mean that the educational groups *differ significantly* in their preference for radio or newspaper.

Let us now see how we use χ^2 to test for significance of difference, using our example in Table 13.2. We start by assuming the null hypothesis; we assume that our two groups were drawn from the same population with respect to method of keeping up with the news. Note that we are not concerned, for either group, with whether the radio is preferred over the newspaper. If we were, we could use χ^2, as was explained earlier, to test a 50:50 hypothesis in each group separately.

Our next step is to determine the expected frequency for each of the four cells of the table. Since we have no a priori hypothesis, we reason as follows: if the null hypothesis is correct, i.e., if the true (expected) frequencies are the same for both samples, then combining the two samples should give us a better estimate of the true frequencies than we could get from either sample alone. Thus we add, within each column, the observed frequencies for the samples to get the marginal column totals of 105 and 101. We use these values as the best estimates of the division in the single assumed population between radio preference and newspaper preference. Since our total sample is 206 cases, the expected percent frequency in the population for radio preference is 105/206, or 50.97%. In other words, our best estimate of what we would obtain if we measured the whole population is 50.97% getting news mostly by radio. In similar fashion, 101/206, or 49.03% of the total frequency, is the expected percent frequency for the newspaper category. All we have to do now, to get the expected raw frequencies for each sample, is divide the sample N on the basis of these expected percent frequencies. Thus, there are 109 college graduates; since we expect 50.97% of them to fall in the radio category, we have 50.97% of 109, or 55.6, as the expected frequency for the upper left-hand cell of the table. This is the value shown in parentheses in that cell in Table 13.2. Similarly, 50.97% of the 97 high school graduates gives us 49.4 as the expected frequency in the radio category for those subjects. The expected frequencies for the newspaper cells are determined by taking 49.03% of 109 and of 97.

Now that we have stated the logic for the method of determining the expected frequencies, we can state a simple rule that may be more easily remembered: simply multiply the marginal total for any column by the marginal total for any row and divide the product by the total N. The result is the expected frequency for the cell common to the row and column whose totals were multiplied together. Thus in our example, $\dfrac{(101)\,(97)}{206} = 47.6$; $\dfrac{(105)\,(109)}{206} = 53.4$, and so forth.

Returning to our problem, now that we have the expected frequencies, we compute χ^2 in the usual manner: each deviation of an observed frequency from its expected frequency is squared, divided by the expected frequency, and the quotients summed. We find that $\chi^2 = 5.77$ for this example. Now, what are the *df*? We shall now state a general rule for determining the *df* for any table that has at least two rows and two columns, and in which the marginal totals are used in determining the expected frequencies. The *df* equals (number of columns -1) (number of rows -1). Thus in a 2×2 table, the $df = (2-1)\,(2-1)$, or 1. The rule applies to tables of any number of rows and columns, as long as there are at least two of each.

With 1 *df*, our χ^2 value of 5.77 is larger than the value given in Table G for the 5% level. We shall therefore reject the hypothesis at the 5% level of confidence that the two groups were drawn from the same population with respect to method of getting the news. We could say the same thing by stating that we reject the hypothesis of independence; the frequencies in the radio *versus* newspaper categories are probably *not* independent of educational level.

Before we leave this example we may note that χ^2 can be computed for a 2×2 table without computation of expected frequencies.[2] Let us schematize a 2×2 table as follows, where the letters in the cells indicate the *observed* frequencies:

A	B	A + B
C	D	C + D
A + C	B + D	N

[2] Reprinted with permission from McNemar, Q. *Psychological statistics* (New York, Wiley, 1949).

With this schema, χ^2 can be computed directly as follows:

$$\chi^2 = \frac{N(AD - BC)^2}{(A + B)(C + D)(A + C)(B + D)}$$

Thus for the data in Table 13.2:

$$\chi^2 = \frac{206[(47)(39) - (62)(58)]^2}{(109)(97)(105)(101)}$$

Significance of Differences among Several Groups

The method of applying χ^2 to test for significance of differences among several groups is identical with the method illustrated in the previous section with two groups. As an example, consider the data in Table 13.3. The data are responses to one of the questions in a public opinion poll.[3] The question, asked in 1949, was: "Is your family more prosperous (better off) today than two years ago, less prosperous, or the same?" The question was asked of samples of people from four socioeconomic levels, identified as A, B, C, and D. Group A is the highest socioeconomic level; Group D the lowest. Table 13.3 shows, for each group, the frequency of response in each of the three categories, "more," "same," or "less," that were asked for in the question, plus an "uncertain" category.

Let us apply χ^2 to the data in Table 13.3. We shall be testing for any overall significance of differences among the groups. The procedure is the same as that previously illustrated with a 2×2 table. The theoretical frequency for each cell is obtained by multiplying the total for the row containing the cell by the total for the column containing the cell and dividing by the total N, which here is 5000. For example, for the cell in row "B" and column "Same" we have: $\frac{(1500)(2295)}{5000} = 688.5$. In Table 13.3 the theoretical frequencies are shown in parentheses. Then χ^2 is computed in the usual way: in each cell subtract the theoretical frequency from the observed frequency to get the deviation, square the deviation and divide by the theoretical frequency of

[3] Link, H. C., and Freiberg, A. D. The psychological barometer on communism, americanism, and socialism. *J. appl. Psychol.*, 1949, **33**, 6-14.

the cell; the sum of the quotients is the value of χ^2. For the data in Table 13.3, $\chi^2 = 6.91$. Since this is a 4×4 table, there are 9 df: $(4-1)(4-1)$. Looking in Table G we see that our value of χ^2 does not even come close to the value (16.92) given at the

TABLE 13.3

Testing Overall Significance of Difference among Several Groups by χ^2

GROUP	MORE	SAME	LESS	UNCERTAIN	TOTAL
A	115(120)	245(229.5)	125(131)	15(19.5)	500
B	375(360)	690(688.5)	375(393)	60(58.5)	1500
C	460(480)	920(918)	540(524)	80(78)	2000
D	250(240)	440(459)	270(262)	40(39)	1000
Total	1200	2295	1310	195	5000

O	E	O − E	$(O-E)^2$	$\dfrac{(O-E)^2}{E}$
115	120	−5	25	.208
375	360	+15	225	.625
460	480	−20	400	.833
250	240	+10	100	.417
245	229.5	+15.5	240.25	1.047
690	688.5	+1.5	2.25	.003
920	918	+2	4	.004
440	459	−19	361	.786
125	131	−6	36	.275
375	393	−18	324	.824
540	524	+16	256	.489
270	262	+8	64	.244
15	19.5	−4.5	20.25	1.038
60	58.5	+1.5	2.25	.038
80	78	+2	4	.051
40	39	+1	1	.026

$$\chi^2 = 6.908$$

5% level for 9 df. We conclude that the groups did not differ significantly in their answers to the question.

Chi square with more than 30 df. Occasionally we may have so many groups and categories that there are more than 30 df. This would be the case in a 6×8 table (35 df), a 9×9 table (64 df), etc. Table G does not go beyond 30 df. To evaluate a χ^2 based on more than 30 df, we convert the χ^2 value to an x/σ value and look up the probability in the normal curve table (Table B).

The following expression is used to convert a χ^2 based on more than 30 df to an x/σ value:

$$x/\sigma = \sqrt{2\chi^2} - \sqrt{2n-1},$$

where $n =$ the number of df for the χ^2 value.

Let us conclude this chapter by reëmphasizing the importance of the restrictions on the use of χ^2 that we discussed. These restrictions are not mere hair-splitting. Actually, we hope you have noticed throughout the whole text that there are limitations on the use of every statistical test. Statistics is not a set of techniques to be applied blindly. At the same time, statistical tests properly applied are valuable and powerful tools. In particular, their importance in research can hardly be overestimated.

APPENDIX

APPENDIX

TABLE A *

Table of Squares and Square Roots of the Numbers From 1 to 1000

NUMBER	SQUARE	SQUARE ROOT	NUMBER	SQUARE	SQUARE ROOT
1	1	1.000	41	16 81	6.403
2	4	1.414	42	17 64	6.481
3	9	1.732	43	18 49	6.557
4	16	2.000	44	19 36	6.633
5	25	2.236	45	20 25	6.708
6	36	2.449	46	21 16	6.782
7	49	2.646	47	22 09	6.856
8	64	2.828	48	23 04	6.928
9	81	3.000	49	24 01	7.000
10	1 00	3.162	50	25 00	7.071
11	1 21	3.317	51	26 01	7.141
12	1 44	3.464	52	27 04	7.211
13	1 69	3.606	53	28 09	7.280
14	1 96	3.742	54	29 16	7.348
15	2 25	3.873	55	30 25	7.416
16	2 56	4.000	56	31 36	7.483
17	2 89	4.123	57	32 49	7.550
18	3 24	4.243	58	33 64	7.616
19	3 61	4.359	59	34 81	7.681
20	4 00	4.472	60	36 00	7.746
21	4 41	4.583	61	37 21	7.810
22	4 84	4.690	62	38 44	7.874
23	5 29	4.796	63	39 69	7.937
24	5 76	4.899	64	40 96	8.000
25	6 25	5.000	65	42 25	8.062
26	6 76	5.099	66	43 56	8.124
27	7 29	5.196	67	44 89	8.185
28	7 84	5.292	68	46 24	8.246
29	8 41	5.385	69	47 61	8.307
30	9 00	5.477	70	49 00	8.367
31	9 61	5.568	71	50 41	8.426
32	10 24	5.657	72	51 84	8.485
33	10 89	5.745	73	53 29	8.544
34	11 56	5.831	74	54 76	8.602
35	12 25	5.916	75	56 25	8.660
36	12 96	6.000	76	57 76	8.718
37	13 69	6.083	77	59 29	8.775
38	14 44	6.164	78	60 84	8.832
39	15 21	6.245	79	62 41	8.888
40	16 00	6.325	80	64 00	8.944

* Table A is reprinted from Table II of Lindquist, E. L., *A first course in statistics* (revised edition), published by Houghton Mifflin Company, by permission of the publishers.

217

Table of Squares and Square Roots—*Continued*

NUMBER	SQUARE	SQUARE ROOT	NUMBER	SQUARE	SQUARE ROOT
81	65 61	9.000	126	1 58 76	11.225
82	67 24	9.055	127	1 61 29	11.269
83	68 89	9.110	128	1 63 84	11.314
84	70 56	9.165	129	1 66 41	11.358
85	72 25	9.220	130	1 69 00	11.402
86	73 96	9.274	131	1 71 61	11.446
87	75 69	9.327	132	1 74 24	11.489
88	77 44	9.381	133	1 76 89	11.533
89	79 21	9.434	134	1 79 56	11.576
90	81 00	9.487	135	1 82 25	11.619
91	82 81	9.539	136	1 84 96	11.662
92	84 64	9.592	137	1 87 69	11.705
93	86 49	9.644	138	1 90 44	11.747
94	88 36	9.695	139	1 93 21	11.790
95	90 25	9.747	140	1 96 00	11.832
96	92 16	9.798	141	1 98 81	11.874
97	94 09	9.849	142	2 01 64	11.916
98	96 04	9.899	143	2 04 49	11.958
99	98 01	9.950	144	2 07 36	12.000
100	1 00 00	10.000	145	2 10 25	12.042
101	1 02 01	10.050	146	2 13 16	12.083
102	1 04 04	10.100	147	2 16 09	12.124
103	1 06 09	10.149	148	2 19 04	12.166
104	1 08 16	10.198	149	2 22 01	12.207
105	1 10 25	10.247	150	2 25 00	12.247
106	1 12 36	10.296	151	2 28 01	12.288
107	1 14 49	10.344	152	2 31 04	12.329
108	1 16 64	10.392	153	2 34 09	12.369
109	1 18 81	10.440	154	2 37 16	12.410
110	1 21 00	10.488	155	2 40 25	12.450
111	1 23 21	10.536	156	2 43 36	12.490
112	1 25 44	10.583	157	2 46 49	12.530
113	1 27 69	10.630	158	2 49 64	12.570
114	1 29 96	10.677	159	2 52 81	12.610
115	1 32 25	10.724	160	2 56 00	12.649
116	1 34 56	10.770	161	2 59 21	12.689
117	1 36 89	10.817	162	2 62 44	12.728
118	1 39 24	10.863	163	2 65 69	12.767
119	1 41 61	10.909	164	2 68 96	12.806
120	1 44 00	10.954	165	2 72 25	12.845
121	1 46 41	11.000	166	2 75 56	12.884
122	1 48 84	11.045	167	2 78 89	12.923
123	1 51 29	11.091	168	2 82 24	12.961
124	1 53 76	11.136	169	2 85 61	13.000
125	1 56 25	11.180	170	2 89 00	13.038

Table of Squares and Square Roots—*Continued*

NUMBER	SQUARE	SQUARE ROOT	NUMBER	SQUARE	SQUARE ROOT
171	2 92 41	13.077	216	4 66 56	14.697
172	2 95 84	13.115	217	4 70 89	14.731
173	2 99 29	13.153	218	4 75 24	14.765
174	3 02 76	13.191	219	4 79 61	14.799
175	3 06 25	13.229	220	4 84 00	14.832
176	3 09 76	13.266	221	4 88 41	14.866
177	3 13 29	13.304	222	4 92 84	14.900
178	3 16 84	13.342	223	4 97 29	14.933
179	3 20 41	13.379	224	5 01 76	14.967
180	3 24 00	13.416	225	5 06 25	15.000
181	3 27 61	13.454	226	5 10 76	15.033
182	3 31 24	13.491	227	5 15 29	15.067
183	3 34 89	13.528	228	5 19 84	15.100
184	3 38 56	13.565	229	5 24 41	15.133
185	3 42 25	13.601	230	5 29 00	15.166
186	3 45 96	13.638	231	5 33 61	15.199
187	3 49 69	13.675	232	5 38 24	15.232
188	3 53 44	13.711	233	5 42 89	15.264
189	3 57 21	13.748	234	5 47 56	15.297
190	3 61 00	13.784	235	5 52 25	15.330
191	3 64 81	13.820	236	5 56 96	15.362
192	3 68 64	13.856	237	5 61 69	15.395
193	3 72 49	13.892	238	5 66 44	15.427
194	3 76 36	13.928	239	5 71 21	15.460
195	3 80 25	13.964	240	5 76 00	15.492
196	3 84 16	14.000	241	5 80 81	15.524
197	3 88 09	14.036	242	5 85 64	15.556
198	3 92 04	14.071	243	5 90 49	15.588
199	3 96 01	14.107	244	5 95 36	15.620
200	4 00 00	14.142	245	6 00 25	15.652
201	4 04 01	14.177	246	6 05 16	15.684
202	4 08 04	14.213	247	6 10 09	15.716
203	4 12 09	14.248	248	6 15 04	15.748
204	4 16 16	14.283	249	6 20 01	15.780
205	4 20 25	14.318	250	6 25 00	15.811
206	4 24 36	14.353	251	6 30 01	15.843
207	4 28 49	14.387	252	6 35 04	15.875
208	4 32 64	14.422	253	6 40 09	15.906
209	4 36 81	14.457	254	6 45 16	15.937
210	4 41 00	14.491	255	6 50 25	15.969
211	4 45 21	14.526	256	6 55 36	16.000
212	4 49 44	14.560	257	6 60 49	16.031
213	4 53 69	14.595	258	6 65 64	16.062
214	4 57 96	14.629	259	6 70 81	16.093
215	4 62 25	14.663	260	6 76 00	16.125

Table of Squares and Square Roots—*Continued*

NUMBER	SQUARE	SQUARE ROOT	NUMBER	SQUARE	SQUARE ROOT
261	6 81 21	16.155	306	9 36 36	17.493
262	6 86 44	16.186	307	9 42 49	17.521
263	6 91 69	16.217	308	9 48 64	17.550
264	6 96 96	16.248	309	9 54 81	17.578
265	7 02 25	16.279	310	9 61 00	17.607
266	7 07 56	16.310	311	9 67 21	17.635
267	7 12 89	16.340	312	9 73 44	17.664
268	7 18 24	16.371	313	9 79 69	17.692
269	7 23 61	16.401	314	9 85 96	17.720
270	7 29 00	16.432	315	9 92 25	17.748
271	7 34 41	16.462	316	9 98 56	17.776
272	7 39 84	16.492	317	10 04 89	17.804
273	7 45 29	16.523	318	10 11 24	17.833
274	7 50 76	16.553	319	10 17 61	17.861
275	7 56 25	16.583	320	10 24 00	17.889
276	7 61 76	16.613	321	10 30 41	17.916
277	7 67 29	16.643	322	10 36 84	17.944
278	7 72 84	16.673	323	10 43 29	17.972
279	7 78 41	16.703	324	10 49 76	18.000
280	7 84 00	16.733	325	10 56 25	18.028
281	7 89 61	16.763	326	10 62 76	18.055
282	7 95 24	16.793	327	10 69 29	18.083
283	8 00 89	16.823	328	10 75 84	18.111
284	8 06 56	16.852	329	10 82 41	18.138
285	8 12 25	16.882	330	10 89 00	18.166
286	8 17 96	16.912	331	10 95 61	18.193
287	8 23 69	16.941	332	11 02 24	18.221
288	8 29 44	16.971	333	11 08 89	18.248
289	8 35 21	17.000	334	11 15 56	18.276
290	8 41 00	17.029	335	11 22 25	18.303
291	8 46 81	17.059	336	11 28 96	18.330
292	8 52 64	17.088	337	11 35 69	18.358
293	8 58 49	17.117	338	11 42 44	18.385
294	8 64 36	17.146	339	11 49 21	18.412
295	8 70 25	17.176	340	11 56 00	18.439
296	8 76 16	17.205	341	11 62 81	18.466
297	8 82 09	17.234	342	11 69 64	18.493
298	8 88 04	17.263	343	11 76 49	18.520
299	8 94 01	17.292	344	11 83 36	18.547
300	9 00 00	17.321	345	11 90 25	18.574
301	9 06 01	17.349	346	11 97 16	18.601
302	9 12 04	17.378	347	12 04 09	18.628
303	9 18 09	17.407	348	12 11 04	18.655
304	9 24 16	17.436	349	12 18 01	18.682
305	9 30 25	17.464	350	12 25 00	18.708

Table of Squares and Square Roots—*Continued*

NUMBER	SQUARE	SQUARE ROOT	NUMBER	SQUARE	SQUARE ROOT
351	12 32 01	18.735	396	15 68 16	19.900
352	12 39 04	18.762	397	15 76 09	19.925
353	12 46 09	18.788	398	15 84 04	19.950
354	12 53 16	18.815	399	15 92 01	19.975
355	12 60 25	18.841	400	16 00 00	20.000
356	12 67 36	18.868	401	16 08 01	20.025
357	12 74 49	18.894	402	16 16 04	20.050
358	12 81 64	18.921	403	16 24 09	20.075
359	12 88 81	18.947	404	16 32 16	20.100
360	12 96 00	18.974	405	16 40 25	20.125
361	13 03 21	19.000	406	16 48 36	20.149
362	13 10 44	19.026	407	16 56 49	20.174
363	13 17 69	19.053	408	16 64 64	20.199
364	13 24 96	19.079	409	16 72 81	20.224
365	13 32 25	19.105	410	16 81 00	20.248
366	13 39 56	19.131	411	16 89 21	20.273
367	13 46 89	19.157	412	16 97 44	20.298
368	13 54 24	19.183	413	17 05 69	20.322
369	13 61 61	19.209	414	17 13 96	20.347
370	13 69 00	19.235	415	17 22 25	20.372
371	13 76 41	19.261	416	17 30 56	20.396
372	13 83 84	19.287	417	17 38 89	20.421
373	13 91 29	19.313	418	17 47 24	20.445
374	13 98 76	19.339	419	17 55 61	20.469
375	14 06 25	19.363	420	17 64 00	20.494
376	14 13 76	19.391	421	17 72 41	20.518
377	14 21 29	19.416	422	17 80 84	20.543
378	14 28 84	19.442	423	17 89 29	20.567
379	14 36 41	19.468	424	17 97 76	20.591
380	14 44 00	19.494	425	18 06 25	20.616
381	14 51 61	19.519	426	18 14 76	20.640
382	14 59 24	19.545	427	18 23 29	20.664
383	14 66 89	19.570	428	18 31 84	20.688
384	14 74 56	19.596	429	18 40 41	20.712
385	14 82 25	19.621	430	18 49 00	20.736
386	14 89 96	19.647	431	18 57 61	20.761
387	14 97 69	19.672	432	18 66 24	20.785
388	15 05 44	19.698	433	18 74 89	20.809
389	15 13 21	19.723	434	18 83 56	20.833
390	15 21 00	19.748	435	18 92 25	20.857
391	15 28 81	19.774	436	19 00 96	20.881
392	15 36 64	19.799	437	19 09 69	20.905
393	15 44 49	19.824	438	19 18 44	20.928
394	15 52 36	19.849	439	19 27 21	20.952
395	15 60 25	19.875	440	19 36 00	20.976

Table of Squares and Square Roots—*Continued*

NUMBER	SQUARE	SQUARE ROOT	NUMBER	SQUARE	SQUARE ROOT
441	19 44 81	21.000	486	23 61 96	22.045
442	19 53 64	21.024	487	23 71 69	22.068
443	19 62 49	21.048	488	23 81 44	22.091
444	19 71 36	21.071	489	23 91 21	22.113
445	19 80 25	21.095	490	24 01 00	22.136
446	19 89 16	21.119	491	24 10 81	22.159
447	19 98 09	21.142	492	24 20 64	22.181
448	20 07 04	21.166	493	24 30 49	22.204
449	20 16 01	21.190	494	24 40 36	22.226
450	20 25 00	21.213	495	24 50 25	22.249
451	20 34 01	21.237	496	24 60 16	22.271
452	20 43 04	21.260	497	24 70 09	22.293
453	20 52 09	21.284	498	24 80 04	22.316
454	20 61 16	21.307	499	24 90 01	22.338
455	20 70 25	21.331	500	25 00 00	22.361
456	20 79 36	21.354	501	25 10 01	22.383
457	20 88 49	21.378	502	25 20 04	22.405
458	20 97 64	21.401	503	25 30 09	22.428
459	21 06 81	21.424	504	25 40 16	22.450
460	21 16 00	21.448	505	25 50 25	22.472
461	21 25 21	21.471	506	25 60 36	22.494
462	21 34 44	21.494	507	25 70 49	22.517
463	21 43 69	21.517	508	25 80 64	22.539
464	21 52 96	21.541	509	25 90 81	22.561
465	21 62 25	21.564	510	26 01 00	22.583
466	21 71 56	21.587	511	26 11 21	22.605
467	21 80 89	21.610	512	26 21 44	22.627
468	21 90 24	21.633	513	26 31 69	22.650
469	21 99 61	21.656	514	26 41 96	22.672
470	22 09 00	21.679	515	26 52 25	22.694
471	22 18 41	21.703	516	26 62 56	22.716
472	22 27 84	21.726	517	26 72 89	22.738
473	22 37 29	21.749	518	26 83 24	22.760
474	22 46 76	21.772	519	26 93 61	22.782
475	22 56 25	21.794	520	27 04 00	22.804
476	22 65 76	21.817	521	27 14 41	22.825
477	22 75 29	21.840	522	27 24 84	22.847
478	22 84 84	21.863	523	27 35 29	22.869
479	22 94 41	21.886	524	27 45 76	22.891
480	23 04 00	21.909	525	27 56 25	22.913
481	23 13 61	21.932	526	27 66 76	22.935
482	23 23 24	21.954	527	27 77 29	22.956
483	23 32 89	21.977	528	27 87 84	22.978
484	23 42 56	22.000	529	27 98 41	23.000
485	23 52 25	22.023	530	28 09 00	23.022

Table of Squares and Square Roots—*Continued*

NUMBER	SQUARE	SQUARE ROOT	NUMBER	SQUARE	SQUARE ROOT
531	28 19 61	23.043	576	33 17 76	24.000
532	28 30 24	23.065	577	33 29 29	24.021
533	28 40 89	23.087	578	33 40 84	24.042
534	28 51 56	23.108	579	33 52 41	24.062
535	28 62 25	23.130	580	33 64 00	24.083
536	28 72 96	23.152	581	33 75 61	24.104
537	28 83 69	23.173	582	33 87 24	24.125
538	28 94 44	23.195	583	33 98 89	24.145
539	29 05 21	23.216	584	34 10 56	24.166
540	29 16 00	23.238	585	34 22 25	24.187
541	29 26 81	23.259	586	34 33 96	24.207
542	29 37 64	23.281	587	34 45 69	24.228
543	29 48 49	23.302	588	34 57 44	24.249
544	29 59 36	23.324	589	34 69 21	24.269
545	29 70 25	23.345	590	34 81 00	24.290
546	29 81 16	23.367	591	34 92 81	24.310
547	29 92 09	23.388	592	35 04 64	24.331
548	30 03 04	23.409	593	35 16 49	24.352
549	30 14 01	23.431	594	35 28 36	24.372
550	30 25 00	23.452	595	35 40 25	24.393
551	30 36 01	23.473	596	35 52 16	24.413
552	30 47 04	23.495	597	35 64 09	24.434
553	30 58 09	23.516	598	35 76 04	24.454
554	30 69 16	23.537	599	35 88 01	24.474
555	30 80 25	23.558	600	36 00 00	24.495
556	30 91 36	23.580	601	36 12 01	24.515
557	31 02 49	23.601	602	36 24 04	24.536
558	31 13 64	23.622	603	36 36 09	24.556
559	31 24 81	23.643	604	36 48 16	24.576
560	31 36 00	23.664	605	36 60 25	24.597
561	31 47 21	23.685	606	36 72 36	24.617
562	31 58 44	23.707	607	36 84 49	24.637
563	31 69 69	23.728	608	36 96 64	24.658
564	31 80 96	23.749	609	37 08 81	24.678
565	31 92 25	23.770	610	37 21 00	24.698
566	32 03 56	23.791	611	37 33 21	24.718
567	32 14 89	23.812	612	37 45 44	24.739
568	32 26 24	23.833	613	37 57 69	24.759
569	32 37 61	23.854	614	37 69 96	24.779
570	32 49 00	23.875	615	37 82 25	24.799
571	32 60 41	23.896	616	37 94 56	24.819
572	32 71 84	23.917	617	38 06 89	24.839
573	32 83 29	23.937	618	38 19 24	24.860
574	32 94 76	23.958	619	38 31 61	24.880
575	33 06 25	23.979	620	38 44 00	24.900

Table of Squares and Square Roots—*Continued*

NUMBER	SQUARE	SQUARE ROOT	NUMBER	SQUARE	SQUARE ROOT
621	38 56 41	24.920	666	44 35 56	25.807
622	38 68 84	24.940	667	44 48 89	25.826
623	38 81 29	24.960	668	44 62 24	25.846
624	38 93 76	24.980	669	44 75 61	25.865
625	39 06 25	25.000	670	44 89 00	25.884
626	39 18 76	25.020	671	45 02 41	25.904
627	39 31 29	25.040	672	45 15 84	25.923
628	39 43 84	25.060	673	45 29 29	25.942
629	39 56 41	25.080	674	45 42 76	25.962
630	39 69 00	25.100	675	45 56 25	25.981
631	39 81 61	25.120	676	45 69 76	26.000
632	39 94 24	25.140	677	45 83 29	26.019
633	40 06 89	25.159	678	45 96 84	26.038
634	40 19 56	25.179	679	46 10 41	26.058
635	40 32 25	25.199	680	46 24 00	26.077
636	40 44 96	25.219	681	46 37 61	26.096
637	40 57 69	25.239	682	46 51 24	26.115
638	40 70 44	25.259	683	46 64 89	26.134
639	40 83 21	25.278	684	46 78 56	26.153
640	40 96 00	25.298	685	46 92 25	26.173
641	41 08 81	25.318	686	47 05 96	26.192
642	41 21 64	25.338	687	47 19 69	26.211
643	41 34 49	25.357	688	47 33 44	26.230
644	41 47 36	25.377	689	47 47 21	26.249
645	41 60 25	25.397	690	47 61 00	26.268
646	41 73 16	25.417	691	47 74 81	26.287
647	41 86 09	25.436	692	47 88 64	26.306
648	41 99 04	25.456	693	48 02 49	26.325
649	42 12 01	25.475	694	48 16 36	26.344
650	42 25 00	25.495	695	48 30 25	26.363
651	42 38 01	25.515	696	48 44 16	26.382
652	42 51 04	25.534	697	48 58 09	26.401
653	42 64 09	25.554	698	48 72 04	26.420
654	42 77 16	25.573	699	48 86 01	26.439
655	42 90 25	25.593	700	49 00 00	26.458
656	43 03 36	25.612	701	49 14 01	26.476
657	43 16 49	25.632	702	49 28 04	26.495
658	43 29 64	25.652	703	49 42 09	26.514
659	43 42 81	25.671	704	49 56 16	26.533
660	43 56 00	25.690	705	49 70 25	26.552
661	43 69 21	25.710	706	49 84 36	26.571
662	43 82 44	25.729	707	49 98 49	26.589
663	43 95 69	25.749	708	50 12 64	26.608
664	44 08 96	25.768	709	50 26 81	26.627
665	44 22 25	25.788	710	50 41 00	26.646

Table of Squares and Square Roots—*Continued*

NUMBER	SQUARE	SQUARE ROOT	NUMBER	SQUARE	SQUARE ROOT
711	50 55 21	26.665	756	57 15 36	27.495
712	50 69 44	26.683	757	57 30 49	27.514
713	50 83 69	26.702	758	57 45 64	27.532
714	50 97 96	26.721	759	57 60 81	27.550
715	51 12 25	26.739	760	57 76 00	27.568
716	51 26 56	26.758	761	57 91 21	27.586
717	51 40 89	26.777	762	58 06 44	27.604
718	51 55 24	26.796	763	58 21 69	27.622
719	51 69 61	26.814	764	58 36 96	27.641
720	51 84 00	26.833	765	58 52 25	27.659
721	51 98 41	26.851	766	58 67 56	27.677
722	52 12 84	23.870	767	58 82 89	27.695
723	52 27 29	26.889	768	58 98 24	27.713
724	52 41 76	26.907	769	59 13 61	27.731
725	52 56 25	26.926	770	59 29 00	27.749
726	52 70 76	26.944	771	59 44 41	27.767
727	52 85 29	26.963	772	59 59 84	27.785
728	52 99 84	26.981	773	59 75 29	27.803
729	53 14 41	27.000	774	59 90 76	27.821
730	53 29 00	27.019	775	60 06 25	27.839
731	53 43 61	27.037	776	60 21 76	27.857
732	53 58 24	27.055	777	60 37 29	27.875
733	53 72 89	27.074	778	60 52 84	27.893
734	53 87 56	27.092	779	60 68 41	27.911
735	54 02 25	27.111	780	60 84 00	27.928
736	54 16 96	27.129	781	60 99 61	27.946
737	54 31 69	27.148	782	61 15 24	27.964
738	54 46 44	27.166	783	61 30 89	27.982
739	54 61 21	27.185	784	61 46 56	28.000
740	54 76 00	27.203	785	61 62 25	28.018
741	54 90 81	27.221	786	61 77 96	28.036
742	55 05 64	27.240	787	61 93 69	28.054
743	55 20 49	27.258	788	62 09 44	28.071
744	55 35 36	27.276	789	62 25 21	28.089
745	55 50 25	27.295	790	62 41 00	28.107
746	55 65 16	27.313	791	62 56 81	28.125
747	55 80 09	27.331	792	62 72 64	28.142
748	55 95 04	27.350	793	62 88 49	28.160
749	56 10 01	27.368	794	63 04 36	28.178
750	56 25 00	27.386	795	63 20 25	28.196
751	56 40 01	27.404	796	63 36 16	28.213
752	56 55 04	27.423	797	63 52 09	28.231
753	56 70 09	27.441	798	63 68 04	28.249
754	56 85 16	27.459	799	63 84 01	28.267
755	57 00 25	27.477	800	64 00 00	28.284

Table of Squares and Square Roots—*Continued*

NUMBER	SQUARE	SQUARE ROOT	NUMBER	SQUARE	SQUARE ROOT
801	64 16 01	28.302	846	71 57 16	29.086
802	64 32 04	28.320	847	71 74 09	29.103
803	64 48 09	28.337	848	71 91 04	29.120
804	64 64 16	28.355	849	72 08 01	29.138
805	64 80 25	28.373	850	72 25 00	29.155
806	64 96 36	28.390	851	72 42 01	29.172
807	65 12 49	28.408	852	72 59 04	29.189
808	65 28 64	28.425	853	72 76 09	29.206
809	65 44 81	28.443	854	72 93 16	29.223
810	65 61 00	28.460	855	73 10 25	29.240
811	65 77 21	28.478	856	73 27 36	29.257
812	65 93 44	28.496	857	73 44 49	29.275
813	66 09 69	28.513	858	73 61 64	29.292
814	66 25 96	28.531	859	73 78 81	29.309
815	66 42 25	28.548	860	73 96 00	29.326
816	66 58 56	28.566	861	74 13 21	29.343
817	66 74 89	28.583	862	74 30 44	29.360
818	66 91 24	28.601	863	74 47 69	29.377
819	67 07 61	28.618	864	74 64 96	29.394
820	67 24 00	28.636	865	74 82 25	29.411
821	67 40 41	28.653	866	74 99 56	29.428
822	67 56 84	28.671	867	75 16 89	29.445
823	67 73 29	28.688	868	75 34 24	29.462
824	67 89 76	28.705	869	75 51 61	29.479
825	68 06 25	28.723	870	75 69 00	29.496
826	68 22 76	28.740	871	75 86 41	29.513
827	68 39 29	28.758	872	76 03 84	29.530
828	68 55 84	28.775	873	76 21 29	29.547
829	68 72 41	28.792	874	76 38 76	29.563
830	68 89 00	28.810	875	76 56 25	29.580
831	69 05 61	28.827	876	76 73 76	29.597
832	69 22 24	28.844	877	76 91 29	29.614
833	69 38 89	28.862	878	77 08 84	29.631
834	69 55 56	28.879	879	77 26 41	29.648
835	69 72 25	28.896	880	77 44 00	29.665
836	69 88 96	28.914	881	77 61 61	29.682
837	70 05 69	28.931	882	77 79 24	29.698
838	70 22 44	28.948	883	77 96 89	29.715
839	70 39 21	28.965	884	78 14 56	29.732
840	70 56 00	28.983	885	78 32 25	29.749
841	70 72 81	29.000	886	78 49 96	29.766
842	70 89 64	29.017	887	78 67 69	29.783
843	71 06 49	29.034	888	78 85 44	29.799
844	71 23 36	29.052	889	79 03 21	29.816
845	71 40 25	29.069	890	79 21 00	29.833

Table of Squares and Square Roots—*Continued*

NUMBER	SQUARE	SQUARE ROOT	NUMBER	SQUARE	SQUARE ROOT
891	79 38 81	29.850	936	87 60 96	30.594
892	79 56 64	29.866	937	87 79 69	30.610
893	79 74 49	29.883	938	87 98 44	30.627
894	79 92 36	29.900	939	88 17 21	30.643
895	80 10 25	29.916	940	88 36 00	30.659
896	80 28 16	29.933	941	88 54 81	30.676
897	80 46 09	29.950	942	88 73 64	30.692
898	80 64 04	29.967	943	88 92 49	30.708
899	80 82 01	29.983	944	89 11 36	30.725
900	81 00 00	30.000	945	89 30 25	30.741
901	81 18 01	30.017	946	89 49 16	30.757
902	81 36 04	30.033	947	89 68 09	30.773
903	81 54 09	30.050	948	89 87 04	30.790
904	81 72 16	30.067	949	90 06 01	30.806
905	81 90 25	30.083	950	90 25 00	30.822
906	82 08 36	30.100	951	90 44 01	30.838
907	82 26 49	30.116	952	90 63 04	30.854
908	82 44 64	30.133	953	90 82 09	30.871
909	82 62 81	30.150	954	91 01 16	30.887
910	82 81 00	30.166	955	91 20 25	30.903
911	82 99 21	30.183	956	91 39 36	30.919
912	83 17 44	30.199	957	91 58 49	30.935
913	83 35 69	30.216	958	91 77 64	30.952
914	83 53 96	30.232	959	91 96 81	30.968
915	83 72 25	30.249	960	92 16 00	30.984
916	83 90 56	30.265	961	92 35 21	31.000
917	84 08 89	30.282	962	92 54 44	31.016
918	84 27 24	30.299	963	92 73 69	31.032
919	84 45 61	30.315	964	92 92 96	31.048
920	84 64 00	30.332	965	93 12 25	31.064
921	84 82 41	30.348	966	93 31 56	31.081
922	85 00 84	30.364	967	93 50 89	31.097
923	85 19 29	30.381	968	93 70 24	31.113
924	85 37 76	30.397	969	93 89 61	31.129
925	85 56 25	30.414	970	94 09 00	31.145
926	85 74 76	30.430	971	94 28 41	31.161
927	85 93 29	30.447	972	94 47 84	31.177
928	86 11 84	30.463	973	94 67 29	31.193
929	86 30 41	30.480	974	94 86 76	31.209
930	86 49 00	30.496	975	95 06 25	31.225
931	86 67 61	30.512	976	95 25 76	31.241
932	86 86 24	30.529	977	95 45 29	31.257
933	87 04 89	30.545	978	95 64 84	31.273
934	87 23 56	30.561	979	95 84 41	31.289
935	87 42 25	30.578	980	96 04 00	31.305

Table of Squares and Square Roots—*Continued*

NUMBER	SQUARE	SQUARE ROOT	NUMBER	SQUARE	SQUARE ROOT
981	96 23 61	31.321	991	98 20 81	31.480
982	96 43 24	31.337	992	98 40 64	31.496
983	96 62 89	31.353	993	98 60 49	31.512
984	96 82 56	31.369	994	98 80 36	31.528
985	97 02 25	31.385	995	99 00 25	31.544
986	97 21 96	31.401	996	99 20 16	31.559
987	97 41 69	31.417	997	99 40 09	31.575
988	97 61 44	31.432	998	99 60 04	31.591
989	97 81 21	31.448	999	99 80 01	31.607
990	98 01 00	31.464	1000	100 00 00	31.623

TABLE B *

Per Cent of Total Area under the Normal Curve between Mean Ordinate And Ordinate at Any Given Sigma-Distance from the Mean

$\frac{x}{\sigma}$	.00	.01	.02	.03	.04	.05	.06	.07	.08	.09
0.0	00.00	00.40	00.80	01.20	01.60	01.99	02.39	02.79	03.19	03.59
0.1	03.98	04.38	04.78	05.17	05.57	05.96	06.36	06.75	07.14	07.53
0.2	07.93	08.32	08.71	09.10	09.48	09.87	10.26	10.64	11.03	11.41
0.3	11.79	12.17	12.55	12.93	13.31	13.68	14.06	14.43	14.80	15.17
0.4	15.54	15.91	16.28	16.64	17.00	17.36	17.72	18.08	18.44	18.79
0.5	19.15	19.50	19.85	20.19	20.54	20.88	21.23	21.57	21.90	22.24
0.6	22.57	22.91	23.24	23.57	23.89	24.22	24.54	24.86	25.17	25.49
0.7	25.80	26.11	26.42	26.73	27.04	27.34	27.64	27.94	28.23	28.52
0.8	28.81	29.10	29.39	29.67	29.95	30.23	30.51	30.78	31.06	31.33
0.9	31.59	31.86	32.12	32.38	32.64	32.90	33.15	33.40	33.65	33.89
1.0	34.13	34.38	34.61	34.85	35.08	35.31	35.54	35.77	35.99	36.21
1.1	36.43	36.65	36.86	37.08	37.29	37.49	37.70	37.90	38.10	38.30
1.2	38.49	38.69	38.88	39.07	39.25	39.44	39.62	39.80	39.97	40.15
1.3	40.32	40.49	40.66	40.82	40.99	41.15	41.31	41.47	41.62	41.77
1.4	41.92	42.07	42.22	42.36	42.51	42.65	42.79	42.92	43.06	43.19
1.5	43.32	43.45	43.57	43.70	43.83	43.94	44.06	44.18	44.29	44.41
1.6	44.52	44.63	44.74	44.84	44.95	45.05	45.15	45.25	45.35	45.45
1.7	45.54	45.64	45.73	45.82	45.91	45.99	46.08	46.16	46.25	46.33
1.8	46.41	46.49	46.56	46.64	46.71	46.78	46.86	46.93	46.99	47.06
1.9	47.13	47.19	47.26	47.32	47.38	47.44	47.50	47.56	47.61	47.67
2.0	47.72	47.78	47.83	47.88	47.93	47.98	48.03	48.08	48.12	48.17
2.1	48.21	48.26	48.30	48.34	48.38	48.42	48.46	48.50	48.54	48.57
2.2	48.61	48.64	48.68	48.71	48.75	48.78	48.81	48.84	48.87	48.90
2.3	48.93	48.96	48.98	49.01	49.04	49.06	49.09	49.11	49.13	49.16
2.4	49.18	49.20	49.22	49.25	49.27	49.29	49.31	49.32	49.34	49.36
2.5	49.38	49.40	49.41	49.43	49.45	49.46	49.48	49.49	49.51	49.52
2.6	49.53	49.55	49.56	49.57	49.59	49.60	49.61	49.62	49.63	49.64
2.7	49.65	49.66	49.67	49.68	49.69	49.70	49.71	49.72	49.73	49.74
2.8	49.74	49.75	49.76	49.77	49.77	49.78	49.79	49.79	49.80	49.81
2.9	49.81	49.82	49.82	49.83	49.84	49.84	49.85	49.85	49.86	49.86
3.0	49.87									
3.5	49.98									
4.0	49.997									
5.0	49.99997									

* The original data for Table B came from, *Tables for statisticians and biometricians*, edited by Karl Pearson, published by Cambridge University Press, and are used here by permission of the publisher. The adaptation of these data is taken from Lindquist, E. L., *A first course in statistics* (revised edition), with permission of the publisher, Houghton Mifflin Company.

TABLE C *

Values of *t* at the 5% and 1% Levels of Significance

DEGREES OF FREEDOM (df)	5%	1%
1	12.706	63.657
2	4.303	9.925
3	3.182	5.841
4	2.776	4.604
5	2.571	4.032
6	2.447	3.707
7	2.365	3.499
8	2.306	3.355
9	2.262	3.250
10	2.228	3.169
11	2.201	3.106
12	2.179	3.055
13	2.160	3.012
14	2.145	2.977
15	2.131	2.947
16	2.120	2.921
17	2.110	2.898
18	2.101	2.878
19	2.093	2.861
20	2.086	2.845
21	2.080	2.831
22	2.074	2.819
23	2.069	2.807
24	2.064	2.797
25	2.060	2.787
26	2.056	2.779
27	2.052	2.771
28	2.048	2.763
29	2.045	2.756
30	2.042	2.750

* Table C is abridged from Table III of Fisher and Yates: *Statistical tables for biological, agricultural, and medical research*, 4th edition 1953, published by Oliver and Boyd, Limited, Edinburgh, by permission of the authors and publishers.

TABLE D *

Values of r at the 5% and 1% Levels of Significance

DEGREES OF FREEDOM (df)	5%	1%	DEGREES OF FREEDOM (df)	5%	1%
1	.997	1.000	24	.388	.496
2	.950	.990	25	.381	.487
3	.878	.959	26	.374	.478
4	.811	.917	27	.367	.470
5	.754	.874	28	.361	.463
6	.707	.834	29	.355	.456
7	.666	.798	30	.349	.449
8	.632	.765	35	.325	.418
9	.602	.735	40	.304	.393
10	.576	.708	45	.288	.372
11	.553	.684	50	.273	.354
12	.532	.661	60	.250	.325
13	.514	.641	70	.232	.302
14	.497	.623	80	.217	.283
15	.482	.606	90	.205	.267
16	.468	.590	100	.195	.254
17	.456	.575	125	.174	.228
18	.444	.561	150	.159	.208
19	.433	.549	200	.138	.181
20	.423	.537	300	.113	.148
21	.413	.526	400	.098	.128
22	.404	.515	500	.088	.115
23	.396	.505	1000	.062	.081

* A portion of Table D is abridged from Table VI of Fisher and Yates: *Statistical tables for biological, agricultural, and medical research,* 4th edition 1953, published by Oliver and Boyd, Limited, Edinburgh, by permission of the authors and publishers. The remainder of the table is from Snedecor, *Statistical methods,* by permission of the publisher, The Iowa State College Press, and the author.

TABLE E *

Values of ρ (rank-order correlation coefficient) at the 5% and 1% Levels of Significance

N	5%	1%
5	1.000	—
6	.886	1.000
7	.786	.929
8	.738	.881
9	.683	.833
10	.648	.794
12	.591	.777
14	.544	.715
16	.506	.665
18	.475	.625
20	.450	.591
22	.428	.562
24	.409	.537
26	.392	.515
28	.377	.496
30	.364	.478

* Computed from Olds, E. G., Distribution of the sum of squares of rank differences for small numbers of individuals, *Ann. Math. Statist.*, 1938, 9, 133-148, and, The 5% significance levels for sums of squares of rank differences and a correction, *Ann. Math. Statist.*, 1949, 20, 117-118, by permission of the author and the Institute of Mathematical Statistics.

TABLE F *
Values of F at the 5% and 1% Significance Levels

(df ASSOCIATED WITH THE DENOMINATOR)		(df ASSOCIATED WITH THE NUMERATOR)								
		1	2	3	4	5	6	7	8	9
1	5%	161	200	216	225	230	234	237	239	241
	1%	4052	5000	5403	5625	5764	5859	5928	5982	6022
2	5%	18.5	19.0	19.2	19.2	19.3	19.3	19.4	19.4	19.4
	1%	98.5	99.0	99.2	99.2	99.3	99.3	99.4	99.4	99.4
3	5%	10.1	9.55	9.28	9.12	9.01	8.94	8.89	8.85	8.81
	1%	34.1	30.8	29.5	28.7	28.2	27.9	27.7	27.5	27.3
4	5%	7.71	6.94	6.59	6.39	6.26	6.16	6.09	6.04	6.00
	1%	21.2	18.0	16.7	16.0	15.5	15.2	15.0	14.8	14.7
5	5%	6.61	5.79	5.41	5.19	5.05	4.95	4.88	4.82	4.77
	1%	16.3	13.3	12.1	11.4	11.0	10.7	10.5	10.3	10.2
6	5%	5.99	5.14	4.76	4.53	4.39	4.28	4.21	4.15	4.10
	1%	13.7	10.9	9.78	9.15	8.75	8.47	8.26	8.10	7.98
7	5%	5.59	4.74	4.35	4.12	3.97	3.87	3.79	3.73	3.68
	1%	12.2	9.55	8.45	7.85	7.46	7.19	6.99	6.84	6.72
8	5%	5.32	4.46	4.07	3.84	3.69	3.58	3.50	3.44	3.39
	1%	11.3	8.65	7.59	7.01	6.63	6.37	6.18	6.03	5.91
9	5%	5.12	4.26	3.86	3.63	3.48	3.37	3.29	3.23	3.18
	1%	10.6	8.02	6.99	6.42	6.06	5.80	5.61	5.47	5.35
10	5%	4.96	4.10	3.71	3.48	3.33	3.22	3.14	3.07	3.02
	1%	10.0	7.56	6.55	5.99	5.64	5.39	5.20	5.06	4.94
11	5%	4.84	3.98	3.59	3.36	3.20	3.09	3.01	2.95	2.90
	1%	9.65	7.21	6.22	5.67	5.32	5.07	4.89	4.74	4.63
12	5%	4.75	3.89	3.49	3.26	3.11	3.00	2.91	2.85	2.80
	1%	9.33	6.93	5.95	5.41	5.06	4.82	4.64	4.50	4.39
13	5%	4.67	3.81	3.41	3.18	3.03	2.92	2.83	2.77	2.71
	1%	9.07	6.70	5.74	5.21	4.86	4.62	4.44	4.30	4.19
14	5%	4.60	3.74	3.34	3.11	2.96	2.85	2.76	2.70	2.65
	1%	8.86	6.51	5.56	5.04	4.70	4.46	4.28	4.14	4.03
15	5%	4.54	3.68	3.29	3.06	2.90	2.79	2.71	2.64	2.59
	1%	8.68	6.36	5.42	4.89	4.56	4.32	4.14	4.00	3.89
16	5%	4.49	3.63	3.24	3.01	2.85	2.74	2.66	2.59	2.54
	1%	8.53	6.23	5.29	4.77	4.44	4.20	4.03	3.89	3.78
17	5%	4.45	3.59	3.20	2.96	2.81	2.70	2.61	2.55	2.49
	1%	8.40	6.11	5.18	4.67	4.34	4.10	3.93	3.79	3.68
18	5%	4.41	3.55	3.16	2.93	2.77	2.66	2.58	2.51	2.46
	1%	8.29	6.01	5.09	4.58	4.25	4.01	3.84	3.71	3.60

* Merrington, M., and Thompson, C. M. Tables of percentage points of the inverted beta (F) distribution, *Biometrika*, 1943, 33, 73-88, by permission of the editor.

TABLE F (*Continued*)

(*df* ASSOCIATED WITH THE DENOMINATOR)		(*df* ASSOCIATED WITH THE NUMERATOR)								
19	5%	4.38	3.52	3.13	2.90	2.74	2.63	2.54	2.48	2.42
	1%	8.18	5.93	5.01	4.50	4.17	3.94	3.77	3.63	3.52
20	5%	4.35	3.49	3.10	2.87	2.71	2.60	2.51	2.45	2.39
	1%	8.10	5.85	4.94	4.43	4.10	3.87	3.70	3.56	3.46
21	5%	4.32	3.47	3.07	2.84	2.68	2.57	2.49	2.42	2.37
	1%	8.02	5.78	4.87	4.37	4.04	3.81	3.64	3.51	3.40
22	5%	4.30	3.44	3.05	2.82	2.66	2.55	2.46	2.40	2.34
	1%	7.95	5.72	4.82	4.31	3.99	3.76	3.59	3.45	3.35
23	5%	4.28	3.42	3.03	2.80	2.64	2.53	2.44	2.37	2.32
	1%	7.88	5.66	4.76	4.26	3.94	3.71	3.54	3.41	3.30
24	5%	4.26	3.40	3.01	2.78	2.62	2.51	2.42	2.36	2.30
	1%	7.82	5.61	4.72	4.22	3.90	3.67	3.50	3.36	3.26
25	5%	4.24	3.39	2.99	2.76	2.60	2.49	2.40	2.34	2.28
	1%	7.77	5.57	4.68	4.18	3.86	3.63	3.46	3.32	3.22
26	5%	4.23	3.37	2.98	2.74	2.59	2.47	2.39	2.32	2.27
	1%	7.72	5.53	4.64	4.14	3.82	3.59	3.42	3.29	3.18
27	5%	4.21	3.35	2.96	2.73	2.57	2.46	2.37	2.31	2.25
	1%	7.68	5.49	4.60	4.11	3.78	3.56	3.39	3.26	3.15
28	5%	4.20	3.34	2.95	2.71	2.56	2.45	2.36	2.29	2.24
	1%	7.64	5.45	4.57	4.07	3.75	3.53	3.36	3.23	3.12
29	5%	4.18	3.33	2.93	2.70	2.55	2.43	2.35	2.28	2.22
	1%	7.60	5.42	4.54	4.04	3.73	3.50	3.33	3.20	3.09
30	5%	4.17	3.32	2.92	2.69	2.53	2.42	2.33	2.27	2.21
	1%	7.56	5.39	4.51	4.02	3.70	3.47	3.30	3.17	3.07
40	5%	4.08	3.23	2.84	2.61	2.45	2.34	2.25	2.18	2.12
	1%	7.31	5.18	4.31	3.83	3.51	3.29	3.12	2.99	2.89
60	5%	4.00	3.15	2.76	2.53	2.37	2.25	2.17	2.10	2.04
	1%	7.08	4.98	4.13	3.65	3.34	3.12	2.95	2.82	2.72
120	5%	3.92	3.07	2.68	2.45	2.29	2.18	2.09	2.02	1.96
	1%	6.85	4.79	3.95	3.48	3.17	2.96	2.79	2.66	2.56

TABLE G *
Values of Chi-square (χ^2) at the 5% and 1% Levels of Significance

DEGREES OF FREEDOM (df)	5%	1%
1	3.84	6.64
2	5.99	9.21
3	7.82	11.34
4	9.49	13.28
5	11.07	15.09
6	12.59	16.81
7	14.07	18.48
8	15.51	20.09
9	16.92	21.67
10	18.31	23.21
11	19.68	24.72
12	21.03	26.22
13	22.36	27.69
14	23.68	29.14
15	25.00	30.58
16	26.30	32.00
17	27.59	33.41
18	28.87	34.80
19	30.14	36.19
20	31.41	37.57
21	32.67	38.93
22	33.92	40.29
23	35.17	41.64
24	36.42	42.98
25	37.65	44.31
26	38.88	45.64
27	40.11	46.96
28	41.34	48.28
29	42.56	49.59
30	43.77	50.89

* Table G is abridged from Table IV of Fisher and Yates: *Statistical tables for biological, agricultural, and medical research*, 4th edition 1953, published by Oliver and Boyd, Limited, Edinburgh, by permission of the authors and publishers.

Index

THE CENTURY PSYCHOLOGY SERIES

Richard M. Elliot, *Editor*

Kenneth MacCorquodale, *Assistant Editor*

Social Psychology, by Charles Bird

Learning More by Effective Study, by Charles and Dorothy Bird

Psychological Counseling, by Edward S. Bordin

A History of Experimental Psychology, 2nd Ed., by Edwin G. Boring

Sensation and Perception in the History of Experimental Psychology, by Edwin G. Boring

Readings in Modern Methods of Counseling, edited by Arthur H. Brayfield

A Casebook of Counseling, by Robert Callis, Paul C. Polmantier, and Edward C. Roeber

Beauty and Human Nature, by Albert R. Chandler

Readings in the History of Psychology, edited by Wayne Dennis

Techniques of Attitude Scale Construction, by Allen L. Edwards

Modern Learning Theory, by William K. Estes, Sigmund Koch, Kenneth MacCorquodale, Paul E. Meehl, Conrad G. Mueller, Jr., William N. Schoenfeld, and William S. Verplanck

Schedules of Reinforcement, by C. B. Ferster and B. F. Skinner

Social Relations and Morale in Small Groups, by Eric F. Gardner and George G. Thompson

Great Experiments in Psychology, 3rd Ed., by Henry E. Garrett

Exceptional Children, by Florence L. Goodenough

Developmental Psychology, 3rd Ed., by Florence L. Goodenough and Leona E. Tyler

Physiological Psychology, by Starke R. Hathaway

Seven Psychologies, by Edna Heidbreder

Theories of Learning, 2nd Ed., by Ernest R. Hilgard

Conditioning and Learning, by Ernest R. Hilgard and Donald G. Marquis

Hypnosis and Suggestibility, by Clark L. Hull

Principles of Behavior, by Clark L. Hull

Development in Adolescence, by Harold E. Jones

The Definition of Psychology, by Fred S. Keller

Principles of Psychology, by Fred S. Keller and William N. Schoenfeld

Psychological Studies of Human Development, by Raymond G. Kuhlen and George G. Thompson

The Cultural Background of Personality, by Ralph Linton

Vocational Counseling with the Physically Handicapped, by Lloyd H. Lofquist

Studies in Motivation, edited by David C. McClelland

The Achievement Motive, by David C. McClelland, John W. Atkinson, Russell A. Clark, and Edgar L. Lowell

Current Studies in Psychology, by F. Joseph McGuigan and Allen D. Calvin

Principles of Applied Psychology, by A. T. Poffenberger

The Behavior of Organisms, by B. F. Skinner

Cumulative Record, by B. F. Skinner

Verbal Behavior, by B. F. Skinner

Diagnosing Personality and Conduct, by Percival M. Symonds

Dynamic Psychology, by Percival M. Symonds

The Dynamics of Human Adjustment, by Percival M. Symonds

The Ego and the Self, by Percival M. Symonds

The Psychology of Parent-Child Relationships, by Percival M. Symonds

Educational Psychology, George G. Thompson, Eric F. Gardner, and Francis J. DiVesta. Also accompanying *Workbook* by the same authors.

Selected Writings from a Connectionist's Psychology, by Edward L. Thorndike

Introduction to Methods in Experimental Psychology, 3rd Ed., by Miles A. Tinker and Wallace A. Russell

The Psychology of Human Differences, 2nd Ed., by Leona E. Tyler

The Work of the Counselor, by Leona E. Tyler

Experimental Psychology, by Benton J. Underwood

Psychological Research, by Benton J. Underwood

Elementary Statistics, by Benton J. Underwood, Carl P. Duncan, Janet A. Taylor, and John W. Cotton. Also accompanying *Workbook* by the same authors.

Persons and Personality, by Sister Annette Walters and Sister Kevin O'Hara